CRITICAL PERSPECTIVES IN PUBLIC RELATIONS

CRITICAL PERSPECTIVES IN PUBLIC RELATIONS

Jacquie L'Etang and
Magda Pieczka
University of Stirling

INTERNATIONAL THOMSON BUSINESS PRESS
I(T)P An International Thomson Publishing Company

London • Bonn • Boston • Johannesburg • Madrid • Melbourne • Mexico City • New York • Paris
Singapore • Tokyo • Toronto • Albany, NY • Belmont, CA • Cincinnati, OH • Detroit, MI

Critical Perspectives in Public Relations

First published by International Thomson Business Press

I(T)P A division of International Thomson Publishing Inc.
The ITP logo is a trademark under licence

British Library Cataloguing-in-Publication Data
A catalogue record for this book is available from the British Library

---

First edition 1996

Typeset in Times by Lisa Williams
Printed in the UK by TJ Press (Padstow) Ltd, Padstow, Cornwall.

ISBN 0-415-12300-3

International Thomson Business Press
Berkshire House
168–173 High Holborn
London WC1V 7AA
UK

International Thomson Business Press
20 Park Plaza
14th Floor
Boston MA 02116
USA

http://www.thomson.com/itbp.html

CONTENTS

NOTES ON CONTRIBUTORS

JACQUIE L'ETANG

Jacquie L'Etang (MIPR) is a Lecturer in Film and Media Studies (Public Relations) at the University of Stirling and has been running the full-time MSc in Public Relations since January 1993. Her public relations experience included internal communications, promotional publications and event management at the British Council and the London School of Economics. Her first degree was in American and English History (University of East Anglia) and she also has postgraduate degrees in Commonwealth History (University of London) and Social Justice (University of Stirling). She was in the first cohort of graduates from the MSc in Public Relations (1988/9), after which she worked as administrator and copy-editor on the distance-learning version of the degree. She has published articles on business ethics and public relations in *New Consumer*, the *Journal of Business Ethics* and the *European Journal of Business Ethics*, and has presented papers at a number of conferences, including the Standing Conference of Organizational Symbolism, Professions and Management Conference, Confédération Européenne de Relations Publiques (CERP), Public Relations Educators' Forum, International Symposia on Public Relations. Her main interest is in the sociology of public relations, but she has recently collaborated with her two colleagues Magda Pieczka and Heike Puchan on a paper which offers a critique of evaluation in public relations. She is currently researching the evolution of public relations in the UK in the postwar era.

MAGDA PIECZKA

Magda Pieczka is a Lecturer in Film and Media Studies (Public Relations) and Course Director of the MSc in Public Relations by Distance Learning at the University of Stirling. She has degrees from Jagiellonian University, Kraków, Poland, where she was a Lecturer in the English Department for six years. She also has postgraduate degrees in English Literature (University of Glasgow) and Publishing Studies (University of Stirling). Her professional experience includes managerial experience obtained while running her own private English Language School in Poland and in freelance publishing. She has presented conference papers at the Public Relations Educators' Forum, the 1st and 2nd International Public Relations Symposia and the 1st International Conference on Marketing and Corporate Communications. She teaches on a wide range of courses on the MSc degrees, including public relations theory and practice, management and organizational theory, communications and research methods. Her main research interests are in the sociology of the professions and organizational ethnography as applied to public relations.

PETER MEECH

Having studied German Language and Literature at the Universities of Wales and Manchester, Peter Meech was a Lecturer at the Universities of Ulster, Stirling and Bochum, Germany. He joined the Department of Film and Media Studies at Stirling after gaining an MA at the Centre for Mass Communication Research, University of Leicester. As a member of the original working party which devised Stirling's MSc in Public Relations, he helped launch both the full-time and the distance-learning versions of the course. For five years he was Assistant Director of the former and he continues to teach and supervise on both courses. His teaching includes units on writing for the media and media training on the MSc and an undergraduate course on journalism. His recent and forthcoming publications include articles on corporate identity and Scottish broadcasting, the structure and regulation of the UK media, the Scottish media and national identity, and tabloid journalism.

BRIAN MCNAIR

Brian McNair is Senior Lecturer in Film and Media Studies at the University of Stirling and Assistant Director of the MSc in Public Relations. He has an MA (Hons) in Sociology, an MPhil in Comparative Communications and a PhD (University of Glasgow). He studied Russian at the Pushkin Institute for the study of Russian Language and Literature, Moscow. He teaches courses on UK media and political and public affairs as well as supervising research in public relations at MSc and PhD levels. He is the author of *Images of the Enemy* (Routledge, 1988), *News and Journalism in the UK* (Routledge, 1994) and *Political Communication* (Routledge, 1995). His main research interests are political public relations and news management strategies.

PREFACE

This book is the result of collaboration between some of those who teach public relations at the University of Stirling, the first institution to teach public relations in the United Kingdom as a postgraduate degree. The book aims to go beyond existing texts in public relations, which largely focus on applied theory, practical skills and case studies. While acknowledging the importance of the applied approach, the editors' ambition in planning a wide-ranging selection of essays was to try and open up the field of public relations to wider debate and analysis. Our motive was to voice many questions that presented themselves in the course of our educational work and, by so doing, first to illustrate how important it is for us as individuals, citizens and members of publics, to understand the potential influence and implications of public relations; and second, to show how the study of public relations can provide an excellent education for its students.

The book is partially, therefore, shaped by the UK public relations educational scene, which is dominated by courses rather than research and based in management or marketing departments which tend to emphasize technical skills and functionalist thought. We hope that this collection of essays will stimulate debate about the boundaries, definitions, functions and effects of public relations and the methodologies that can be brought to bear upon the subject.

The book aims to explore key concepts, themes and theories in public relations from a variety of critical perspectives (hence the title), thus challenging the increasingly taken-for-granted view that public relations is a management discipline, which seems to mean 'applied science', aimed at improving organizational effectiveness. The book sets out to encourage creative and lateral thinking in this new and exciting field. It consists of a collection of interdisciplinary essays written by some of the academics from the course team of the MSc in Public Relations (full time and distance learning) at the University of Stirling. Two of the authors teach media studies both at the undergraduate level and on the postgraduate MSc in Media Management at Stirling. Their backgrounds are in languages, communications and media studies. Two authors teach predominantly on the MSc degrees in public relations and have interdisciplinary backgrounds which include postgraduate degrees in history, applied philosophy, public relations, publishing, languages and literature.

The book is theoretical since we believe that the ancestry of the public relations discipline has remained inadequately explored. We have sought to make connections, to broaden thinking and to provoke. While the essays are complementary in terms of themes and specific links are made between some chapters, each essay works as an independent piece of writing. The style of the essays varies in scope and presentation: some present literature reviews of an area, others present critiques of existing public relations concepts and literature.

We are indebted to a number of people who have contributed knowingly or unknowingly to the present volume. We are grateful for the contributions and enthusiasm of Brian McNair and Peter Meech for their willingness to entrust themselves to untried editors. We received encouragement and support for this project from other colleagues, especially from Philip Schlesinger, Professor of Media Studies and Director of the Media Research Institute at Stirling, and from Mike Cormack, Film and Media Department, University of Stirling. The project would never have got off the ground without the advice and enthusiasm of Francesca Weaver at Routledge and of Caroline Law at International Thomson Business Press; and the project would never have appeared without the diligence of Lisa Williams. Reviewers' comments were also useful in helping us to refine ideas and arguments.

We also want to express our gratitude to Stuart Jones, who spent a lot of time reading the manuscript and making careful and helpful comments.

An acknowledgement is also due to the full-time and distance-learning students – especially the 1994/5 full-time cohort with whom we debated many of the ideas in this book.

The book would never have been written without the personal support of our partners, who commented on drafts and put up with many late-night phone calls and weekend absences.

Jacquie L'Etang and Magda Pieczka
University of Stirling 1996

INTRODUCTION

This book was inspired by our desire to explore new and diverse themes we thought might be useful in thinking about public relations. We approached the subject with a mind-set that combined curiosity and creativity, which we hope are communicated in the various chapters. As we began the process of writing and thinking we were confronted with a variety of conceptual problems which we believe are of importance in the development of the field of public relations. At present there is no obvious outlet for publishing such material. One of the authors has already had the experience of having an article rejected from one of the public relations journals on the grounds that it was too radical (the article was subsequently published by another refereed journal outside the field). Yet, as the history of almost any discipline can prove, development needs challenge as much as it needs consensus. In public relations, consensus seems currently quite strong; therefore, we feel we should set out to challenge.

Much of the material has been tested on students on the MSc in Public Relations at Stirling (full time and distance learning), many of whom are experienced practitioners. We found that students enjoyed some of these more critical ideas as a contrast to the standard theories in public relations in the core curriculum. We were encouraged by their response and that of our colleagues in the Film and Media Department at Stirling to communicate our approach to a wider audience.

Some of the material has, along with some of our other critical work, been presented at conferences – with varying responses, some of which have been quite hostile. While this has not always been a pleasant experience, we firmly believe, journalistically, that if people appear not to want you to say something, then there is all the more reason to say it. In a field as new as public relations there is plenty of room for academics to pursue a range of interests using the full panoply of methodologies. There is surely no one way of researching or teaching public relations, and doubtless in time there will be a range of courses, approaches and even 'schools'. At present, however, we feel that the area is quite limited and so consciously chose to use our academic backgrounds in the humanities to develop different ideas.

Themes that emerge from the collection of essays in this volume could be summarized as critique, social effects and education. The critical approach adopted is, we believe, an important and necessary step in the development of public relations as an academic area. We also argue that public relations should be taught in an interdisciplinary and integrated way and not purely as an instrumental discipline. We discuss the limitations of instrumentalism expressed through the major paradigm in the field but we hope that the range of questions explored in this collection demonstrates the creative potential of public relations as a discipline. Such an approach is likely to attract criticism from many quarters, but we hope that many of our academic colleagues will receive this volume with sympathetic interest.

Chapter 1, Public Relations Education, reviews educational developments in the context of professionalization. It discusses the nature of the public relations discipline, the appropriate location of courses and proposes a radicalization of the curriculum. The chapter suggests that the functionalist nature of courses in the United States and the United Kingdom can be linked to pressures from the industry, and argues that this emphasis might threaten the academic freedom and credibility of the subject. It is suggested that public relations education needs instead to be rooted more firmly in its conceptual origins and to resist being equated with basic training. It is argued that public relations academics should be producing a wide variety of theoretical and applied research. Students should be educated to think independently and critically, not simply taught to conform to existing industry norms and values. This first chapter thus sets the tone for the remaining chapters, which aim to be thought-provoking.

Chapter 2, Public Relations as Diplomacy, continues the educational theme, drawing comparisons between the emergence of public relations and of diplomacy as areas of academic study. The author compares the practical and professional functions of diplomats and public relations practitioners and the underlying assumptions of theory in the respective fields. As a result of the analysis the chapter offers a critique of the concept of 'symmetry' in public relations theory, both for its lack of content and its apparent potential for hegemony.

Chapter 3, Performance in Politics and the Politics of Performance, is a polemical essay which develops the political and international themes of the previous chapter. In particular the chapter explores the ways in which public relations 'manages' public opinion. The chapter seeks the answer to the question 'Is public relations a necessary element of contemporary political performance or simply another stage in the degradation of our political life and culture?' In the process of addressing this question the chapter explores the relationship between public relations and democratic politics as pursued by parties and governments in domestic and international arenas. The chapter provides a number of recent and contemporary national and international examples of public relations used in support of politicians and political parties, including commentary on recent allegations of corruption in government. The chapter includes extensive comment on the effects on political processes of the professionalization of opinion management in a complex media environment and, especially, on its impact on the ability of the citizen to make informed judgements about politics. The author concludes that the contemporary media scene creates many opportunities for democratic participation and debate, and that criticisms of the practice are based on overly romantic views of democracy. The chapter thus provides an optimistic analysis of the role of public relations in political processes.

Chapter 4, Public Opinion and Public Relations, fills a gap in public relations literature by reviewing debates in the field from a public relations perspective. The chapter introduces the main concepts and gives some background as to their origins and philosophical underpinning. The second part of the chapter looks at applications of the concepts in research, an area which is important for public relations in its bid for professional and academic (social scientific) credibility. The chapter highlights the empiricist stranglehold on the concept of public opinion and explores the connections between public opinion and mass communication. The essay concludes with a discussion of the conceptual and methodological links between public opinion and public relations research to demonstrate the assumptions implicit in current public relations theory. As part of this discussion, the chapter reveals the source of public relations' claim to be a neutral and enabling function in society (a position supported by McNair in chapter 3), as well as proposing that the close link between public relations and political science should be articulated more openly.

Chapter 5, Corporate Identity and Corporate Image, presents an overview of terminology and the historical development of the field. Particular attention is given to oversimplified accounts of corporate image and the process involved in a corporate identity exercise. The discussion is related to concepts of corporate culture and the process of representing this symbolically. The chapter concludes with a case study of one less-than-successful corporate identity exercise.

Chapter 6, Public Relations and Corporate Responsibility, is a long chapter which is wide-ranging in its scope. It explores the relationship between public relations and corporate social responsibility by means of discussions of crisis management and community programmes. Utilitarian and Kantian moral theory are used as analytical tools to expose contradictions in these two practices. The analysis draws out the motivation behind corporate social responsibility, crisis management and issues management to expose the essential tension that lies between the fight for organizational survival and concern for the public interest. There is also an analysis of the claim that public relations itself is intrinsically ethical and socially responsible, and points that emerge from the discussion are linked to broader questions about relationships between government, society and business.

Chapter 7, Public Relations: A Rhetorical Perspective, explores classical and contemporary ideas in rhetoric for insights into the role and ethics of public relations. The chapter reviews some key ideas in the work of classical authors such as Plato and Aristotle and relates these to ideas about public relations, persuasion, ethics and public opinion. The chapter reviews recent work in the rhetorical tradition conducted within public relations and argues that questions of ethics in public relations cannot be addressed without consideration of recent and contemporary intellectual debates in rhetoric, epistemology and postmodernism.

Chapter 8, Paradigms, Systems Theory and Public Relations, is the longest chapter in the book and is monographical in style. It begins with a detailed review of three clearly defined manifestations of systems thinking in sociology and organizational studies. The chapter carefully traces the development of systems ideas, showing how these ideas came to be adopted in public relations theory. In the second half of the chapter the author takes a critical look at the emerging discourse of public relations within academia in relation to important debates which have emerged within organizational studies. It is argued that the adaptation of the systems approach in public relations has become a way of thinking that excludes other ways of thinking and thus prevents certain questions from being asked. In conclusion it is suggested that despite the current claims of the paradigm struggle in the field, public relations would benefit from more theoretical variety and a greater range of research interests and perspectives. This chapter thus presents a major challenge to the dominant perspective in the field.

Acknowledgements are due to the following authors and publishers for permissions:

Dr Jon White for his generous permission to quote from the unpublished paper co-authored with John Blamphin (1994), 'Priorities for research into public relations practice in the United Kingdom' and from his co-authored chapter (with Professor James Grunig) 'The effect of worldviews on public relations theory and practice', in *Excellence in Public Relations and Communications Management* (Lawrence Erlbaum, 1992);

Dione Morris for her generous permission to quote from her unpublished Master's dissertation (1994) 'Public relations in the UK: an overview of the marketing/public relations debate';

Professor James Grunig for permission to quote from *Excellence in Public Relations and Communications Management* (Lawrence Erlbaum, 1992);

Penguin Books for permission to quote from *Phaedrus* by Plato, translated by Walter Hamilton (Penguin Classics, 1973) © Walter Hamilton, 1973, and from *Gorgias* by Plato, translated by Water Hamilton (Penguin Classics, 1960) © Walter Hamilton, 1960, and from *The Art of Rhetoric* by

Aristotle, translated and introduced by H.C. Lawson-Tancred (Penguin Classics, 1991) © H.C. Lawson-Tancred, 1991;

Sage for their permission to quote from *Images of Organisation* (Morgan 1986) and *Rethinking Organization* (M. Reed and M. Hughes 1992);

Butterworth Heinemann for their permission to quote from *New Thinking in Organizational Behaviour* (Tsoukas 1994);

Routledge for their kind permission to reproduce text from M. Ruse (1993) *The Darwinian Paradigm: Essays on its History, Philosophy and Religious Implications* and from Hill and Beshoff (1994) *Two Worlds of International Relations*;

Sage for their kind permission to reproduce material from Enos and Brown (1993) *Defining the New Rhetorics*;

Lawrence Erlbaum for their kind permission to reproduce material from Grunig (1992) *Excellence in Public Relations and Communications Management*;

First Magazine for their kind permission to publish extracts from their special report on Corporate Social Responsibility published in association with the Prince of Wales Business Leaders Forum, vol. 8, no. 4, 1995.

Thanks are also due to the History of Advertising Trust, Beccles, Norfolk, which holds the IPR archive, and to John Lavelle, Executive Director of the IPR, who gave permission for access to the archive in summer 1995.

Every effort has been made to trace all copyright holders, but if any have been inadvertently overlooked the publishers will be pleased to make the necessary arrangement at the first opportunity.

Jacquie L'Etang and Magda Pieczka
University of Stirling, 1996

1

PUBLIC RELATIONS EDUCATION

Jacquie L'Etang and Magda Pieczka

INTRODUCTION

The practice of public relations has aspirations to professionalize itself, and public relations education is a tool which can help achieve that status. However, the nature of curricula and the purpose of courses is a matter for discussion, and sometimes difference, between academics and practitioners. The context of the debate in the United Kingdom is one in which Government explicitly encourages vocational education. Education is thus increasingly required to serve business and industrial interests.

This chapter explores the relationship between public relations practice, education and research. The discussion includes an overview of educational developments in the United Kingdom, which are contrasted with developments in the United States and continental Europe. The essay presents an argument for academic freedom in the design and delivery of courses.

REVIEW OF EDUCATIONAL DEVELOPMENTS IN THE CONTEXT OF PROFESSIONALIZATION

Professional status is important to public relations because such recognition could achieve social respectability and satisfy social aspirations as well as facilitate a clear separation from propaganda. The drive for professionalism in the UK has been articulated to a certain degree through debates over the structure and content of academic syllabuses and their location, aspects of which we will be discussing later in this chapter.

Within public relations literature concerned with the concept of professionalism there is a strong tendency to treat it as something which is applied to the individual rather than the occupation as a whole. Grunig and Hunt claim that

> we could say that an occupation becomes a profession when a majority of its practitioners qualify as professionals.
>
> (Grunig and Hunt 1984: 66)

This leaves wide open the question of what exactly is the size of majority required and also seems a convenient way of moving debate away from important questions about the role of public relations in society. The process of individuation carried out here by Grunig and Hunt is similar to that in the area of public relations ethics, which is often narrowed down to questions of individual behaviour. It is not that such an approach in itself is not of interest; the problem lies in the lack of alternatives, which creates a substantial gap in the literature on the sociology of public relations. Doubtless this gap will in due course be filled, by those academics in public relations whose backgrounds or interests in sociology, politics and media studies equip them better to address such questions.

Many of those writing about professionalism claim that public relations can already be described as a profession on the grounds that

> Public relations [in the US] has a body of knowledge, a professional society, a code of ethics, a system for accreditation of practitioners by examination, a process for reporting violations including reviewing and censuring, a foundation for furthering public relations research and education, specified curricula at university level.
>
> (Wright 1979: 20)

Others simply describe public relations as though it had already achieved professional status, sometimes ignoring key criteria that emerge from sociological literature, for example:

> Although public relations is often dismissed as a young profession and therefore not to be taken too seriously as an academic discipline, the professional practice of public relations can be dated logically from 1923 when Ed Bernays published the first textbook on public relations and taught the first university course.
>
> (Public Relations Education Trust 1991: 9)

The published record of educational developments in the field of public relations has been dominated by the American experience. In part, this reflects the fact that the two academic journals in public relations to date, *Public Relations Review* and *Journal of Public Relations Research*, are based in America and largely devoted to American research and academic orientations. The representation of the European scene has been very general and not always as accurate as it might be; publication in refereed journals about the British scene is limited to one article (Hatfield 1994: 189–201) published eight years after its submission and consequently so outdated as to be very inaccurate. Another article (Hazleton and Cutbirth 1992: 187–97) generalizes about the 'European system of education' on the basis of research in Austria, Hungary and Germany. Both of these articles are written by Americans, not Europeans.

Educational developments in the United Kingdom seem to have been stimulated in the first instance largely by professional bodies. The Institute of Public Relations (IPR) set up its own courses and examinations in the 1950s. Teachers were recruited from the band of existing practitioners who delivered teaching at the Department of Management Studies, Regent Polytechnic, London, and the first Intermediate Examination was taken in July 1957. In the late 1950s the Education Committee of the IPR reported the early awakenings of interest in the University sector at the University of Sheffield, where there was talk of a Chair in Public Relations; at the London School of Economics, where there was to be a Lecturer in Advertising; and at Keele College (later University), where it was proposed that a Chair in Communications be appointed (IPR Education Committee Minutes IPR 3/7/2 History of Advertising Trust). At this stage there was an emphasis on technical skills such as film-making, photography, typography and advertising, and the most theorctically driven topic appeared to be opinion research. Examiners' reports and minutes of the Education Committee indicate concern over the scope of teaching of 'Public relations principles' and the absence of appropriate texts. Assessment was by two-stage examination (Intermediate and Final), including a viva voce examination designed to 'enable the Board of Examiners to assess a candidate's personality and his ability to think and express himself clearly and concisely on a specific public relations problem' (Education Committee Minutes 24/4/59 IPR 3/7/2).

In the late 1970s and early 1980s IPR Education Committee members explored the possibilities for degree-level education with a number of educational institutions, largely in the then polytechnic sector. The International Public Relations Association (IPRA) produced two policy documents on education (Gold Papers 4 and 7) which reviewed the role and scope of public relations education in relation to the professionalization of the practice and made a number of specific recommendations in relation to the content and level of degree courses and the appropriate qualifications for those teaching the subject.

We shall concentrate our attention here on the second, more recent, of these papers. The main themes emerging can be summarized as concern over the academic and professional standards of those who teach public relations, the establishment and maintenance of independence from other disciplines, the role for practitioners in making contributions to education, the balance between academic and practical work and the importance of education in contributing to the professionalization of the field. The paper presents a model which places public relations theory and practice as an academic subject at the centre of two concentric circles (the Wheel of Education) containing topics, such as editing, research and advertising, which can be seen as developing relevant skills; and in the outer circle, a number of subjects, such as business administration, humanities, natural sciences and statistics, which could be drawn on to develop theoretical underpinnings for public relations and furnish future practitioners with knowledge rather than just skills. The model offers an enlightened view of what is required of a good public relations practitioner and a good educational programme; at the same time, it is revealing about the authors' perspective. We shall reflect on a few points which can be inferred from the model or which are directly stated in the paper itself, in order to provide an educational and academic response.

The main focus of the paper is on what is needed in terms of developing academic courses and research for public relations to be able to achieve the status of 'more traditional professions' (IPRA 1990: 5). There is no definition of what such a profession is, but the examples provided are law, medicine and theology (lawyers, medics and clergy). This is an interesting selection, revealing perhaps more about the aspirations of public relations than about the concept of profession or professionalism. The three professions chosen have traditionally been highly respectable middle-class occupations; entry to each of them has required formal academic qualification, and additional vocational training for lawyers and medics, in effect a period of often hard and exploitative apprenticeship. The nature of these professions is also of some interest here: in general terms, they seem to be concerned with correction and prevention of physiological, spiritual or social malfunctions. The nature of the service these professions provide, and therefore the professionals' relationship with clients, puts the professionals in a position of power based either on the specialized knowledge possessed or the special social status accorded to the system of beliefs they represent (clergy). In brief, one does not normally tell the doctor or the lawyer how they should go about providing the service that is being paid for. Perhaps it is the aspiration to this kind of social position and relationship with the client that underlies some of the current ideas in public relations, such as the need, expressed in many definitions, to be counted as a management function (Grunig 1992; White and Mazur 1994; Cutlip et al. 1994); as a member of the dominant coalition (Grunig 1992); or the organizational conscience (see chapter 6).

More importantly perhaps from our own point of view, the paper is also very revealing about what the authors understand to be a sound methodology, how public relations theory is supposed to be built and, finally, how academics work. In terms of methodology the paper notes that

> Insofar as public relations is concerned, 'basic research' is of the type conducted by sociologists, psychologists and other social scientists . . . research in the social sciences seldom produces the same kinds of definite statements of principle that are evolved in the 'hard' sciences.
>
> (IPRA 1990: 19)

The paper also recommends 'that public relations be taught as an applied social science with academic and professional emphasis' (ibid.: 13) and that there is a need in public relations for a balance between theory and the requirement of acting on 'solid, empirically tested foundations and concepts' (ibid.: 7). There are two obvious questions that must be asked at this point. If producing 'definite statements' is not really possible for the social sciences, where are the 'solid, empirically tested foundations' supposed to come from? If basic research for public relations is to be done by other disciplines, if public relations is to be 'an applied social science' where is public relations theory supposed to come from? It appears that public relations aspires to the status of a social science, but at the same time is not ready to conduct basic research or accept that positivism is not the only worldview. This position, in our view, is symptomatic of a young discipline eager to graduate to long trousers and grow a moustache.

The IPRA paper speaks of 'theory of public relations', thus assuming its existence. To date, it would seem more appropriate to speak of *a* theory – represented by the research effort of Professor Grunig and the 'Excellence' team (see chapter 8) – and a growing body of empirical and critical research, as conducted by Broom, Dozier, Pearson, White, to mention just a few prominent names. However, the use of theory to indicate a well-developed discipline combining a diversity of theories and approaches, such as communication studies, seems to be an aspiration rather than a factual statement.

The above inconsistencies or overgeneralizations could be attributed to the rather simplistic understanding of the academic environment. True, the authors admit that education and consultancy require different skills, and that suitable teachers coming directly from the practice 'will be exceptions', but in the same breath they talk about substituting 'lengthy and appropriate years of experience for academic credentials' (ibid.: 11). The move from consultancy to teaching and research is seen as unproblematic, based purely on consulting experience, and presumably intellectual ability combined with the acceptance of a likely salary cut. In fact, it represents a major career change: to become a professional academic one probably needs several years to become a fully trained and competent lecturer, catch up on reading in a number of disciplines in the case of public relations, and start producing and supervising research – all this on top of a normal routine of teaching, student counselling and academic administration. To achieve this transition successfully requires at least high motivation on the part of the new recruit and a sympathetic academic environment.

The respect for public relations in academia which the paper calls for can only come from a sufficient body of academics performing the duties described above to standard academic performance indicators and, much more importantly, from a large volume of respectable published research. This in turn is facilitated by a culture which encourages research; in practical terms this means manageable teaching loads, senior colleagues sympathetic to the discipline, financial support to attend conferences, opportunity to tackle doctoral and postdoctoral research, a structure of appropriate academic appointments and, of course, the infrastructure mentioned in the Gold Paper. How many of those teaching and researching public relations can claim to have such support? In reality it seems that many colleagues in the area are employed to teach lucrative undergraduate programmes with little thought being given to their academic development or the future of the discipline.

Differences between academics and practitioners with regard to the development of theory and research in public relations have already been debated in published research. Typical empirical studies of this nature include Terry's (1989) study of educator and practitioner differences on the role of theory in public relations and research into the gap between professional and research agendas in public relations journals (Broom et al. 1989). These studies clearly illustrate a major difference in interest, and in understanding of and use of research. Recently a study (White and Blamphin 1994) has been conducted in the United Kingdom to explore practitioner and academic perceptions in relation to the research agenda.

The Delphi study, carried out in May, June and July 1994, replicated a similar American study carried out in 1992 by Professor McElreath of Towson State University with the help of John Blamphin, who collaborated with Jon White on the British study. The report produced contains the following general summary:

> Among the Delphi group, most felt that the important research topics were those dealing with the scope of practice, the contribution public relations makes to strategic management, and measurement and evaluation of the practice. A number of people felt that the list was focused too much on the professional concerns of public relations practitioners, and further study was needed of management and client expectations. One academic commented on the list [of research topics generated] as one of subject headings rather than a true guide to research. The overriding conclusion at the Symposium [held in November 1994] was that there is a need for a translation service, or research digest, which would interpret findings from the social sciences so as to make them relevant for practitioners.
>
> (White and Blamphin 1994)

(For further discussion of relationships between academics and practitioners or policy makers see chapter 2.)

There was a fair degree of disagreement and a wide range of opinions were expressed by the participants both in the research paper and at a meeting held in November 1994 which one of the authors (Pieczka) attended. If one can at all generalize from the results presented, it would appear that people in public relations are searching for a confirmation of their professional identity (scope of practice; management and client expectations); of their status and perceptions of the practice (contribution to organizational strategy, evaluation, and client expectations); and of their own professionalism in terms of working on the basis of scientific findings.

Published literature has highlighted the different perspectives of educators and practitioners with regard to the role, scope and content of public relations education. There appears to be some lack of clarity among some practitioners and some teachers regarding the distinction between education and training. Practitioners are naturally keen that relevant practical skills should be taught but often express doubts about the value of underpinning theory as noted in the preceding section. Some practitioners (and even some academics) are uncomfortable with the notion that academics may adopt critical perspectives. The lack of critical work in public relations has already been noted:

> considerably more work is needed to enhance our understanding of the 'sociology' of public relations . . . the role of public relations in this process and the 'manufacturing' of PR communications is an important area of future research . . . critical research has been virtually non-existent.
>
> (Pavlik 1987: 123)

> most critical researchers tend to be Marxist Europeans, with few Americans embracing the challenge to engage in a process that is by definition disruptive. Perhaps American public relations scholars, working to promote a positive image of public relations, find that challenge problematic.
>
> (Cottone 1993: 169)

Practitioners are keen that those teaching public relations should not only already possess practical experience but also 'continue to develop their professional experience while they hold teaching appointments' (IPRA 1990: 11). Such comments reveal a lack of understanding not only of the educational role but of the educational culture and the professional requirements and priorities for academics. Academic performance indicators in the United Kingdom consist of research, teaching and administration, and every academic is evaluated yearly against preset objectives; failure to achieve in any of these fields can result in the termination of an individual's contract. It perhaps has not been fully realized that educators and practitioners inhabit different cultures and attempts to maintain or impose public relations occupational roles and norms within the academy are likely to be frustrated. Attempts by industry to dictate or control the research agenda may well be resisted once academics realize the potential threat to academic freedom and the subsequent loss of academic credibility within education. Too cosy a relationship between education and practice threatens the development of the academic discipline:

public relations is compromised when educators allow practitioners to view universities as production houses for business interests, rather than as entities that should engage in critical research.

(Cottone 1993: 173)

Morris (1994) found that there was a difference of opinion as to the role of the Institute of Public Relations and the extent to which it should lead educational developments. Whereas some expressed the view that education should reflect practice, a number of interviewees in her study thought it was important for a clear distinction to be made between academia and practice and that part of the educational role was to challenge and critique the practice. One academic was quoted as saying,

> It's up to academics to challenge the definitions set by the people who are practising public relations . . . we shouldn't have limitations in education . . . We're not here to produce clones, we're here to educate people . . . One of the things that industry has got wrong is thinking that we're a training school, because we're not, so there's bound to be a discrepancy, because if there weren't we'd be doing something wrong – we're not teaching to serve practice, we're educating and it's quite a different thing.
>
> (Morris 1994)

Perhaps the appropriate metaphor for understanding the relationship between educator and practitioner is that of artist (practitioner) and critic (educator); both are expert but have to be judged on different criteria. Education goes beyond training, and to fulfil their role in academic life educators must move beyond the purely pragmatic.

Educators in the United Kingdom have been slow to cooperate with one another and to develop an agenda of their own. While a number of educators in the UK are tackling PhDs in public relations, none have so far been publishing regularly in refereed articles in their chosen field. Morris found that most academics in the field had practical experience in public relations and commented that

> it is problematic that so few have postgraduate qualifications . . . without input from credible academics, public relations will not be accepted as an academic discipline, certainly not at postgraduate level. If public relations degrees are being taught by those who only have practical experience – no matter how extensive that experience may be – not only may public relations be ridiculed for the lack of faculty's 'necessary academic requirements' (IPRA 1990: 11) but research will suffer. A lack of public relations educators with Ph.D.s means there is an absence of faculty qualified to supervise public relations students undertaking postgraduate study and Ph.D.s. Thus, a lack of research will not facilitate growth of the body of knowledge.
>
> (Morris 1994)

One aspect which does not appear to have received much attention in the literature is the appropriate role of practitioners in education. It is clearly very important for students to receive teaching from practitioners. Such sessions can be quite inspirational for students, as well as conveying invaluable practical information attractively packaged in anecdotal form. However, the nature of such presentations tends to be very different from academic lectures and students need to be prepared for this so that they can get the most out of the experience; for them the practitioners themselves are as much an object of study as the content of the presentation. To give one example of the differences between academic and practitioner approaches, the IPRA Gold Paper (No. 7) specifically recommends 'the use of guest lecturers . . . to keep professors updated on developments in areas such as case studies' (IPRA 1990: 12).

Guest lecturers offer an invaluable link to the practice though their understanding and presentation of, for example, 'case studies' is very different from that of an academic. For a practitioner, 'case study' tends to mean 'story' told as a narrative and usually ending with a moral. An academic understanding of 'case study' is considerably more demanding methodologically, requiring demonstration of triangulation and explanation of the multiple methodologies applied.

The drive to professionalization evident in IPRA Gold Paper no. 7, and which has been referred to in this chapter, has led to educational developments but there is a long way to go before academic credibility and autonomy are achieved.

ACADEMIC DEBATES: DEVELOPMENT AND POSITIONING OF THE DISCIPLINE

Public relations in the United Kingdom has developed largely in the former polytechnic sector, which has traditionally specialized in more vocational and innovative courses. A Diploma in International Public Relations was set up in 1987 at Watford College, followed by a Master's degree in 1988 at a traditional university, Stirling, in Scotland (in 1991 the Stirling degree was made available via distance learning to meet the needs of practitioners). Undergraduate degrees followed in England at Bournemouth, the College of St Mark and St John (University of Exeter), and Leeds Business School. The College of St Mark and St John (University of Exeter) also participated in an innovative master's degree jointly with a number of European institutions. On this degree students from participating institutions study in a variety of languages and universities. By 1994 these courses had been added to by two more postgraduate qualifications, a degree in public relations at the new university Manchester Metropolitan and a diploma in journalism at the University of Wales.

As indicated earlier, little attention has been given to the educational scene in the United Kingdom in the existing literature. Hatfield's (1994) article was published several years after it was written and gives a journalistic overview mostly of practitioner views about what public relations education should consist of and achieve for its graduates. The article is interesting from a couple of points of view in the light of subsequent developments. First, it is quite noticeable that the American author has sought practitioner rather than academic perspectives. Ten practitioners were interviewed but the views of only one academic (Dr Jon White, then of Cranfield Institute of Technology, now Visiting Professor at City University) are represented. It is quite clear that the assumptions of the author and those she interviewed are that the role of education is to produce qualified people for industry: 'The British public relations profession has recognized that through the development and support of a sound educational programme it can direct and shape its own future' (Hatfield 1994: 198).

There is considerable emphasis on skills and the legitimation of public relations as a profession. In contrast to literature recording the American scene, there is no discussion or debate about the academic content or the location of courses as the appropriate home is presented as being business and management.

American academics Hazleton and Cutbirth (1993) also survey the European scene with a view to exploring educational paradigms. Much of what they say, however, relates to continental Europe only and not to the European Community in general. For example, British academics, like their American counterparts, are under extreme pressure to publish in refereed journals, especially since the introduction of governmental research exercises which review all departments and allocate funding according to research productivity. Another point of difference is that academics in Britain are not referred to as 'Professor Doctor', neither are they accorded the respect accorded to continental Europeans. In terms of public relations education the British model has tended to follow the American rather than the continental European model of education. This has led to an emphasis on skills and business education rather than the rigorously academic teaching which is available in countries such as Germany, Denmark and the Netherlands. In continental Europe, as opposed to Britain, public relations is generally studied in departments of mass communication. In contrast to the situation in America, where public relations courses tend to be housed in Schools of Journalism, the majority of public relations courses in Britain are housed in business schools and departments of marketing or advertising. Morris (1994) argued that the placement of public relations courses in marketing and business departments was likely to inhibit, not facilitate, the professionalization process. Therefore, there seems to be a strong argument for placing public relations education in departments which facilitate an interdisciplinary style of teaching encompassing communications, media studies and cultural studies, management and organizational behaviour and public relations theory and practice.

TOWARDS A RADICALIZATION OF THE CURRICULUM

Public relations offers an opportunity for developing stimulating and broad curricula producing graduates with good skills and an understanding of a range of subjects from psychology, politics, sociology and organizational behaviour to media and cultural studies. Public relations practitioners must be generalists and a wide-ranging curriculum helps to ensure that they are; it also has another educational aim in developing a habit of flexibility and a sensitivity to different ways of seeing the world, as different subjects bring their own conceptual frameworks and cultures. There are, however, also clear dangers: inviting a range of subject specialists to contribute to teaching may produce a fragmented and confusing course. It is therefore necessary for public relations educators to develop a required level of expertise in a number of subjects to ensure that the delivery of the curriculum does take public relations as the focal point.

Public relations courses are expected to produce graduates who can 'hit the ground running', i.e. fit in smoothly into any public relations operation without Account Directors and Managers having to spend too much time on training or supervising junior staff. They are also expected to produce graduates with good analytical skills and capable of developing into seasoned 'counsellors'; and, finally, public relations courses are where research is supposed to come from. All this should happen, well, preferably now. It seems that public relations has waited to become a 'traditional profession' for so long that it is running out of patience.[1] While this is understandable, the attitude also produces undesirable effects by pushing towards research agendas geared to instantaneous solutions and is responsible for some confusion as to what exactly a curriculum should do. While the opinions of practitioners are a valuable guide to many decisions that educators need to take in designing their courses, it is ultimately the professional educator who should be trusted with the task.

We suggest that a sensible course of action for academic institutions which offer public relations courses to take under these demanding circumstances is to start with educational aims rather than a checklist of techniques and applications suggested by the Gold Paper no. 7. The difference of approach can be best illustrated by an example. Let us imagine a situation where a pupil needs to be taught perfect table manners to last a lifetime in a rather short space of time. There are two approaches that could be taken. A simple way would be to compile a list, as comprehensive as one can make it or as comprehensive as one knows the pupil will need to be familiar with, of things to do and not to do. The time of instruction would be spent on making sure the pupil has memorized the rules, applies them appropriately, is familiar with all the types of implements and has rehearsed all the useful conversation topics to be tried on, for example, a young female stranger who is the hostess' cousin, or an old family friend who might be a lawyer or doctor.

While pupils with a natural gift and better memory could do quite well, one can easily imagine the less confident ones getting the rules embarrassingly mixed up. An alternative is to leave all the three- and four-pronged forks till later and spend some time first of all talking about the history of table manners, the dynamics of a social interaction at a dinner party, food, maybe amuse the student with some well-chosen reading; and, having in this way mastered the 'why', progress to the 'how'. No doubt the pupil would make mistakes, but at the same time would be much better prepared to deal with a wider range of problems and be confident in confronting completely unknown situations which might arise – for example, in different cultures.

A similar approach is influencing some changes in medical education in the United Kingdom. Although medical syllabuses have, of course, always differed between the various medical schools, traditionally students have been required to undergo an intensive course of factual learning. Now some medical schools are adopting an approach in which students will be working in small groups with a facilitator to focus on particular problems and analytical concepts. The idea underlying this approach is twofold: first, students will be required to carry out research in their chosen field from an early point in their career; and second, they will understand that their career will consist of continual research, updating and problem-solving. Students may possess less factual knowledge when they qualify, but they will have been given the ability to think for themselves, conceptualize problems and find things out for themselves. This represents a fundamental shift in educational practice from a system of intensive cramming of facts, many of which may be forgotten once finals are over, and where academic or conceptual learning is thought to be something which occurs between the ages of 18 and 25 or 26, to a system where it is clearly understood that the graduate may not know all procedures but has a greater capacity for identifying problems.

Curricula in medical schools in the UK are determined by individual universities; there is no attempt by the General Medical Council (GMC) to prescribe a list of skills that students must acquire beyond two or three core skills such as cardiopulmonary resuscitation and the ability to set up an intravenous line. Instead, the GMC make very broad recommendations which the universities consider and take into account as they revise and update educational aims, objectives and curricula. The latest GMC recommendations propose moves away from departmentally focused teaching to integrative system-based teaching which avoids factual overload and facilitates the intellectual development of research, conceptual and communication skills as discussed above.

Whatever approach one chooses in education it can only succeed if the pupil is willing to trust the teacher's judgement and, as it were, willingly suspend disbelief. It is also to some extent a question of a pupil's personality. Some will be happy to engage with your way of teaching, even if the engagement is rebellious and demands proof every stage of the way; some will take the attitude that they know what is needed and refuse to engage with what they perceive as academic rubbish. It is a perfectly reasonable reaction, the trouble is it is only reasonable on the basis of what the student knows at the time; consequently, the student, impatient to learn 'useful stuff', limits his or her own potential for future development.

If public relations practice chooses to look up to medicine or law it should also be prepared at least to tolerate the study of some seemingly non-practical subjects such as Roman law or Latin. This is not to say that choices made by educators about curriculum details should go unquestioned; but a more liberal attitude and an understanding that every graduate will still need on-the-job training would be a constructive and beneficial approach.

It is our view that public relations education should be integrated and interdisciplinary, taught by academics who can move comfortably between the traditional disciplines as they help students learn to see different perspectives and the varied implications of any particular situation. If this approach is taken students can be encouraged to be curious, to play 'devil's advocate', question received truths and develop moral courage – all qualities they will need as public relations counsellors.

Public relations taught in an interdisciplinary way demands intellectual flexibility from academics and students. As such, it is a field in which there is the potential to deliver an excellent education regardless of whether its young graduates decide to pursue careers in public relations or not. It is a subject with opportunities to connect students with the challenging and important ideas which will confront them not only as public relations practitioners but as citizens.

It is our view that the responsibility of academics in the field of public relations is to define and unpack concepts in use in practice and to identify the sources of ideas in order to reflect upon their significance to the world we inhabit. While it is the case that public relations has only recently become an area of study in Europe, it is not the case that the ideas underpinning it are unique and that the subject has to be invented from scratch. The educator's role is surely to bring to bear upon public relations ideas from moral philosophy, epistemology, philosophy of language, sociology, communications and media studies, as well as from some of the more technical subjects such as psychology, management and marketing. This we see as education's contribution to the process of the professionalization of public relations.

2

PUBLIC RELATIONS AS DIPLOMACY

Jacquie L'Etang

INTRODUCTION

This chapter contrasts the practice and academic disciplines of public relations and international relations and illustrates the point that such a comparative-approach can yield many ideas of use in understanding the immature discipline of public relations. Three main themes are pursued: practical or craft concerns, the evolution of the academic disciplines and, finally, the conceptual convergence of the two areas. The last-named theme is given most emphasis and detailed explanation.

The discussion of the practical similarities in the role of public relations and diplomacy is explored partly through the somewhat limited existing academic literature and partly through practitioner perspectives which illustrate that aspiration to diplomatic status could offer public relations the kudos it currently lacks. The discussion of the emergence of the academic disciplines illustrates common sources and similar problematics such as tension between academics and practitioners and methodological debates. The review of conceptual convergence describes the overlap between the framework in international relations and the dominant framework in public relations and attempts to draw out possible implications for public relations theory from the more developed international relations model. In drawing out the implications from this analysis, the author critiques the concept of symmetry as it is presented in the public relations model and suggests that assumptions about its positive benefits may not be justified.

It will be shown that, rather than being underpinned by separate and distinct theoretical and philosophical frameworks, existing traditions in international relations, which have tackled diplomacy from a theoretical rather than a purely practical perspective, can also be applied with validity to public relations. It will be seen, therefore, that public relations theories are linked to well-established philosophical positions not currently referred to in the standard literature in the field and, consequently, that public relations can be seen neither as unique nor neutral, as is often implied in standard texts. Rather its degree of disinterestedness is contingent upon any one of a range of specific philosophical positions that may be applied to it.

It should be noted that diplomacy is sometimes identified as an aspect of 'international theory', which is usually seen as falling within the field of international relations, also known as international affairs. In general I have used the term 'diplomacy' when I am discussing the practical application and role. However, in referring to broader theoretical issues I allude to international theory and when referring to schools of thought or the broad academic domain I make reference to international affairs or international relations following sources used. The emergence of public relations and diplomacy as fields of academic study is also briefly discussed, highlighting the conflicts which have arisen during the evolutionary process.

A METAPHORICAL APPROACH

Following organizational and communication literature and particularly Morgan (1986, 1989, 1993), I have chosen a metaphorical approach to public relations because I believe that it can offer a fresh perspective on emerging public relations theory and practice as well as allowing the subject to be usefully linked with a relevant body of theory and analysis. The use of metaphor helps one to explore similarity and difference and thus aids sense-making.

It is possible to trace a number of related functions in public relations and diplomacy in the existing public relations literature: rhetoric, oratory, advocacy, negotiation, peacemaking, counselling, intelligence gathering. There appear to be three orders of function here: representational (rhetoric, oratory, advocacy), dialogic (negotiation, peacemaking), advisory (counselling). The function of intelligence gathering describes research and environmental scanning and underpins the issues management function. This is a very interesting function because it carries with it connotations of a military function carried out at least partly secretly (L'Etang 1996). The representational functions acknowledge self-interest and suggest strategies of promotion and persuasion. They also imply processes of planning and impression management, and possibly a degree of rigidity in terms of maintaining one's own position.

The dialogic metaphors, those of negotiation, peacemaking and, to an extent, counselling, imply some degree of neutrality or objectivity. This seems to be linked to public relations' aspiration to professional status and its desire to sanitize its generally sleazy image: there is a substantial qualitative difference in terms of status and respectability between a 'spin doctor' and a 'corporate diplomat'.

Public relations as counsellor explains the advisory role to management. In diplomatic circles the post of counsellor is a senior embassy post, junior to minister or ambassador but senior to the first secretary. Another potential metaphor that can be derived from this terminology is a legal one, since 'counsel' is a British term for a barrister or advocate, as in 'Queen's Counsel', and 'counselor' is the American term for a lawyer, particularly one who conducts cases in court. Both imply the 'asymmetrical' advocacy role. Examples of how this may be represented in the literature emphasize the advisory role; for example, 'Advice on the presentation of the public image of an organisation' (Black and Sharpe 1983: 19), 'Advise management on policy' (Wilcox et al. 1986: 7) and the very term originally promoted by Bernays (1955), 'PR Counsel'.

Clearly these various functional approaches to public relations practice may not necessarily be applied in isolation from one another and several might be used in the course of a relationship, but the strategy adopted at any one moment builds in different assumptions about the nature of the relationship between sender and receiver and this, in turn, will affect the quality and process of subsequent communication acts. Sensitivity to such issues is clearly important to public relations but difficult to express in a single definition or mission statement.

Many definitions of public relations are all-encompassing, including both advocacy and mutual understanding within the same framework. A seminal article on the many definitions by Rex Harlow (1976: 34–42) set an unfortunate precedent for those that followed, in that the article at no stage makes clear whether definitions are descriptive or normative – he does not distinguish these as different orders of definition, neither does he attempt to classify these in any way. The effect of all this is that public relations definitions are apparently constructed in an attempt to be all things to all people simultaneously.

CORPORATIONS: THEIR POLITICS, DIPLOMACY AND DIPLOMATS

At a personal and functional level there are clear similarities in the work of diplomats and public relations practitioners. Theoretical support for this comes from various studies in communication which highlight the stressful 'boundary-spanning' role of both parties, which sees them crossing cultures (whether organizational or national) and bridging cultural gaps. Both parties have interpretative and presentational roles and both attempt to manage communication about issues. Both diplomats and public relations practitioners conduct much of their business via the media and are media-trained to provide appropriate 'sound-bites' on the issues of the day. In communications literature, the political role of organizational diplomats is recognized:

> there is now a substantial level of international business diplomacy.
>
> (Fisher 1989: 407)

> numerous large organisations today explicitly act in a political manner and see themselves as doing so.
>
> (Cheney and Vibbert 1987: 188)

The political role for diplomats and public relations practitioners has come to depend increasingly upon the management of public opinion. Conventional diplomats have long recognized the power of public opinion and the diplomat Sir Harold Nicolson credited Richelieu as being the first to do so, realizing that 'no policy could succeed unless it had national opinion behind it' (Nicolson 1954: 51). According to Nicolson's interpretation, Richelieu also recognized the concept of 'opinion leaders' or 'opinion formers' since he sought to 'inform, and above all to instruct, those who influenced the thoughts and feelings of the people as a whole. He was the first to introduce a system of domestic propaganda' (ibid.: 51–2). Richelieu wrote and circulated pamphlets which were intended to educate and 'create a body of informed opinion favourable to his policies' (ibid.: 52).

Techniques of political communication are therefore fundamental to the diplomatic role. While the term 'diplomacy' normally implies a political role and context, its application to the organizational context reveals a number of insights. First, it implies a specific interest in power-broking at an elite level; and second, it implies the need for representative agents (Mitnick 1993: passim).

Organizations are active in seeking to influence national and international political decisions in their favour and also to manage the way in which issues are perceived and media agendas set. Cheney and Vibbert suggest that organizations are faced with a dilemma, in that while they act politically and consciously develop their own political goals they also have to

> direct political influence without being identified as political groups. They must proclaim political messages without at the same time being represented as political bodies in the discourse of other corporate and political rhetors.
>
> (Cheney and Vibbert 1987: 188)

It is also in organizations' interests to identify their opponents as political actors in order to position them both as ideologically motivated and as solely self-interested (ibid.), which is surely what lies behind pejorative terms such as 'activist groups', 'single-issue publics', 'social activists'. Such groups are often presented as being the reason why organizations need public relations.

Organizational politics targeted externally is conducted through the public relations specialities of public affairs, issues management and lobbying. The ambitions of practitioners to lay claim to strategic high ground in terms of their own political positions within organizations can match the needs of organizations for reliable agents or diplomats to act on their behalf. Mitnick argues that corporate political activity is thus a game of agents in a democracy which can be seen as a system of competition as to whose agents will govern and which goals of which principals those agents will seek to advance (Mitnick 1993: 1). It is clear, however, that some principals have more resources than others and can therefore buy more or better agents than others, so that a free-market system will invariably favour some actors over others. It may also be argued that the creation of a corporate political elite which is effectively shadowing legitimate accountable political elites, both national and international, is a move which leads not only to an institutional domination of the public sphere (see chapter 3 for a review of this concept) but also to the creation of a particular elite culture sharing privileged information and thus power. Since elite persons and groups are always 'newsworthy', the chance of these groups being able to shape communication and political agendas is considerable. Organizational agents negotiate space for the organizational mission partly through the symbolic management of meaning. This influence may not always be obvious: the agents may effectively be secret, as is argued in Gandy's (1982) analysis of source-media relations and 'information subsidies'.

While one is likening the collectivity of an organization to a country in adopting the diplomatic metaphor, it is a truism that many multinational organizations are economically as big as or bigger than small or developing countries. However, they are not as accountable politically. Although they are ostensibly limited by national and international law, the relationship between themselves and governments is one of collusion; governments are highly dependent upon industries and industry agents can use government agents as their own to secure their ends. In other words, the relationship between government and business elites may lead to the formation of a wider diplomatic culture within which an extended chain of agency relationships exists; these agency relationships may not be formalized or even recognized.

At a practitioner level, there is only limited anecdotal evidence that the term 'corporate diplomacy' is beginning to creep into use. Perhaps this is the result of aspiration and status-building to compensate for a lack of professional status and a desire to highlight 'important' elite aspects of the work that may help to distinguish public relations from marketing. The trade journal *PR Week* described the current Director-General of the British Nuclear Industry Forum as 'every bit the corporate diplomat' (*PR Week* 1993: 16). The Director-General described his own role thus:

> I think the real role of a public affairs PR person like myself is to act as a catalyst, helping corporations play a much bigger role in setting the agenda of our society. That's what I call corporate diplomacy. That's my mission.
>
> (ibid.: 16)

It is interesting to speculate about the degree to which public relations practitioners, as they take the first steps along the road to professionalization, share such sentiments. Certainly, views expressed at professional meetings such as the UK Institute of Public Relations (IPR) Conference appear to be based on the assumption that the role of public relations is to act on behalf of business against the interests of activist groups. For example, one speaker at the 1995 IPR Conference declared that business was 'too nervous' in dealing with pressure groups. He also suggested that whereas businesses relied on 'cool description' in their communication strategies, the 'direct action industry . . . started by Greenpeace' relied on 'emotion and religious effects'. These views, which were not questioned by those present, could be seen as part of the norms and values of the occupational culture.

If we turn to the diplomatic field, it is clear that Nicolson saw the evolution of shared values between diplomats as significant in the political process. He points out that officials in capitals around the world had similar levels and standards of education and similar peripatetic lifestyles, and that they shared objectives. Often, members of this international diplomatic corps had served in the same foreign capitals together. In short, they shared a professional culture and camaraderie which, according to Nicolson, meant that

> They desired the same type of world . . . they tended to develop a corporate identity independent of their national identity . . . they all believed, whatever their governments might believe, that the purpose of diplomacy was the preservation of peace. This professional freemasonry proved of great value in negotiation.
>
> (Nicolson 1954: 75)

The precise delineation of occupational culture is beyond the scope of this chapter, but the concept is important in considering its effect on the overall political and social system. I am not, of course, suggesting that public relations practitioners only work for business – clearly they do not – but I am suggesting that the dominant coalition, both in academia and in practice, who see the role as a management function are 'buying in' to a particular worldview that excludes certain questions from being asked. In short, the key question is: 'What kind of "professional freemasonry" is developing and what social and political costs and benefits result?'

LITERATURE

Public relations and diplomacy

Considering the degree of at least superficial similarity between the roles of diplomacy and public relations, there has been little discussion comparing the two functions. What there has been has focused on the role that public relations, specifically in its media relations role, can play in facilitating diplomacy and international relations rather than focusing on the role itself.

Indeed, on the specific topic of public relations and diplomacy I have traced only three sources (Traverse-Healy 1988b; Grunig 1993a; Signitzer and Coombs 1992),[1] two of which (Grunig 1993a; Signitzer and Coombs 1992) are academic journal articles. I shall be giving most attention to the journal article (Signitzer and Coombs 1992), which attempts to analyse the conceptual relationship between public relations and diplomacy. The authors note the lack of attention given to diplomacy by public relations academics and observe that the main focus of public relations texts which tackle 'international public relations' is purely practical, focusing on the problems which arise for multinational organizations in communicating with multinational publics. The article identifies a gap in public relations literature arguing that

> How nation-states, countries or societies manage their communicative relationships with their foreign publics remains largely in the domain of political science and international relations. Public relations theory development covering this theme has yet to progress beyond the recognition that nations can engage in international public relations.
>
> (Signitzer and Coombs 1992: 138)

Another way of approaching this is offered by writers in international relations, two of whom have pointed out that the revolution in communications and technology means that nation-states can also be seen as activist groups:

> A senior British practitioner, the diplomat Brian Crowe . . . argued in an academic journal recently that 'in our new global village and with the spread of *intermestic* issues . . . domestic opinion on domestic matters in individual countries is becoming more and more a matter for concern to others.[2]
>
> (Hill and Beshoff 1994: 223; italics mine)

Therefore the scope of diplomacy and public relations becomes broader as technology facilitates communication across national frontiers and creates more publics. This approach is well reflected in Traverse-Healy's paper (1988b), which provides a practitioner's perspective and documents a number of international examples of politicians and governments achieving credibility and influence with foreign publics through careful impression and media management.

Signitzer and Coombs focus on the concept of 'public diplomacy' or the way in which activist groups (which they define as including governments as well as pressure groups) influence public opinion to shape a government's foreign policy decisions, rather than on 'traditional diplomacy', which, they suggest, 'conjures up images of nation-states sending formal documents to other nation-states' (Signitzer and Coombs 1992: 138). In particular, Signitzer and Coombs show how public diplomacy may be used to exert an influence on foreign audiences 'using persuasion and propaganda' (ibid.: 138) through the dissemination of political information via the news media, which is designated the 'tough-minded' approach. The alternative, traditionally referred to as cultural diplomacy, is designated the 'tender-minded' approach, which, through the use of cultural, educational and artistic exchanges can transmit 'messages about lifestyles, political and economic systems and artistic achievements'. The authors argue that in the 'tough-minded' approach

> Objectivity and truth are considered important tools of persuasion but not extolled as virtues in themselves . . . the supreme criterion for public diplomacy is the raison d'état defined in terms of fairly short-term policy ends.
>
> (ibid.: 140)

The article goes on to contrast the 'tough-minded' approach with information and cultural programmes, the aim of which 'is not necessarily to look for unilateral advantage'; rather they 'must bypass foreign policy goals to concentrate on the "highest" long-range national objectives. The goal is to create a climate of mutual understanding . . . truth and veracity are considered essential, much more than a mere persuasive tactic' (ibid.: 140). Signitzer and Coombs proceed to compare the motivation of these two 'schools' of thought with the four models of Grunig and Hunt (1984) and to argue that basic concepts and motivations are shared.

While both Signitzer and Coombs and Traverse-Healy acknowledge overlap between the fields of public relations and diplomacy, their respective analyses fail to uncover deeper similarities between the two occupations in terms of international and national political structures and competition. Traverse-Healy comes closest to this where he acknowledges that 'international competition between states is comparable to commercial competition between business organisations in one national setting' (Traverse-Healy 1988b: 3). This interpretation, however, heavily underplays or negates the political role of business organizations and fails to acknowledge the degree to which economics and politics are intertwined.

I would argue that Signitzer and Coombs's review of public diplomacy, especially cultural diplomacy, implies a de-formalization of diplomacy and the involvement of non-governmental organizations and their personnel in the diplomatic process. They argue that the purpose of such exchange is 'mutual understanding' (a phrase which used to be part of the British Council's mission statement). However, their argument here is dependent upon one key source, Mitchell, a professional cultural diplomat whose distinguished career saw him reach Assistant Director-General level of the British Council and whose analysis is thus necessarily from the perspective of a participant-observer. While Signitzer and Coombs suggest that cultural relations has a 'nobler goal, that of information exchange' (Signitzer and Coombs 1992: 142), which is broadly equated with that of Grunig and

Hunt's (1984) symmetrical communication, they fail to explore the implications of this position in the context of international relations or the degree to which national goals may really be adjusted. The relationship between traditional diplomacy and cultural diplomacy remains under-explored – for example, the funding arrangements between central government and cultural agencies may be crucial in determining the 'real' goals of the latter, which could be considerably more tough-minded than the publicly expressed statements of such organizations. Signitzer and Coombs's presentation of cultural organizations emphasizes artistic and academic exchanges rather than the scientific, medical, technical and language work that many such organizations carry out. Increasingly, too, such agencies are having to prove their worth, and this might increasingly be linked to trade agreements.

Another difficulty in Signitzer and Coombs's analysis is an underlying but unacknowledged instrumentalism which is at odds with their stated aim to explore conceptual links between 'the' (sic) public relations models and ideas drawn from public or cultural diplomacy. While on the face of it the authors seem to be exploring shared concepts in public relations and diplomacy, they demonstrate a concern for 'what works' and for whether the tough- or tender-minded school 'function[s] best' (Signitzer and Coombs 1992: 141). The authors' definitions of and assumptions about what is best or ideal are not stated. The heavily deductive approach becomes clear towards the end of the article, where it is stated that

> the exact ideas/concepts which can be transferred from one area to the other have yet to be fully delineated and tested . . . researchers should test which concepts best transfer . . . Only a series of theory-based empirical studies will facilitate this convergence of research traditions.
> (ibid.: 145–6)

Grunig's article addressing diplomacy and international affairs sets out to 'analyse the effects and ethics of . . . international campaigns and derive recommendations for how public relations can contribute to global diplomacy without obfuscating or corrupting the process' (Grunig 1993a: 139). It is argued that asymmetrical and unethical public relations has been 'prevalent in international public relations throughout history' (ibid.: 147) with a view to influencing political events and public opinion. Asymmetrical public relations is associated with, if not actually defined as, propaganda: 'The terms "promoters, propagandists, and lobbyists" seem to describe the press agentry, two-way asymmetrical and personal influence models of public relations, respectively' (ibid.: 149). This view presents a role for public relations of facilitating international relationships which are 'ethical'. Grunig does not define what is meant by 'ethical', but it looks as though it is the dialogic aspect of symmetry which makes communication moral rather than immoral.[3] Grunig's view is that

> when practised symmetrically, public relations is a valuable component of the public communication systems of a country and of the world . . . If public relations is practised according to the principles of strategic management, public responsibility and the two-way symmetrical model, it is an important element of the global communication system.
>
> (Grunig 1993a: 149)

This quote clearly indicates the importance given to the role of public relations in influencing the political architecture. The role for public relations can be seen as influential and interventionist in national policies. Depending on one's political position, one's culture and the case in hand, such intervention might not 'obfuscate' or 'corrupt' (ibid.: 130) international communication but it clearly is intended to effect change and influence public relations practice in one way rather than another. We must surely ask ourselves: 'what is the fundament of this position and what does it imply both for public relations and international relations?'

If international relations is the discipline which tries to explain political activities across state boundaries (Taylor 1978), it is difficult to see how public relations can be entirely separated from this. Public relations is profoundly concerned with the establishment and maintenance of the reputation and credibility of client organizations and this is done explicitly to maintain the client's ability to influence key publics and to be identified by the media as a contributor to debate on particular issues. Furthermore, as has been noted, governments themselves employ such techniques – though in this case these are sometimes referred to as information or propaganda.

Development of the discipline of diplomacy

Literature on diplomacy falls within the field of international relations, which is a relatively new area of study in itself. There is some potential confusion in the terminology since the terms 'international theory' and 'diplomacy' are sometimes used interchangeably, as are the terms 'international affairs' and 'international relations'. The term 'international theory' is used to define the theoretical as opposed to historical or applied aspects of the field of international relations, and the term 'international relations' may be used metonymically to stand as representative of any of these more specialized aspects. The inconsistent use of terminology appears to arise from continued debate over the definitions and boundaries of the field, a feature shared by public relations, where analogous discussions dispute the relationship between public relations, public affairs and corporate communications. I shall continue to refer to the specific role of diplomacy but in the remainder of the chapter will reflect the literature and refer to theories of diplomacy and international theory interchangeably, following the sources used in the discussion. When discussing the emergence of diplomacy as an area of study I shall do so largely under the umbrella term of international relations because this describes the academic area and degrees awarded by universities.

Within the field of international relations there has been surprisingly little theoretical work specifically on diplomacy. Diplomacy, it seems, is only interesting insofar as it contributes to specific political decisions or crises and is treated descriptively rather than analytically. It is not, therefore, seen as a field of study in itself, but as a technique used to achieve certain ends, similar in some respects to a marketing view of public relations. Such work as there is on diplomacy is very much of the 'how to do it' variety, a feature it has in common with public relations. *Satow's Guide to Diplomatic Practice* (Gore-Booth 1978), first published in 1917, is still used by the British Foreign and Commonwealth Office and describes in great detail diplomatic customs and precedent but contains no theoretical debate. The other key British source is Nicolson, who again adopts an uncritical approach, asserting that the 'essence' of diplomacy is common sense (Nicolson 1954: 50, 132, 144), a view apparently shared by a number of public relations practitioners. A theoretical study of public relations or diplomacy must go beyond practical guidance and consider the motivations, values, beliefs and conventions of the practice, its organizational and social effects, as well as the underlying assumptions and political configurations that go along with these practices.

Important common ground is shared by international relations and public relations partly because they are relatively new fields of study and relate to clearly defined areas of practical application. There are a number of common concerns: the relationship between academics and policy-makers or practitioners; debate over the purpose and appropriate orientation of the discipline; debate over epistemology and methodology; and questions of ethics. Some of these similarities confront any new discipline: questions of boundaries, legitimacy, credibility and methodology. Other similarities arise from a response to similar intellectual currents; for example, systems theory was important to international theory in the 1970s. By the 1980s systems theory was not a significant force and academics in the field responded to work developing in anthropology and psychology and became focused on debates emerging around structuralism, critical theory and postmodernism. Public relations appears to have become fossilized at the systems theory stage and academics seem to find it difficult to escape the totalizing net of systems theory. Even ideas taken from different intellectual traditions, such as critical theory, are used to support a systems perspective (see chapters 7 and 8 for detailed discussion). Interestingly, the aspect of Habermas's work which has received most attention from public relations academics, that of the Theory of Communicative Action, has also been the focus of interest in international theory, the two possibly unconsciously sharing a motive to

> reinscribe the emancipatory potential within IR [PR] – both as a discipline and a social practice. Much of this work is informed by Habermas's arguments regarding communicative rationality as the basis for discourse ethics which allows the uncovering and construction of 'truths'.
>
> (Hoffman 1994: 38)

The relationship between academics and practitioners is debated in both international relations and public relations (see chapter 1 for a discussion of the issue in relation to public relations). Because both areas are practice-based it can be difficult for academics to obtain access to certain types of information or activity regarded as politically or commercially sensitive. The relationship between academics and practitioners may be difficult because of their differing perspectives on the purpose of the discipline. One very eminent academic in the field of international relations, Christopher Hill, Montague Burton Professor of International Relations at the London School of Economics, identified the following key questions arising from the relationship between academics and practitioners in international relations:

- How far do academics and policy-makers define problems in the same way? Can the theoretical debate about competing 'paradigms' illuminate policy choices?
- Do decision-makers increasingly rely on outside sources of expertise, whether technical, historical or regional?
- Is theory, as Friedrich von Hayek once suggested, the ultimate source of power because new ideas promote change?
- Do International Relations academics take too many cues from politicians? What are the proprieties which should govern the agenda and conduct of research?
- How can academic findings be conveyed to the world of action? Is the indirect route (i.e. via scholarly publication) enough, or should knowledge be mobilised through the use of media, conferences and political contacts?

(Hill and Beshoff 1994a: 4)

These questions have considerable resonance in public relations and are at least beginning to be properly aired; White and Blamphin's study (1994), which is reviewed in chapter 1, was the first attempt to draw out some of these issues in a UK public relations context.

Hill presents a dichotomous choice for academics between the role of popular commentator and that of traditional academic. He argues that the existence of this choice means that the academic world of international relations is divided between the 'ivory-tower' academics and those actively involved in contemporary affairs. This picture is reflected in the nature and scope of professional and academic journals, which can largely be divided between those that are policy-driven and those that are academic. In the light of the International Public Relations Association's recent (1994) decision to include an 'academic' section in its journal on a regular basis, it is salutary to note Hill and Beshoff's comments on similar attempts to encompass both perspectives in the international relations arena, where they refer to publications which 'work heroically back and forth across the divide . . . respected by all, but followed by none' (Hill and Beshoff 1994a: 7).

Hill and Beshoff rightly point out the dangers posed to academics by pursuing the latest *Zeitgeist* or by overdependence on research funded by policy-makers:

> The point is not that scholarship should not respond to major changes in the world; it is rather that the opportunity costs of so doing are not always appreciated in terms of the atrophying of important but suddenly unfashionable areas where the lack of expertise may indeed be keenly felt once the wheel eventually turns again in their favour . . . academics [may] become, almost without noticing it, reactive to the initiatives of others, rather than pursuing their own professional concerns, which would otherwise intersect with policy issues only occasionally . . . Creativity is thus attenuated . . . It is difficult indeed to free oneself from the pressures and conventional wisdoms of one's own time. But that is exactly what is supposed to characterise a good academic; the ability to pursue an independent line of thought.
>
> (Hill and Beshoff 1994a: 8)

The debate over the degree of mutual involvement and shared focus between academics and practitioners which has been articulated in international relations is only just beginning in public relations, but it is clear from the views articulated that similar themes are emerging. Indeed, one could see the very concept of 'a research agenda' as typifying practitioner rather than traditional professional academic concerns. (See chapter 1 for further discussion of these points.)

The debate over the purpose of a discipline involves broader epistemological, metatheoretical and methodological issues which are only just beginning to be addressed in public relations. Assumptions that academics are there to service industry tend to lead to positivistic thinking and the application of the scientific method. To date there has not been a great epistemological or methodological debate in public relations but it is hard to believe that this state of affairs can continue for much longer.

Another area of convergence for public relations and international relations lies in a number of ethical and political issues which arise from a number of their practitioners servicing large and powerful collectivities. The questions about the relative rights and responsibilities of these collectivities and their relationships to their citizens and publics takes international relations and public relations into the realms of political philosophy; and thus requires those writing in these fields to deal with questions of ideology, something that some practitioners might prefer to remain between the covers of books. Like their cousins in public relations, practitioners in international relations would much prefer to believe that their work and decisions are scientifically based and value free, and they may be supported in such beliefs by the more positivist and instrumentalist academics in their respective fields.

The development of both subjects within academia shows interesting similarities. Both subjects can trace their 'roots' back to classical literature – in the case of diplomacy to Thucydides' *History of the Peloponnesian War*, Machiavelli's *The Prince* and *The Art of War*; in the case of public relations useful reference can be made to Aristotle's *The Art of Rhetoric*, and Plato's *Gorgias* and *Phaedrus* (see chapter 7 for a discussion of *Rhetoric* and *Gorgias*). The first Chair in International Relations in the UK was created at the University of Aberystwyth in the 1920s. The first Chair in Public Relations in the UK was created at the University of Stirling in 1993 but was still unfilled when this book went to press in 1996 because of the shortage of candidates fulfilling academic as opposed to professional criteria. The early years of both subjects were marked by uncertainty and hostile debate over the extent and role of the areas under review. Critics claimed that International Relations was not a subject in its own right because it lacked unity of knowledge and depended on many other disciplines. Not only were the boundaries of the international relations discipline in dispute but it was claimed that there were 'no obviously valid theories nor self-evident methods of obtaining them' (Taylor 1978: 8).

A bitter methodological debate then ensued between the Traditionalists, who argued that accurate prediction was impossible in international relations and who produced explanations centred on concepts of power and national interest, and the Behaviouralists, who advocated that all assumptions should be clearly spelt out and only empirically verifiable hypotheses should be produced. The field expanded dramatically post-World War II, fuelled by the Cold War and work in strategic studies focused on case studies, computer modelling of game theory, theories of deterrence, theories of crisis management and an increasing amount of action research by peace researchers. There are some similarities to be noted here with regard to public relations, for example the use of case studies both as a teaching tool and as a research method and a clear overlap in subject matter in the area of crisis management. Both public relations and diplomacy deal in trust and use strategies of negotiation and impression management while guarding the reputation of their clients. Thus it can be seen that diplomacy and public relations are comparable occupations and have certain similarities in their development as disciplines. The degree to which they share common problems in terms of theorization and justification will be explored in the remainder of this chapter.

JACQUIE L'ETANG

THEORIES OF DIPLOMACY – WIGHT'S FRAMEWORK

One of the few examples of a substantial attempt to theorize about diplomacy was made by Wight in the 1950s. His series of lectures at the London School of Economics (LSE) have remained a landmark although there have been few attempts since to develop such work further. Wight's approach was that of political philosophy and he pursued it in defiance of the Behaviouralists, who 'sought a kind of theory that approximated to science' (Wight 1991: x). The Behaviouralists sought to exclude moral issues from the subject matter of international relations on the grounds that they lay beyond the scope of scientific behaviour, whereas Wight placed these questions at the centre of his enquiry (ibid.: x).

Wight conceptualized diplomacy as consisting of three main approaches in terms of diplomatic style and underlying assumptions about political intercourse and international society. Wight identified these three positions as Machiavellian (characterized as pragmatic but one-sided), Grotian (after Hugo Grotius, the Dutch diplomat, whose *De Jure Belli et Pacis* was published in 1625 and whose style of diplomacy was moderate negotiation) and Kantian (diplomacy based on the sentiments expressed in Kant's *Perpetual Peace*, published in 1795 and which basically argued that the human condition could only be overcome by belief that it had the potential for transformation). Somewhat confusingly he also referred to these three types of diplomacy as Realist, Rationalist and Revolutionist. These positions did not have rigid boundaries and occasionally collapsed into one another. Wight's method was to analyse historical ideas and events in relation to political philosophy in order to reveal the fundamental sources of the positions adopted.

The Machiavellian or Realist position was based on the assumption that international politics was equal to international anarchy and that each state should therefore pursue its own interest in a free-market Hobbesian world where the only relationships that count are those based on contract. The authority, dignity and coherence of individual states was emphasized at the expense of any concept of international society or the suggestion that the state is a member of a wider society of states (Wight 1991: 33). In other words, the Realist sees international relations as an arena for competition and conflict rather than a society. The Realist assumes that interests will conflict and that the intelligent position to adopt is therefore that of the application of pressure and the offering of inducements in pursuit of one's own interests. The approach is supported by assumptions that the world is constantly in flux and transformation, that people and states are driven by fear and greed, and that the sensible way to respond is to use all the techniques of bargaining to negotiate from a position of strength. The characteristic Realist response to political change can be summed up as 'adapt, forestall, facilitate and control', and the basic quality for a diplomat is argued to be that of adaptability to change (ibid.: 189). The following quotation could easily be from a public relations book on issues management: 'the capacity to adapt oneself to change is the minimum diplomatic requirement. A higher achievement is to anticipate change, to see the dirty weather ahead and avoid it or outflank it' (ibid.: 190).

The Machiavellian or Realist position is clearly represented in the public relations literature. This position is clearly self-interested and seeks to persuade publics to fall into line and governments to accommodate organizational interests. In this there are similarities with much of the writing on issues management, where military terminology is readily used. It assumes a hostile, difficult, changeable and competitive world in which strategic alliances and sympathetic agents are sought out to enhance the organizational position. The specific public relations role is to secure 'the willing acceptance of attitudes and ideas' (Black 1989: 7); the public relations person must be a 'professional persuader' (Hayward 1984: 3). The approach might be characterized by the title of Edward Bernays's book *Engineering Consent* (1955). Hiebert acknowledged directly that 'too much public relations is Machiavellian' (Hiebert 1966: 317). The approach is also rhetorical in its focus on the persuasive function and the intention to seek and develop arguments that will persuade publics to change their views in line with organizational wishes.

The Rationalist or Grotian tradition focuses on continuous international and institutional intercourse based on concepts of mutuality. The Grotian style was based on building relationships through truthfulness and promise-keeping, which helped to build a good reputation for reliability and trustworthiness. Diplomacy is seen as something akin to commerce and international society is defined as the sum of customary (and often commercial) exchanges. It acknowledges, therefore, that there is something called international society but that its form is distinct from that of a state. The principle of reciprocity is important and was used to justify colonialism, which was argued not to be pure philanthropy but of reciprocal benefit (Wight 1991: 79). The paternalistic concept of trusteeship was also important. Both these arguments are of a similar nature to those often employed in the justification of corporate social responsibility (see chapter 6 for a detailed discussion of this concept). The position of enlightened self-interest raises problems, in that it presupposes that you can estimate the interests of other parties. This problem is clearly shared by public relations practitioners claiming to be working in the public interest. The Grotian or Rationalist tradition emphasizes enlightened self-interest and reciprocity and can be likened to claims in the public relations literature which emphasize mutual understanding as an organizational goal. Much literature emphasizes that the role of public relations is to achieve mutually beneficial acts for both organization and public. Leading writers (Grunig and Grunig 1990) have latterly been recommending 'Negotiation, collaborative mediation' as the prime role in two-way public relations. Grunig goes so far as to claim that 'the two-way symmetrical model bases public relations on negotiation and compromise' (Grunig 1993a: 146) and it is clearly an important element of his approach. It is an appealing ideal, emphasizing dialogue, truth and 'win/win' end-states, but possibly underplays negative outcomes such as lying and manipulation, defence–attack spirals and so on. It also ignores the possibility of organizational hegemony and the domination of the public sphere.

The third tradition, that of the Kantian or Revolutionist, is based on the assumption that the multiplicity of sovereign states form a moral and cultural whole. This whole is imbued with an authority which transcends that of individual states but which, in a somewhat Rousseauian way, represents the will of the people. It conceives of an international society comprised of a world-state empowered by individuals in a world where nation-states have diminished influence. Concepts of ideological homogeneity and doctrinal imperialism (whether Stalinism or capitalism) are of importance in the creation of an international citizenship. International tension is seen as an irrational obstacle to the fulfilment of human potential and the assumption is clearly made that existing national governments manipulate public opinion to their own ends.

The Revolutionist or Kantian approach emphasizes a peacemaking approach in which the public interest is served by a world order which limits the influence of nation-states. In public relations this is represented by the strong emphasis on public relations' potential to achieve transcendental mutual satisfaction and understanding between peoples. For example, J. Carroll Bateman, President of IPRA in 1980, 'referred frequently to public relations professionals as "peacemakers" of world society.. He appropriately did so in recognition of public relations' value and importance to world peace in facilitating communications and understanding between the governments and the publics that constitute nations' (Black and Sharpe 1983: vii). The late DeWitt C. Reddick, Dean Emeritus of Journalism and Communications at the University of Texas at Austin, called public relations 'the lubricant which makes the segments of an order work together with the minimum friction and misunderstanding' (ibid.: vii).

This type of aim and argument seems clearly linked to the Revolutionist tradition and it raises similar questions over what counts as peace or mutual understanding and who defines this. The approach may lead to the complacent imposition of traditional orders with little space for those who wish to deviate from the accepted norm. The following quotations give examples of perceptions of the peacemaker function in public relations:

> In the two-way symmetric model, finally, practitioners serve as mediators between organisations and their publics. Their goal is mutual understanding between practitioners and their publics.
>
> (Grunig and Hunt 1984: 22)

> I believe the more we understand one another, the more we will reduce the chances of war, or terrorism, and of man's violence against man. Fortunately, public relations can aid us in that understanding.
>
> (Hiebert 1988: 1)

> Public relations must be a two-way activity and is all about creating both goodwill and understanding.
>
> (Hayward 1990: 4–5)

> Public relations serves society by mediating conflict . . . PR plays a major role in resolving cases of competing interests in society . . . Blessed are the peacemakers.
>
> (Black and Sharpe 1983: vii)

> Public relations . . . should be ethical in that it helps build caring – even loving – *relationships* with other individuals and groups they affect in a society or the world.
>
> (Grunig 1992: 38)

These idealistic goals are utilitarian, in that they maximize happiness, but in instances of irreconcilable difference between organization and public it is likely that organizational interests will prevail. This is not to say that majority interest is not taken into account, but it may only be considered to the degree that is prudent for the organization. In such circumstances the notion that the aim of organizational public relations is to create goodwill, understanding and peace suggests that the concept of what constitutes goodwill, understanding and peace may be determined principally by the organization. There is also something slightly unreal and a little sinister in the idea that agreement can always be reached and that this is a desirable state of affairs. Given that public relations largely represents organizations, it seems that the potential for individual or minority interests may be compromised. In short, I am suggesting that the very notion of symmetry or understanding can be doctrinally imperialist.

Another characteristic which can be found in justifications offered for public relations and which can be interpreted as Revolutionist thought in action is that of the public relations obsession with democracy. Arguments in public relations literature highlight the contribution that public relations makes to 'democracy', in terms of enhancing the free flow of information in society. It is significant that the nature of this 'democracy' is never clearly articulated and defined since public relations very clearly enhances the flow of subsidized institutional information. It may claim to 'serve the public interest by providing a voice in the public forum for every point of view, many of which would not otherwise be given a hearing because of limited media attention' (Hayward 1990: 4–5).

The implications of this view are that public relations facilitates the articulation of various and possibly conflicting points of view and also manages to increase the media's attention span. However, in reality the public relations industry clearly does not take upon itself responsibility for ensuring that all views are heard – it simply represents those who pay for its services.

IMPLICATIONS

At a societal level there are clear overlaps between public relations and diplomacy since they both have to do with concepts such as power, negotiation, coercion, manipulation, propaganda, principal, agent, publics and public opinion, with issues management and lobbying functions bearing perhaps the closest relationship to diplomacy. Cultural or 'soft' diplomacy could be likened to corporate social responsibility.

Thus the three positions identified by Wight can be identified in the public relations literature. The Machiavellian or Realist position overlaps with both the 'Press Agentry' and 'Asymmetrical' models. The Grotian or Rationalist position overlaps with the 'Public Information' and 'Asymmetrical' models. The Kantian or Revolutionist position seems to have strong similarities with the 'Symmetrical' model. These overlaps suggest that the problems of public relations are not unique but relate to particular views about the way the world operates and how collectivities, whether organizations or countries, ought to behave. The overlap also suggests that the public relations models should not be presented as some discrete form of historical development; on the contrary, they relate to existing but heretofore unacknowledged, unresearched roots. They arise from a particular interpretation of events leading to the evolution of the public relations industry in one country (the United States), but it is not self-evident that they have the normative power often ascribed to them. The presentation of historical development as necessarily logical and progressive has long been controversial and a matter for intense debate.

The 'Symmetrical' or Revolutionist position is the one of most interest here because the meaning and implications of this position have not been exhaustively debated. Symmetry is presented as being a noble (and more effective) organizational goal which can result in peaceful coexistence. The question that is neither raised nor answered is 'What kind of peace do you want?'[4] Symmetry implies an open form of negotiation, something that Nicolson criticized in his historical sweep of diplomatic practice, where he argued against Wilsonian democracy and its imposition on international practice because transparency inhibited genuine negotiation as it led to posturing and propaganda speeches for media consumption. Furthermore, Nicolson suggests, Wilson's view of the conduct of international relations was both naive in its understanding of human nature and imperialistic in its imposition of American doctrine.

The claims made for the potential of symmetrical public relations are quite substantial: 'Symmetrical public relations would eliminate most ethical problems of international public relations. More importantly, it would make public relations more effective in producing international understanding and collaboration' (Grunig 1993a: 162). The argument seems to imply an extremely powerful role for public relations advisers in the international scene while underplaying the strong desire for gain of those involved in international relations.

Revolutionist doctrine in international relations posits an international state or community which can override nation-states. Symmetrical doctrine in public relations does not currently propose an equivalent body which can override organization-states. The implications of the convergence of public relations theory and international theory may be that we have to rethink our concept of organizations, organizational goals and organizational boundaries. Public relations and diplomacy both deal with an ensemble of interpenetrating relationships and overlapping publics, principals, agents and cultures in a social world which is the product of creative human activity undergoing continuous transformation. For these reasons it is important to see diplomacy and public relations in structural contexts which have the potential for change. Of crucial importance is the relationship between international society and the State, the status of corporate actors in these contexts and the perception of these by public relations practitioners. It seems that the diplomatic function of public relations is to perform a political role on behalf of organizations in national and international society.

In theoretical terms I am arguing that the concept and implications of 'symmetry' in public relations theory has been insufficiently delineated and justified. It is said that the symmetrical approach is both ethical and effective, but these terms are not fully unpacked. The definitions and practice of symmetry are presented as unproblematic, and the social and political impact of the approach is not explored. Drawing the contrast between the frameworks of Wight and Grunig demonstrates some theoretical convergence but also shows that the critical implications of symmetrical thought are more developed in international theory than in public relations theory.

It is also clear that in international theory the Revolutionist (symmetrical) position implies fundamental change in political architecture but the potential for transformation is not explored in public relations theory. This raises a problem for the public relations theory where there seems to be a tension between achieving the goal of symmetry and retaining existing structural and organizational frameworks. The concept of 'symmetry' has implications for the potential disintegration of organizations as we know them and their possible transformation as they reintegrate in some different form.

Public relations and diplomacy negotiate with publics on behalf of principals. The ways in which each is conducted and the aims they profess to have are based on particular positions about how organizations should be organized and how they should relate to one another, and the extent to which they should order our political and social affairs, both nationally and internationally. Through 'boundary-spanning', the functions of public relations and diplomacy also have a role in maintaining boundaries and thus in protecting the status quo. This was represented symbolically in diplomacy between the fifteenth and nineteenth centuries, when on occasion European princes met each other at the centre of a bridge and spoke to each other through a stout oaken lattice (Nicolson 1954: 38). The attempt to participate in or define symmetrical public relations threatens those boundaries and raises the prospect of an as yet undefined but rather different organizational and political life. What could be described as the 'pax symmetrica' is itself based on the imposition and acceptance of a particular worldview of common sense, and is thus intrinsically hegemonic in that one overall framework may be applied and the potential for disagreement may be restricted. For example, Heath (1992: 318) sees the value of public relations as 'its ability to contribute to the collective shared reality that brings harmony, a shared perspective that leads people to similar compatible conclusions'. Because there is so little content to the concept of 'symmetry', the term appears to have become a euphemism for 'good'. 'Symmetry' appears to offer liberation and free expression simultaneously, but it is also a potentially totalitarian ideology.

This chapter argues that public relations should properly be considered in tandem with international relations, not simply because it performs a (publicity) function in the process of diplomacy and international relations, but because it is linked to fundamental positions about the way individuals organize themselves into collectivities (whether publics or nations), form identities and relate to other collectivities. Assumptions about what is considered appropriate in organizational and international intercourse and about the rights of organizations and nations to define and fulfil their destinies are as important as the communicative acts that are undertaken in the name of those represented.

Finally, this chapter reveals shared normative conceptions with ideas in international theory. These frameworks and the intellectual currents they sprang from are a rich potential source for public relations academics which will enable them to connect public relations with what will surely come to be recognized as an associated discipline, international relations.

3

PERFORMANCE IN POLITICS AND THE POLITICS OF PERFORMANCE

Public relations, the public sphere and democracy

Brian McNair

INTRODUCTION

Seventy-five years have passed since the publication of Walter Lippmann's *Public Opinion*. In it he heralded the coming of a new age of opinion management, in which 'the art of creating consent among the governed' (Lippmann 1954: 245) would be developed beyond anything seen before in the political organization of human affairs. Lippmann was right, and as we approach the end of the century 'consent creation' has become an integral part of the political process.

Those professionals whose services are employed in the creation of popular consent for the actions of government (or those who aspire to govern) go under a variety of names – 'news managers', 'spin doctors', 'minders' and 'media gurus', to name but four in current usage. Although many of the best known, such as Sir Bernard Ingham and Tony Blair's media adviser Alistair Campbell, come from careers in journalism, they are all engaged in the business of public relations, where the politician is the client and the electorate is the public. And as Ingham showed repeatedly during his time as Margaret Thatcher's Press Secretary, their role in the political process is one of the most pressing issues facing the still-emerging profession of public relations.

For some, public relations is a wholly legitimate, indeed essential, input to modern politics. For others, the development of political public relations has signalled the sinister corruption of democracy. Among the conditions required for authentic democracy to exist, it is argued, is a knowledgeable electorate, supplied with objective information on which rational choices about politics can be made. Public relations is the antithesis of rational discourse, insofar as it represents the conscious management of opinion, image and symbol.[1]

This essay examines the relationship between public relations and democratic politics, as they are pursued by parties and governments in both the domestic and international arenas. At its end, we shall hope to have provided some contribution to answering the question: 'Is public relations a necessary element of contemporary political performance or simply another stage in the degradation of our political life and culture?'[2]

A SHORT HISTORY OF PUBLIC RELATIONS

In *Public Opinion* Lippmann observed that the communication of political information to the citizenry was more or less constrained by four factors: censorship, secrecy, media bias and selectivity, and the ability of citizens to assimilate and assess information rationally. Consequently, 'the common interests very largely elude public opinion entirely, and can be managed only by a specialized class whose personal interests reach beyond the locality' (Lippmann 1954: 310).

This 'specialized class' of opinion managers were referred to by Lippmann as press or publicity agents, and by Edward Bernays as public relations counsellors. To them fell the task of making sense of a complex world, initially for the journalists and then, through the media, for the people. As Bernays put it in his classic text *Crystallizing Public Opinion*, the public relations counsellor had to 'isolate ideas and develop them into events so that they [could] be more readily understood and so that they may claim attention as news' (Bernays 1923: 171).

By the 1920s, when these 'founding fathers' of public relations were writing, a sizeable industry of opinion managers already existed in the United States, employed largely by the big corporations to represent their interests before a public becoming increasingly educated and politically active. In the early years of the twentieth century, with expanding suffrage and trade union organization, the big coal, steel and transport corporations were finding it necessary to pay increasing attention to how their activities were reported in the media and to the views of politicians in Congress. As the rapacious activities of the 'robber barons' were forced to adapt to such newfangled ideas as corporate responsibility and workers' rights, the new profession of public relations played a key role in securing positive media coverage, with all that that meant in terms of congressional lobbying and industrial relations. For example, when the steel industry was affected by strikes shortly after the World War I, the public relations profession contributed significantly to the manufacturing of 'Red Scares' designed to portray striking workers as dupes and agents of the Communist Party and the newly established Bolshevik state in Russia.

If such 'propagandistic' activity was not representative of public relations as a whole, the success of these and other campaigns in managing US corporate image and identity was soon noted by politicians, who proceeded to import the techniques and methods of corporate public relations (as they were later to adopt commercial advertising techniques) into their governmental and campaigning activities. President Wilson established a federal

Public Information committee to manage public opinion during World War I. In 1928 the Democrats became the first political party to set up a permanent public relations office, with the Republicans following suit in 1932.

Campaigns Incorporated, based in Los Angeles, became the first political public relations consultancy in 1933, since which time the industry has expanded throughout America and the rest of the democratic capitalist world. Now, as we enter the twenty-first century, it is axiomatic that no serious contender for public office can afford to do without the services of his or her 'spin doctor' or media adviser. Once the politician is in government, the role of the political public relations specialist becomes even more important, as the careers of Bernard Ingham in Britain, and Pierre Salinger and Richard Wirthlin in the United States show.

What, then, does political public relations do? To answer that question we will consider examples drawn from both the domestic and the international political arenas.

POLITICAL PUBLIC RELATIONS IN PRACTICE

Political public relations, like other branches of the profession, has proactive and reactive dimensions. On the one hand (whether contracted or in-house) it seeks to initiate change in such variables as public opinion, voting behaviour and journalistic agendas. On the other it reacts to events with potentially negative consequences for the organization, limiting the potential damage which may occur. It may also be involved in the effort to prevent certain information from reaching the public domain. We shall discuss each aspect of 'consent creation' in turn.

Parties and public relations

The history of party political public relations in the post-war period is one of gradual recognition by the clients (the parties) that they no longer inhabit an environment in which interpersonal communication matters all that much. If parties wish to win government, to govern effectively and to retain power, they must successfully communicate their messages to a mass electorate through the media. The few examples of interpersonal political communication one now sees, such as John Major's 'soapbox' performances in the 1992 general election campaign or Tony Blair's Clause Four campaign of early 1995, are constructed largely as media spectacles, for the purpose of swaying a far wider audience than those in the actual proximity of the politician at the time when he or she is performing.

The rise of Tony Blair marks the final stage in the British Labour Party's full and uninhibited acceptance of public relations as a tool of opinion management. The British Conservatives, on the other hand, did so almost as soon as television became a truly mass medium, as did the Republicans in the United States. Parties of unapologetic, aggressive capitalism both, the Conservatives and the Republicans were, unsurprisingly, well attuned to the power of television to sell ideas and programmes, as well as commercial goods and services, to mass audiences. An early success in this respect was Richard Nixon's 1952 'Checkers' speech, in which he rescued his vice-presidential candidacy, and possibly his future career as president, by appealing directly to the American public, through television, and saying that he was innocent of political corruption charges (Checkers was the name of the dog claimed by Nixon to have been his only political gift). In Britain, a successful early employer of public relations was Harold Macmillan, who pioneered the manufacturing of what Daniel Boorstin called 'pseudo-events' (Boorstin 1962), such as Eisenhower's 1959 visit to Chequers (Cockerell 1988).

While Macmillan and his successors in the Conservative Party were at ease employing the services of commercial public relations companies to shape public opinion in their favour, Labour (notwithstanding some early successes in political advertising engineered by Tony Benn) harboured, throughout the 1960s, 1970s and early 1980s, an ideological commitment to 'authentic' political discourse. This was paralleled by a distrust of the opinion management industry and a reluctance to be guided on matters of style and presentation by anything so tainted with capitalist principles as a public relations agency.

Although Labour won three elections after the (as yet never to be repeated) landslide of 1945, all under the leadership of Harold Wilson (who, despite the party's overall reluctance to adopt public relations techniques, displayed an instinctive feel for the sound-bite and the photo-opportunity), the Conservatives won seven, under four different leaders. While one should of course be cautious in attributing a party's electoral performance to the skill (or incompetence) of its public relations and other campaigning efforts, few would dispute that Labour's post-war defeats have been in large part failures of presentation, as exemplified by the disaster of the 1983 campaign, when the party lost 25 per cent of its voting share. Leader Michael Foot, formidably intellectual but lacking elementary dress sense and political nous, became the butt of merciless abuse from Conservative and SDP opponents, while the party's managers failed to prevent senior figures arguing in public with each other, rather than the opposition, about what Labour policy was or should be (McNair 1989).

The trauma of the 1983 defeat, and the success a little later of Ken Livingstone's Greater London Council in persuading largely Conservative voters that they should support Labour's campaign against abolition, provoked Labour's national leadership into a fundamental overhaul of their political communication strategy. In 1985 former television producer Peter Mandelson became head of the Campaign and Communications Directorate, and shortly afterwards the Shadow Communications Agency was formed.

The new structure sought to encourage coherence and presentational skill both in public campaigning activities and in the internal communications which underpinned the public effort (Shaw 1993). By the late 1980s, and not without resistance from many on the left, Mandelson and his colleagues had succeeded in transforming Labour from a doggedly 'cloth-cap', 'grim-up-north' social democratic party into a (post)modern, communicatively adept organization. In the 1987 and 1992 election campaigns, the Conservatives frankly acknowledged the superiority of Labour's efforts in this regard.

Labour lost on both occasions, however, so was it worth it? As this essay went to press, the answer appeared to be a tentative 'yes'. Following the 1983 defeat, and Labour's subsequent adoption of a communications strategy with public relations at its heart, the party slowly climbed back from the abyss of electoral oblivion to emerge, by 1995, as a credible government once more. With careful image and issue management, orchestrated by Mandelson, Philip Gould, Patricia Hewitt and others, Labour gradually reasserted its status as a 'natural' party of government. While it was far too early, in the first months of 1995, to predict which party would win the next British general election, Labour had for several months enjoyed historically high opinion poll ratings, far ahead of the Conservatives. The leader, Tony Blair, and his close advisers had moved on from the progress made during John Smith's leadership to reposition Labour as a government-in-waiting, seizing back from the Conservatives terms – such as community, responsibility, patriotism – which had since 1979 been associated with Thatcherite values. While the symbols of 'new Labour' and the debate around the future of Clause Four were not substitutes for worked-out policies and a coherent election manifesto, they were – most observers agreed – a successful first step towards Labour usurping the Conservatives' post-1979 hold on government.

Public relations in government

The proactive public relations pursued by parties as they campaign for election (or re-election) represent the visible, truly *public* dimension of political communication. Much political public relations work remains hidden from public view, however. Aware that information, and access to it, is a power resource, parties in government have become enthusiastic custodians of a vast machinery for suppressing, censoring and at times falsifying information which, it might be thought, the citizenry of a democratic state has a right to receive in relatively unadulterated form. In this respect the British government, in both its Conservative and Labour variants, has been an exemplar amongst western democracies, developing over the decades an especially secretive system of information management (if compared, for example, with that in the United States).

The relatively closed system of information management enjoyed by

British governments dates back to the 1911 Official Secrets Act, passed to censor information about the Boer War. This was supplemented by the establishment of an Official Press Bureau to control information about World War I, from which time the British state has operated on the principle of secrecy rather than disclosure (Cockerell et al. 1984). Ever since the 1914–18 war governmental media management (as opposed to the actual censorship of information on national security grounds) has grown increasingly sophisticated.

The apparatus comprises three institutions: the Government Information Service (the centre of the civil service public relations machine), the Central Office of Information, which supplies the press and broadcast media with 'the spine of each day's news agenda' (ibid.: 59), and the Meeting of Information Officers (MIO) a committee accountable to the Cabinet and which contains the senior public relations officers in Whitehall. The head of the MIO is the Prime Minister's Press Secretary.

In the post-war period two developments affecting the Whitehall public relations system have been particularly notable. First, as governments have grown increasingly conscious of the importance of media relations and public opinion, the 'quality' of the personnel employed to carry out the key public relations functions has increased. Second, the information organizations – technically part of the civil service and thus politically neutral – have been politicized to suit the needs of the party in power. Both processes culminated in the government of Margaret Thatcher (1979–90), and the figure of Bernard Ingham in particular. By the end of Thatcher's time in office her press secretary Ingham had centralized the Whitehall information management system under his own control, and thus that of the Prime Minister, to an unprecedented degree, becoming by 1989 head not only of the governmental public relations apparatus (the Meeting of Information Officers), but also of the Government Information Service, with its huge advertising budget. So great was Ingham's power perceived to be that he became known as the 'Minister of Information', a title accurately reflecting his authority and influence, as reflected in the many occasions when he dispatched opponents of Thatcher from the Cabinet.

At the same time, under the Thatcher–Ingham regime an ever-larger portion of information services and resources were devoted to the business of 'selling' key government policies, such as the privatization of gas, telecommunications and other nationalized industries, and to conducting covert propaganda campaigns against pressure groups like the Campaign for Nuclear Disarmament. While Ingham strongly denied any suggestion that his role as the government's public relations manager was different in kind from that of Joe Haines (Harold Wilson's Press Secretary) or other successful occupants of the post (Ingham 1991), by November 1989 even former Conservative Cabinet minister Nigel Lawson was accusing him of using 'black propaganda techniques' (quoted in Harris 1991: 176).

Perhaps the most distinctive and idiosyncratic aspect of British governmental public relations is the institution known as 'the Lobby', established informally in 1884 and officially recognized in 1929, since when it has been the principal means by which a Prime Minister may communicate, over the heads of his or her Cabinet ministers, directly to the country's media. The Lobby comprises those correspondents of the main media organizations accredited to cover parliamentary affairs. In regular meetings with the Prime Minister's Press Secretary and those of ministers they are kept informed not only of what the government is doing and when (a necessary organizational function on which the media depend), but also of the 'spin' which they are to adopt on particular issues and events. Through the Lobby, in short, the Prime Minister can seek to manage the political news agenda.

The system is complicated somewhat by the fact that, although all the Lobby correspondents know who the ultimate source of their stories is, they must agree not to name that source, thus preserving the politician's 'deniability' should a story backfire and generate negative publicity. Failure to honour the agreement on non-attribution means expulsion from the Lobby and a media organization's consequent inability to cover major political events at firsthand.

Detractors of this system, of whom there are many, argue that it amounts to a form of blackmail against journalists, who must go along with the use (and abuse) of the system by Prime Ministers to conduct Machiavellian political intrigues, precisely as Bernard Ingham and Margaret Thatcher were accused of doing on several occasions. While the news releases and statements of US presidents are often publicly made and open to question, live on national television, the British Prime Minister can fall back on the confidentiality of a statement if it looks like generating unwelcome controversy. It also weakens the independence of the Cabinet and centralizes power in the Prime Minister's office, 'enabling Number 10 to impose its interpretation of events on the news' (Harris 1991: 76).

Lobbying

A different kind of lobbying, and one of considerable importance to the integrity of politics, is that which made British media headlines in 1994, amid accusations of 'sleaze' levelled against the Conservative government and its supporters in Parliament. Following revelations that several Conservative MPs (in 1995 peers were similarly accused) had accepted financial payments in return for asking questions in the House of Commons, the governing party was compelled to defend itself against charges of corruption and conflict of interest. While a certain amount of lobbying on behalf of extra-parliamentary groups (commercially or politically motivated) is not new, and is indeed wholly proper in a parliamentary system, here it was seen to be going beyond the boundary of acceptability. The issue, as Mark Hollingsworth put it, was simple: 'should elected public servants also be the paid advocates of outside organizations?' (Hollingsworth 1991: 22).

Organizing and facilitating corporate advocacy is one of the functions of political public relations companies, many of them run and owned by present and former MPs such as Michael Forsyth, Sir Marcus Fox and Keith Speed. In 1991 Hollingsworth estimated that there existed in the UK fifty political lobbying companies, with an annual turnover of some £10 million. Three hundred and eighty-four MPs had commercial interests, comprising 522 company directorships and 652 consultancies.

As the 'sleaze' scandals of 1994 showed, lobbying has increased since Hollingsworth's research, becoming, because of some key exposures in the press, a major political issue. Indeed, ongoing revelations of Conservative corruption have played a large part in the rise of the Labour Party's opinion poll ratings discussed earlier.

PUBLIC RELATIONS AND INTERNATIONAL POLITICS

The pursuit of politics takes place not only on the domestic stage, but also in the international arena, where nation-states vie for influence and advantage in territorial disputes, trade wars and access to scarce strategic resources. Here, no less and indeed perhaps more than in any other sphere, governmental action is premised on popular consent, if not necessarily always active support. Democratic governments which neglect such support, as the Americans did in Vietnam and the Russians in Chechnya, pay a heavy price. And domestic public opinion is not the only kind which matters. The media environment within which international relations are conducted is a global one, bringing images and information instantaneously to a planetary audience of billions. The speed and reach of contemporary news-gathering technologies have made diplomatic negotiation and the fighting of wars a public process, that public consisting not only of one's own and other countries' populations, but also of international actors such as the United Nations and the World Bank. As Edward Bernays put it more than seventy years ago, in words which are hardly less relevant today:

> governments act upon the principle that it is not sufficient to govern their own citizens well and to assure the people that they are acting wholeheartedly in their belief. They understand the public opinion of the entire world is important to their welfare.
>
> (Bernays 1923: 44)

In securing the consent of those publics in pursuing foreign policy, the activities of public relations professionals have become increasingly important throughout the twentieth century. We noted above that the origins of governmental public relations lay in the period just before and during World War I when, with growing suffrage and expanding media, the opinions of mass publics were beginning to matter. Then and since, governments have recognized the importance of manufacturing consent behind international policy (and military action especially) and have employed professionals to do so on their behalf. As Walter Lippmann put it in 1922: 'where masses of people must cooperate in an uncertain and eruptive environment, it is usually necessary to secure unity and flexibility without *real* consent' (Lippmann 1954: 238; italics mine). This, he noted, is done by the manipulation of symbols which can 'obscure personal intention, neutralise discrimination, and obfuscate individual purpose' (ibid.: 238).

In his or her capacity as the producer and disseminator of symbols which can contribute to the building of unity and consent around governmental policy, the public relations worker is, of course, a propagandist. The word is not used in this context as a pejorative term, which it has become in western democratic culture, but as a statement of the obvious: at times of international tension and conflict, governmental public relations becomes part of the state's wider propaganda effort, seeking to manage public opinion and permit what may be extremely difficult and potentially unpopular decisions to be taken.

Public relations professionals performed this function in both world wars, in both Britain and the United States. In Britain, for example, when the Soviet Union joined the western alliance against Hitler in 1941 government information officers played an important part in the symbolic transformation of the Russians from baby-eating, nun-raping Bolsheviks (which had been their officially encouraged image since 1917) to honest, hardworking sons of toil whom the British could happily fight alongside in the fight against fascism. Feature films and documentaries portraying the new image were made, and establishment figures such as Lord Beaverbrook were enlisted to reassure the people that the Soviets were allies and not class enemies.

Following the Allies' victory, of course, the reality of ideological conflict was permitted to replace the symbols of anti-Nazi unity, and western governments opened an anti-Soviet propaganda campaign which lasted, with varying degrees of severity, for more than forty years. I have written elsewhere on the origins of the Cold War, and how it was reflected in the British media in particular (McNair 1988). Here we will note that governmental publicity and information establishments on both sides of the Atlantic played key roles in manufacturing consent around an image of the USSR as the 'enemy', portraying the Soviet armed forces as overwhelmingly superior to those of NATO (always a ludicrous suggestion, but only acknowledged as such after the ignominious collapse of the Soviet Union), Soviet society as uniquely hostile to and contemptuous of human rights (while the United States and British governments cheerfully supported death squad juntas in Central and South America), and Soviet foreign policy as inherently expansionist (despite the rarity, if compared to the record of NATO countries, of Soviet military expeditions beyond the USSR's own borders in the post-World War II period). Insofar as these myths were prepared and circulated to the media by information officers working for military and governmental agencies, they were political public relations aimed at public opinion management.

The value of a public opinion which was solidly, if irrationally, anti-Soviet was obvious: to facilitate the US and its own allies' military interventions in the Middle East, Central America, Southeast Asia and elsewhere; to lend credibility to massive military programmes which, in the absence of a Soviet threat, had no rationale (a continuing public relations problem for the western defence establishment in the post-Cold War era); and to counteract domestic anti-nuclear sentiment, such as that represented by the British Campaign for Nuclear Disarmament. We have already noted that Bernard Ingham, as head of the Government Information Service in the 1980s, authorized anti-CND publicity to be carried out using taxpayers' money. In the early 1980s the British government was forced to abandon a £1 million anti-CND propaganda campaign after its existence was disclosed by the Liberal opposition. Since 1917, indeed, anti-Soviet propaganda, or 'public relations' as it was described by one American historian in the 1950s (Murray 1955), has been used frequently by western governments to combat domestic left-wing groups. In short, throughout the twentieth century governments have manipulated symbols of the enemy in propaganda wars directed against sections of their own people.

It is then fitting, given what we have said about the role of public relations in perpetuating it, that the process which led to the end of the Cold War – the policies of *glasnost* and *perestroika* implemented by the Soviet government in the late 1980s – was largely public relations-led. As I have described in detail elsewhere (McNair 1988, 1991) Mikhail Gorbachev's international campaign to halt the arms race and his domestic campaign for reform were battles for public opinion. Gorbachev successfully employed – for the first time in the Soviet context – many of the techniques of political public relations familiar to western governments, such as live news conferences, media briefings, public walkabouts and the manufacturing of pseudo-events. The acknowledged success of Gorbachev's efforts in this regard allows us to claim that public relations played a major role in overcoming the West's preferred image of the USSR as an 'evil empire', and thus in allowing the superpower rapprochement which had taken place by the end of the 1980s.

Public relations during wartime

One of the most striking developments of the post-World War II period has been the increased use of public relations in conflicts which, though not necessarily 'wars of national survival', nonetheless present governments with potentially fatal (for them) problems of opinion management. When a state is threatened with annihilation, as was the United Kingdom in the 1939–45 war, populations are likely to endorse the information policies of their governments, even when these involve disinformation and secrecy, since such evils are correctly judged to be outweighed by the necessity of defeating the common enemy. In limited wars, however, of which there have been many in the post-war period, governments are required to be more sensitive to public opinion and the media serving it. As Mercer et al. note, 'in a limited war, the relationships between politicians and the media will be particularly sensitive; the government's interest will not necessarily be construed as identical to the national interest' (Mercer et al. 1987: 161). The importance of public opinion in this context is further heightened as each advance in news-gathering technology makes the reportage of war more immediate and compelling for the domestic audience. When war becomes, indeed, media spectacle, beamed live around the world by CNN or the BBC, those who conduct it cannot afford to ignore the views of their citizens. Consequently, public relations has become an increasingly important instrument of warfare, managed in the big armies of the western powers by echelons of military public relations officers.

In conflict situations military public relations personnel use the full battery of proactive and reactive techniques to shape media coverage. Proactively, 'enemies' must be constructed in the public imagination, whether they have an objective reality or not. Hence, the Americans manufactured the 'Gulf of Tonkin' incident in the early 1960s, alleging that a North Vietnamese warship had attacked a US boat in the area, to provide legitimation for what eventually became the Vietnam War. In the run-up to the Gulf War Kuwaitis in exile employed US public relations firm Hill and Knowlton to manufacture the 'incubator story', alleging that the Iraqi invasion forces in Kuwait City had removed new-born babies from their incubators and left them to die on hospital floors. Although there was no shortage of real atrocity stories concerning Saddam Hussein and his army, this one was false – 'black propaganda', as it was described afterwards[3] – invented to mobilize American politicians and public behind military action at a time when support for such action was still half-hearted.

Having manufactured public support for war, governments must then seek to manage media relations in such a way as to maximize positive coverage of the conflict. The experience of Vietnam, in which American journalists enjoyed relative freedom to roam the front lines and battlefields photographing and writing about whatever seized their interest, led to a much more restrictive approach in subsequent conflicts, since the images of war seen nightly on American television were blamed for the population's and the military's loss of morale. Media sociologist Daniel Hallin rejects the widely held view that Vietnam War coverage was 'anti-American' as opposed to merely reflecting splits in the US politico-military establishment on Vietnam policy (Hallin 1986). Nevertheless, it has been perceived as such, and this has strongly influenced the development of military public relations. The British in the Falklands, for example, used the geographical isolation of the war zone to limit the numbers of journalists covering the conflict and to censor closely the reportage of those allowed to accompany the military. In the Gulf War, too, the allies imposed strict conditions on journalists, herding them around the front line in 'pools' chaperoned by military public relations personnel. During the Gulf War, as in the Falklands (and in sharp contrast to the Vietnam experience), such restrictions meant that domestic audiences were not subjected daily to images of dead or dying soldiers, nor indeed of civilian casualties (Macarthur 1992).

In both conflicts, news-hungry journalists were supplied with a regular diet of 'good-news' stories. In the Falklands, British bombers were reported to have destroyed an important Argentine-held airbase when they had not; and in the Gulf, global audiences were given a hugely exaggerated picture of the allies' success rate in air strikes against Iraq, reinforced by the video footage – shot by allied pilots – which led to the conflict being dubbed in some quarters 'the Nintendo war'.

No matter how skilful and all-embracing media management may be, however, governments at war are inevitably required to deal reactively with some bad news. In the Falklands the British had to manage the news of the sinking of HMS *Sheffield* and other setbacks which seriously threatened to undermine official images of Britain's military superiority and control over the Argentinians. In this respect, observers agreed afterwards, Britain did not have a good public relations war. The British policy of secrecy and minimal release of information adopted throughout the conflict led journalists to speculate, exaggerate and misreport important facts, which, had the Argentines proven to be more of a match militarily than turned out to be the case, could have been politically disastrous for the government.

In the Gulf War, again, the virtual absence of major setbacks for the allies meant that the military's reactive public relations was rarely tested. Only when an allied bomb struck an air-raid shelter in Baghdad, killing hundreds of Iraqi civilians under the noses of CNN, did any threat to the 'clean war' image of the conflict which had been prevalent up until then emerge. As it was, the allies' line that an unfortunate mistake had occurred was generally accepted.

PUBLIC RELATIONS, THE MEDIA AND THE DEMOCRATIC PROCESS

The emergence of public relations as a key specialism in the conduct and management of political affairs – at home and abroad – is not in dispute. What concerns observers and analysts, as we noted at the outset, is the impact which this development has had on the political process – in particular, on the ability of the citizen to receive objective information about politics and to act rationally upon that information. Does the increasing centrality of public relations in politics signal the inevitable professionalization of opinion management in a complex media environment, or does it lead inexorably to the manipulation of public opinion and the propagandization of public discourse? Does it contribute to or detract from the efficient functioning of democracy?

Not so long ago there was no need to pose such questions, since there were neither mass media nor citizens with political rights. Until the revolutions of the seventeenth century European societies were run as despotic autocracies, with absolute power residing in the (divinely ordained) personage of the feudal monarch. When, with the development of capitalism and the rise of a class which enjoyed economic wealth but not political power, notions of democracy, freedom and citizenship began to gain ascendancy, the extension of electoral rights to any more than a small minority of propertied, educated men was a slow, hesitant process punctuated by many bloody put-downs of popular protest. As Karl Marx noted in the nineteenth century (in terms which have remained relevant for women and ethnic minorities in many countries until well into the twentieth century), the concept of democracy was an ideological fiction designed to secure the political, and hence economic, domination of the bourgeoisie, while excluding from representation the great mass of working people. The bourgeois attitude to genuine democracy was best revealed, for Marx, in the massacre of the Paris Communards.

Whatever the reality of democracy in early capitalism, however, its normative principles as defined in the writings of More, Rousseau, Jefferson and others were clear. Against the background of recently deposed feudal overlords, democratic political systems would guarantee individual rights and liberties, and would give legitimation (mandates) to elected governments and prevent the abuse of political power by making government, as Jeremy Bentham put it, 'frequently removable by the majority of all the people' (quoted in Macpherson 1976: 35).

Among the conditions required for these benefits to accrue from democracy were, first, the participation of a substantial proportion of the people in elections and, second, the ability of these citizens to make rational choices between competing parties and candidates. This latter required, in turn, institutions for educating the people and a means of disseminating 'objective' information to them.

In the early phase of capitalist and liberal democratic development such conditions did not exist. In Britain and other countries there was no system of public education and no mass media. Voting rights were dependent on property, education and other qualifications, which thus excluded the vast majority. The 'public' referred only to a very small group consisting of the bourgeoisie and aristocracy. For this elite, early forms of print media began to perform the function of providing the information and analyses on which political attitudes and behaviour could be formed. In the mid-eighteenth century the term 'public opinion' began to be used, signifying the 'critical reflections of a public competent to form its own judgments' (Habermas 1989: 90). Politicians began to acknowledge the importance of public opinion, and a 'public sphere' emerged.

For Jürgen Habermas, the most influential theorist of the public sphere, the term refers simply to that 'sphere of private people come together as a public' (ibid.: 27) in the coffee houses and salons of late seventeenth- and early eighteenth-century London. There, and thereafter in France and Germany, fuelled by the expanding number of political journals and newspapers, these first citizens would debate public affairs, form opinions and exercise their political rights to influence government. While in practice, as already noted, access to this system was denied to the vast majority, it was in theory available to all with the required qualifications. In this sense it was, for Habermas, an institution (both in reality and in the abstract) bound up with capitalist social relations and class distinctions. The public sphere both reflected and contributed to the continuation of 'dominance by one class over another' (ibid.: 88). It served the interests of the bourgeoisie, while claiming to represent the public as a whole.

Yet, in articulating a liberal philosophy of universal access (irrespective of how divergent from reality the ideal was) bourgeois democracy contained within it the potential for a more authentic, truly representative system of politics and government. While some (mainly Marxist) critics of liberal democratic government doubted its capacity ever to function as anything other than a 'committee of the ruling class', an alternative view, expressed in the work of Antonio Gramsci and his neo-Marxist followers, stressed the possibility of extending mass participation to the point at which the liberal ideal was transformed into real, popular democracy – a system in which the people as a whole, rather than a bourgeois minority, would enjoy meaningful powers and rights.

The genuine democratization of bourgeois politics would be, from this point of view, the result of a process of struggle for access to the system fought by the organizations of the labouring masses – their trade unions and political parties. And indeed, the nineteenth and twentieth centuries have witnessed many successful examples of such struggles, up to and including the final winning of citizenship rights by the black people of South Africa in 1994.

But the potential for real democracy has also arisen, it is clear, from the need of capitalism for an ever more educated, technically proficient workforce and from the fact that to secure legitimacy bourgeois parliaments have had from the outset to acknowledge the rights of the masses, even if these were withheld. As capitalist industry increased its technological sophistication in the eighteenth and nineteenth centuries and societies became more disciplined and organized, the expansion of education was essential. With education came literacy and the growth of mass-circulation print media, followed then by popular agitation for, and eventual access to, citizenship rights for a growing proportion of the people. By the early twentieth century governments found themselves confronted, for the first time, with *mass* publics, forming their collective opinions in an expanded public sphere comprising first print media, then radio and eventually television.

For Habermas, and others who have been influenced by his account of the development of the public sphere, what might appear to be a progressive movement towards 'true' democracy has been impeded by the changing nature of the public sphere itself. As media expanded in the nineteenth and twentieth centuries they evolved, Habermas argues, from institutions for the rational public discussion of political affairs into privately controlled, privately motivated organs. The press became profit-making businesses, editors became the tools of proprietors, newspapers became 'the gate through which privileged private interests invaded the public sphere' (Habermas 1989: 185).

At the same time as the public sphere was being privatized, and media outlets increasingly concentrated in the hands of a few individuals and conglomerates, it was expanding rapidly and moving from the servicing of public opinion to the management of it. While the extension of suffrage gave public opinion an enhanced role in legitimizing and checking political elites, the expanding public sphere provided opportunities for the management and manipulation of that opinion. Thus, as advertising emerged to manage the process of commodity distribution, public relations became the means by which politicians could be represented in the public sphere and access the vote-wielding public.

Crucially, for Habermas, the nature of the evolving mass media, and the activities within it of the public relations industry working on behalf of political actors, transformed the public sphere from its original status as a forum for rational debate into an arena dominated by the values of entertainment and consumption. Parties began to organize themselves like businesses, marketing and 'selling' their ideas and programmes in the name of the public interest. The style of a political performance, shaped and honed by public relations, began to have more importance than the substance of policy. Henceforth, 'important political decisions [would be] made for manipulative purposes, and introduced with consummate propagandistic skill as publicity vehicles into a public sphere manufactured for show' (Habermas 1989: 221).

Equally pessimistic analyses can be found in the work of such as Nicholas Garnham, who argues that 'the rise of public relations [represents] the direct control by private or state interests of the flow of public information in the interest, not of rational discourse, but of manipulation' (Garnham 1986: 41).

From this perspective the early, bourgeois ideal of the public sphere has been corrupted by the commercialization and trivialization of mass culture and the increasing sophistication of the opinion management industry. The contemporary public sphere is comprised of ideologically biased, self-interested media on the one hand, and orchestrated by sinister public relations professionals on the other, rendering any belief in the authenticity of democracy hopelessly naive. Moreover, the argument continues, since the Thatcherite assault on that last bastion of the ideal public sphere – public service broadcasting – and similar movements towards the commercialization and deregulation of broadcasting in other countries, the process has accelerated.

The pessimism of such views is not universal, however. For American political scientist Stanley Kelley, writing more than forty years ago (when this debate was already underway), the 'problem' of political public relations was one which resulted from 'the closer approach of democracy to its ideal' (Kelley 1956: 219). From this perspective (shared, naturally enough, by the practitioners themselves) the rise of political public relations is the inevitable consequence of the process whereby mass media have become ever more central to opinion formation and political decision-making. Mass participation in politics is only possible, indeed, through the involvement of mass media, since with the best political will in the world, interpersonal forms of communication such as door-to-door campaigning, rallies and public speeches could never permit the level of contact between citizens and politicians which is provided by appearances on *The Jimmy Young Show*, *Question Time* or *Frost on Sunday*.[4]

An extension of this argument points to the possibilities of 'subversive' political communication opened up by the expansion of the media and their growing requirements for information. Early Marxism, as we noted above, viewed democracy and the media of capitalist societies as almost wholly tied to the interests of the economically dominant class. Opportunities for dissenting voices to be heard were so few as to be negligible in the overall scheme of things. Consequently, the primary definitions of public issues, as represented in the journalistic agendas of media organizations, tended to reflect dominant interests, thus contributing substantially to the ideological reproduction of capitalist societies (Hall et al. 1978).

As media outlets have proliferated, however, competition for audiences has required them to seek out information and events for transformation into news, current affairs and documentary. Moreover, increased competition puts a premium on 'scoop' journalism and the uncovering of information which challenges and threatens ruling groups. Both trends reduce the power of ruling groups to define issues and set the media's agendas. Subordinate groups may find themselves with increasing opportunities to have their issues, interests and definitions represented in the media.

Optimists and pessimists agree, however, that mediatization (if we may call it that) changes the nature of political discourse. Television studios, as Richard Nixon discovered to his cost in the groundbreaking live presidential campaign debates of 1960, throw a harsh light on the candidate. On that occasion Nixon's choice of suit (light grey, against a light studio background), the 'five o'clock shadow' on his face and the fact that he was a little underweight due to a period of illness contrasted sharply with the dashing figure of John Kennedy, suntanned, clean-shaven and dressed in a crisp dark suit. While the majority of radio listeners, according to opinion polls taken at the time, perceived Nixon to have won the debate on the issues, television viewers 'gave' the bout to Kennedy. Whether Kennedy's narrow victory in the 1960 election can be attributed to that incident or not, there can be no doubt that Kennedy *looked* better than Nixon and that this was judged – by voters, pundits and most subsequent candidates for high office in the United States and elsewhere – to have mattered. This perception, well founded or not, was real in its consequences, establishing the importance of image management – a key specialization within public relations.

Other aspects of media production have influenced the form and content of political discourse. The simple but inescapable fact that broadcast media can communicate less information than print, and that airtime is an extremely scarce and valuable resource, has imposed on politicians the need to craft their programmes and ideas into 'sound-bites' which can be slotted neatly into ninety-second news items. Failure to do this results in a lack of the news coverage on which contemporary politics depends. As Roderick Hart has observed in his trend analysis of US presidential rhetoric, 'the presidency has been transformed from a formal, print-oriented world into an electronic environment specialising in the spoken word and rewarding casual, interpersonally adept politicians' (Hart 1987: 14). The observation is equally true of executive leadership throughout the advanced capitalist world.

For Hart, and those who think like him, this development, and the many others encouraged by the emergence of the media at centre stage in politics, is almost wholly to be regretted. For Hart, as for Habermas, the increased role of the media, and of public relations professionals, has undermined the rationality of political discourse: 'What used to be a broad, bold line between argument and entertainment, between speechmaking and theatre, now has no substance at all' (Hart 1987: 152).

Political discourse, as Daniel Boorstin suggested in the early 1960s, has been reduced to a sequence of 'pseudo-events' manufactured for the purpose of attracting media – and particularly television – attention (Boorstin 1962). The professionals of public relations have become the image-builders, manipulators and event-manufacturers.

The leading postmodernist Jean Baudrillard adopts a different position in the debate – neither optimistic about the democratic potential of mediatized politics (and, within that, of public relations) nor pessimistic about its degenerative effects on the public sphere. In an essay published in the early 1980s Baudrillard accepts that the masses of advanced capitalism have become a 'silent majority', apparently passive and unwilling to participate fully in the process of government. This, however, is not a consequence of the narcotizing, cynicism-inducing impact of mediatized politics, but a conscious (if unarticulated) strategy of resistance to bourgeois political structures. For Baudrillard, as for Marx one hundred years before, liberal democracy is merely a symbol signifying the will of the people but falling far short of the 'real thing'. The people know this and resist incorporation into the ritual of participation, which they come to view (correctly) as mere spectacle. Despite the best efforts of political communicators (through advertising, public relations and other vehicles for the dissemination of political messages) at 'injecting them with information' (Baudrillard 1983: 25), the masses exercise the only real power which they have: the power not to participate and thereby to deprive the system of its legitimacy. As Baudrillard has it, this rejection is not 'a flight from politics, but rather the effect of an implacable antagonism between the class which bears the social, the political culture – master of time and history – and the un(in)formed, residual, senseless mass' (Baudrillard 1983: 38).

CONCLUSION

Notwithstanding the varieties of optimism, pessimism and nihilism which separate the perspectives described in this section, they have in common the positioning of opinion management, of public relations, at the centre of the political process. In assessing whether this is a good or a bad thing for democracy, I would like to end with the following observations.

First, the expansion of the media, and the enhanced role of public relations, has increased the quantity of political discourse routinely circulating in the public sphere beyond the most utopian dreams of the early democratic theorists. The *quality* of that discourse has also changed, undoubtedly, and not always for the better. 'Trivial' aesthetic judgements about style and performance have perhaps become more important to many citizens than one would wish. Yet, it is naively romantic to think that there was ever a 'golden age' of rational, objective discourse beyond the narrow elites of the early bourgeoisie. Mass democracy is inevitably *populist* democracy, in which appearance and image, as well as policy substance, have a role to play. To argue otherwise is to propose a return to the view of John Stuart Mill and the early classical theorists (Mill 1975) that only those with sufficient education should be permitted to have full voting rights.

Second, the dynamics of the contemporary media system have opened up the public sphere to many groups which were previously excluded. As British TV screens showed dramatically in early 1995, pressure groups – such as those active on animal welfare and the environment – can and do shape the news agenda, often forcing politicians to behave in ways they would not otherwise behave. Organizations such as Sinn Fein have also proven to be effective media managers, applying familiar public relations techniques with skill and innovation over a number of years (D. Miller 1994). Traditional left-wing notions of a capitalist media closed off to all but the representatives of dominant groups are clearly inadequate for explaining the diversity of the contemporary public sphere and the unpredictability of the media environment within which elites must operate. Limits to access remain, of course. Money continues to matter, since wealth buys (or should be able to) better public relations, and those with wealth thus have an in-built advantage on entering the contemporary media environment. Certain groups and individuals enjoy more status and credibility (from the journalistic viewpoint) than others, and thus have privileged access to the means of disseminating their views. But a knowledge of how public relations works, and the entrepreneurial skill to apply that knowledge, has never been the monopoly of the establishment.

What, then, of the wider, Habermasian view that public relations represents the illegitimate manipulation of public opinion, rather than the mere professionalization of its management? It seems enough to say that one citizen's persuasion will always be another's manipulation, one's public relations another's propaganda and that clear-cut distinctions can be drawn only with difficulty. Even where public relations is used unambiguously to make 'black propaganda', as it was during the Gulf War, we might wish to argue that the objective in that case – to unseat a modern fascist dictator guilty of genocide against his own people – was some mitigation (even if the ultimate motivation of the allies was economic rather than humanitarian). The ethics of using public relations in a particular context cannot be divorced from the ethics of the cause for which it is enlisted.

Public relations is like electricity and the atomic bomb. Having been invented, it cannot be uninvented. The public relations function is a necessary dimension of the modern political process, which has overall become more democratic, and not less, in the course of the twentieth century. The price of media-assisted mass democratic participation, imperfect as it is, is an enhanced tendency for politicians to seek to 'manufacture our consent'. Our best defence against such efforts is, as it has always been, to gain knowledge and understanding of the process (including, crucially, those aspects of it which the politicians would rather keep secret).

The media, it should be acknowledged, play their part in this by increasingly approaching public relations and news management as political issues in themselves, during and between the coverage of campaigns, in their exposure of cover-ups, in their routine rating of politicians' 'star' qualities. Public relations' age of innocence (assumed or otherwise), it might be said, is over, and the self-reflexive, meta-discursive era has begun. As citizens we should welcome that fact.

4

PUBLIC OPINION AND PUBLIC RELATIONS

Magda Pieczka

INTRODUCTION

This chapter aims to review the concept of public opinion and the research traditions in the field in order to discuss their relevance to public relations. The first part of the chapter concentrates on definitions and the development of public opinion research. The main focus of the second part is the concept of 'public' itself and the implications for public relations practice of the various definitions employed.

The literature on all aspects of public opinion with which this chapter is concerned is quite extensive; much of it is well known and often cited. The difficulty, therefore, is in balancing the requirements of a useful review accessing this literature for a public relations student against the danger of being merely repetitive. Oddly, while public relations literature demonstrates awareness of both the concept and the reality of public opinion it has not been very attentive to the debates in the field of public opinion research. This chapter attempts to fill this gap for students and to reflect on exactly why the concept of public opinion is relevant to public relations.

As in chapter 8, I have cited a substantial range of useful references to show the origins and development of the concept. The citation of sources is also intended to help the student see which concepts public relations writers have borrowed and which have become absorbed into public relations literature, sometimes without question. It should also be noted that the section on public opinion research assumes some familiarity with methodological terminology.

WHAT IS PUBLIC OPINION?

Traditionally, definitions of public opinion have been seen as falling into two categories: those which view public opinion as akin to Rousseau's 'general will'; and the majoritarian definitions in which public opinion is the opinion that matters, i.e. the majority opinion in a democracy (Price 1992: 13; Herbst 1993: 49).[1] The first type of definition derives from the work of the Enlightenment thinkers, such as Rousseau, who were preoccupied with the problem of how a state should be governed in the age when the institution of monarchy based on the monarch's divine right was gradually getting out of step with a society transformed by a range of economic, cultural and religious factors. This process of transformation, with its attendant rise of public opinion, is discussed in detail by Habermas, who conceptualized it as the rise of the 'public sphere' (Habermas 1989; Speier 1980).[2] Chapter 3 defines the concept of public sphere and discusses its relevance in considering the role of public relations in democracy.

From its beginning the concept of public opinion has been rooted in political science and it has remained so despite the extensive interest it has aroused throughout the twentieth century among sociologists, psychologists and communication experts. If one reviews the history of the concept, it appears to have been created in its early form by the English (Locke, Hume), then taken over by the French (Rousseau) and Americans (Madison), and again by the English (Mill, Bentham). The cross-Channel, indeed cross-Atlantic, nature of the endeavour can be easily explained by the timing of the political and social changes taking place in England, its American colonies and France from the 1640s to the mid-nineteenth century.

It is generally accepted that Locke's law of opinion or reputation is the first explicit recognition of the mechanism of public opinion. The philosopher worked on this, and other ideas contained in his *Essays Concerning Human Understanding*, in the 1670s, although it appeared in print for the first time in 1690. The work was inspired, perhaps very appropriately for the subject of public opinion, by a discussion with friends on human knowledge and principles of politics, which must have been influenced by the political struggle taking place in England. The next generation of thinkers developed Locke's ideas further: Hume, in his *Treatise of Human Nature* (1740), formulated his basic principle that 'It is . . . on opinion only that government is founded' (quoted in Noelle-Neumann 1979: 146); the principle was subsequently endorsed in 1788 by Madison in the Federalist paper No. 49 (ibid.: 146) as the basis for the emerging American democracy.

English politics was watched keenly from across the Channel in France, which around the 1750s started moving quite clearly towards 'a politics of contestation' (Baker 1990a: 168). Montesquieu, in *De l'Esprit des lois* (1748), admired the type of 'modern state, free and individualistic' (ibid.: 177) that England had become; and that was his inspiration for proposing the 'theory of separation and balance of powers' (ibid.: 173) which lies at the foundations of the modern democratic state. It is Rousseau, however, who is credited with using the term public opinion (*opinion publique*) for the first time, in his *First Discourse* (1750) (ibid.: 186).[3] For him, public opinion was a social rather than political phenomenon which could be defined as 'the collective expression of the moral and social values of a people, the shared sentiments and convictions embodied in a nation's customs and manners and applied in its judgements of individual action' (ibid.: 186).

This was very much how the phenomenon was conceptualized and used until the 1780s in France, when the definition changed and public opinion was no longer seen as the 'generalized social practice', but as

> the enlightened expression of active and open discussion of all political matters, the free exercise of the public voice regarding the daily conduct of affairs, the institutional remedy for the administrative secrecy and arbitrariness that was threatening France with despotism.
>
> (ibid.: 188)

It is impossible to overestimate the influence not only on the development of modern democracy, but also on the debate about public opinion, of the political storms of the late eighteenth century – American Independence and the French Revolution – with the role that constitutional debates played in them, and with the resulting declarations of basic philosophical principles, in the form of the Bill of Rights (1791) and the Declaration of the Rights of Man and Citizens (1789). Both declarations were based on the firm belief in the rational nature of men, the equality of all men and therefore their ability, and right, to govern themselves and their equals through a process of communal decision-making, whatever the particular structure of that process might be.

In the debates of the French National Assembly on the exact shape of the constitution to be adopted evidence can be found of strong interest in the current American and English solutions, but equally in Rousseau's social contract and the concept of the general will. In fact, the solution finally adopted in 1791 was a compromise between different opinions and factions. The 'Rousseauian principle of the inalienable sovereignty of the general will' (Baker 1990a: 303) was upheld: the constitution was not a pact between the king and the people, but an expression of the laws of the nation binding the king as much as any other citizen. On the other hand, the general will as a discursive process taking place in the Assembly was abandoned in favour of the practice of representation, in which individual wills had to be balanced, a solution that created a danger of subverting the general will by partisan interests. In the course of the deliberations many points were raised, such as whether the general will (i.e. the public opinion) can err and the clear possibility of the majority oppressing minorities in a representative form of government based on opinion – doubts echoed by later commentators and public opinion researchers.

A few decades later, within the context of rapid economic and social changes, utilitarian philosophers, most famously Mill and Bentham, provided ethical justification for the rule of majority. Their basic premise was that society consists of self-interested individuals, and a way of managing the unavoidable conflict was, in accordance with the general happiness principle, to govern by listening to the majority opinion.[4] It appears, then, that within roughly one hundred years public opinion evolved from being first conceptualized as the general will through a complex process of political, economic and social change in America, England and France into the widely accepted nineteenth century definition of public opinion as the opinion of the majority of citizens.

It could be argued that the writers whose ideas have been discussed so far concerned themselves with establishing the concept of public opinion and deliberating on how it was present in the principles and effort of government. However, as the practice of popular government was becoming well established, the critical interest turned perhaps more towards observing complexities and paradoxes of government and public life in democracies. This is not to say that the concept itself had become finally clarified and defined – in fact, this aim has yet to be achieved – but conceptual ambiguities were considered alongside the practicalities, or for that matter impracticalities, of the relationship between public opinion and democratic institutions.

One of the best-known and most quoted works of that nature is Bryce's *The American Commonwealth*, published in 1888. The author's insight is impressive and, despite all the technological and social changes of the last hundred years and the staggering amount of public opinion research published in the last sixty years, many of Bryce's points are easily compatible with the contemporary scientific knowledge in the field. For example, Bryce postulated a five-stage process of opinion formation which included elements such as – to use twentieth-century terminology – the agenda-setting role of the mass media, group influence, simplification of the opinion in the process of a 'yes' or 'no' electoral choice, and the apparent 'uniformity', meaning possibly generalizability, of public opinion, equated again with a vote outcome.

Equally interesting are Bryce's comments on definitions of public opinion:

> The difficulties . . . arise from confounding opinion itself with the organs whence people try to gather it, and from using the term to denote, sometimes everybody's views, – that is, the aggregate of all that is thought and said on the subject, – sometimes merely the views of the majority.
>
> (quoted in Berelson and Janowitz 1966)

This points to yet another type of definition in addition to the original historical distinction suggested at the beginning of this chapter. A useful discussion of the dilemma and a typology was presented by Herbst (1993), who proposed four definitional categories: aggregation, majoritarian, discursive/consensual and reification. The most common understanding of the term 'public opinion', that of aggregation, underlies polling, surveys, elections and referenda. It assumes 'that public is an atomized mass of individuals, each with a set of opinions' (Herbst 1993: 439) and consequently sees public opinion as the sum of opinions people hold. The majoritarian view also depends on counting individual opinions, but it assumes that opinions are not equal in weight. Earlier in this discussion we saw how it was decided in modern democracy that it was the opinions of the majority that counted. An important condition was added to this definition by Lowell, who believed that numerical supremacy was not sufficient in itself and that there had to be willingness on the part of the minority to accept the majority opinion as a binding solution (ibid.: 439). The discursive/consensual approach concentrates on the role of communication in the process of opinion formation. Similarly to Rousseau's, such definitions assume that public opinion emerges in the process of rational public discourse (Habermas). Paradoxically this approach can also focus on the censorial nature of such public discourse (Locke, Noelle-Neumann). Finally, the last type of definition is based on the assumption 'that public opinion does not exist at all – it is a reification or fictional entity' (Herbst 1993: 440). Lippmann expressed such a view in *The Phantom Public* (1925); as did Bourdieu (1979), who came at the problem from a Marxist perspective.

This typology represents the knowledge of some two hundred years of reflection before the empirical tools of public opinion were developed in the twentieth century, as well as the cumulative knowledge that sixty years of such empirical research has produced. The following section will provide an overview of public opinion research as a social-scientific activity and facilitate a sideways move to the consideration of some relevant aspects of public relations at a time when clear aspirations to a social-scientific status have been expressed in the field (Grunig 1992; Pavlik 1987; Broom and Dozier 1989).

PUBLIC OPINION RESEARCH

Writing in 1957 Lazarsfeld (1981) commented on the fierce antagonism in public opinion research since the late 1940s between the supporters of what he called the classical tradition and the modern empiricists.[5] Following Berelson, he defined the classical stage in the development of public opinion research as 'a general feeling that something called public opinion was important. As a result, prominent writers developed broad speculations about it' (Lazarsfeld 1981). Modern empiricists, in contrast, had been able to learn from earlier attempts at gathering empirical data, from debates about a suitable methodology and from 'intellectual neighbours' such as psychology and anthropology. This made possible a phase 'in which systematic propositions on public opinion [were] being developed: public opinion [had] become an empirical social science' (ibid.).

The turning point between these two traditions, or perhaps more appropriately stages in the development reminiscent of the different stages in the scientific of 'hypothetico-deductive' method, came in the 1930s. By that time attempts at opinion polls had become quite popular in America, but it was the success of the 1936 poll conducted by Gallup, Roper and Crossley which predicted 'the Roosevelt landslide' in the presidential elections that gave such a strong impetus to the survey approach (Converse 1987: S12).

Nineteen thirty-seven saw the publication of the first issue of *Public Opinion Quarterly*, which was founded by prominent academics who 'hoped to promote the scientific study of interrelationships among three potent new social forces: *mass opinion* . . . *mass communication* . . . and *public opinion measurement and reporting* . . . based on scientific sampling' (Beniger 1987: S46). The editors decided to dedicate the journal to these new social forces, which they summarized as public opinion, and to study them from 'the perspective of "scholarship, government, business, advertising, public relations, press, radio, motion pictures"' (ibid.: S46).

However, the journal did not develop quite in this way and a short digression here might provide a useful illustration of the development of the public opinion research in general. Davison, writing in the fiftieth anniversary special issue, commented on the long-term trends from such content analyses of the journal as were available. It appears that since the late 1940s the proportion of articles devoted to propaganda and public relations has steadily declined, while the number of articles either based on quantitative methods or devoted to their discussion has risen (Davison 1987: S6). There is, it seems, an interesting set of questions here for public relations researchers: was the journal's mission statement based on an overoptimistic assessment of public relations' potential for academic development, or was the early promise unfulfilled?; is there, perhaps, a completely different explanation capable of dealing sensibly with this apparent non-engagement of public relations with public opinion research?

What the above digression confirms is the empiricists' hold over the field of public opinion. This was by no means a unanimously applauded development. At the 1947 annual meeting of the American Sociological Society, Herbert Blumer presented a paper which articulated the nature of the disagreement between the two factions. The empiricists were criticized for a mistaken approach to the problem: they started from the premise that public opinion was what the polls measured rather than from a generic definition from which systematic propositions could be derived – in short, they reversed the accepted order of scientific enquiry, or at least seemed to have omitted an important initial stage. Their narrow instrumentalism could 'leave or raise the question of what the results meant. Not having a conceptual point of reference the results [were] merely disparate findings' (Blumer

1954: 71). It is fair to say that the other major criticism Blumer made referred to the practice of weighting all opinions in a survey equally, whereas in reality some opinions, he believed, were more important, or effective, than others. His own definition attempted to capture both the social dynamics of the process and its effectiveness: 'the character of public opinion in terms of meaningful operation must be sought in the array of views and positions which enter into the consideration of those who have to take action on public opinion' (ibid.: 73). Public opinion as defined by opinion poll outcomes appears out of its natural social context: because it captures only the views of disparate individuals, it appears static. Blumer's direct attack provoked equally direct responses, the main arguments of which as well as the flavour of the debate might be gathered from Newcomb's and Woodward's comments (Katz et al. 1954: 78–84).[6]

A way to reconciliation was opened in 1957 by Lazarsfeld (1981), who suggested that the empiricists had learnt from the classics and returned the favour, as it were, by sharpening conceptual tools that might allow further development of the classical ideas. Converse (1987) offered support to Lazarsfeld's views on the matter; and Noelle-Neumann's 'Public opinion and the classical tradition: a re-evaluation' (1979) provided an example of how modern research could both be inspired by classical writers and provide a scientifically backed reworking of their ideas.

So far this chapter has looked at the origins of the classical tradition and at the debate between the supporters of this tradition and the modern empiricists. It should be clear how the battle started and what it was all about, but what has not been explained is where the empiricists came from in the first place. Lazarsfeld gives the following account of the beginnings:

> The empirical tradition in opinion and attitude research began . . . in Germany with . . . laboratory experiments on problem solving . . . [then came] the work of the Chicago school of sociologists, which brought the study of attitudes and values into play . . . thereafter, the psychometricians . . . introduced the . . . problem of measurement.
>
> (Lazarsfeld 1981)

Another important early influence was the theme of mass society, apparent in the first issue of *Public Opinion Quarterly*. Beniger (1987: S46–S48) offered a succinct discussion of how the interest in mass society developed among American scholars. He pointed to the European influence, which reached America in the 1930s through translations of works such as Ortega y Gasset's *The Revolt of the Masses* (1930), Durkheim's *Division of Labor in Society* (1933) and Parsons's synthesis of the work of European mass theorists in *The Structure of Social Action* (1937), assimilating the work of Toennies and Weber into the English-speaking sociology even though the actual translations appeared in the US in the 1940s. Last but not least, the Frankfurt school moved to New York in 1933. Beniger, however, also pointed to the already existent American interest in mass society: Lippmann's *Public Opinion* (1922/1954) and *The Phantom Public* (1925); Bernays's *Crystallizing Public Opinion* (1923); Dewey's *The Public and its Problems* (1927); and Lasswell's *Propaganda Techniques in the World War* (1927).

The concept of mass society, in very general terms, grew out of the intense process of industrialization and bureaucratization, which were accompanied by increasing scepticism about traditional liberal values. The mixture of angst and exhilaration at the possibilities offered by this urban industrial civilization were vividly captured by Modernist art: alienated individuals in the midst of a mass of their likes, like the voice of T.S. Eliot's poetry; the Futurists' fascination with the city and the machine; the anarchy of Dada; and the bizarre alliance of ideology and the subconscious in Surrealism, to mention just a few examples.

> Born in this intellectual context, on the advent of world war involving several totalitarian states, the mass society model of public opinion formation and change continued to dominate the field for almost three decades [i.e. until the 1960s].
>
> (Beniger 1987: 345)

Central to this model was the belief that the mass media influence individuals, rather than people as members of social groups, and that such influence is direct. Similar assumptions, of course, underpinned the 'large-scale probability sampling model used in public opinion surveys' (Beniger 1987: S49), which could therefore be criticized for reducing social science to 'aggregate psychology', an argument offered by Coleman in 1964 (ibid.: S49). Klapper's intervention in 1960, 'codifying' (Katz 1987: SS6) the model of limited effects, turned the tide against the notion of the passive, atomized audience and the powerful media. The new trend coincided with communication studies being abandoned by sociologists and political scientists when it could no longer offer a theory clearly linking public opinion and mass communication (Beniger 1987: S50).

Despite mounting criticism, the direct effects model was not entirely discredited or abandoned. McQuail points to the arrival of television as a new popular medium in the 1950s and 'the revival of (new) left thinking in the 1960s' (McQuail 1987: 254–5) as being responsible for the return of the concept of the all-powerful media and consequently the view of 'public opinion as an effect of mass communication' (Beniger 1987: S51). The old model, however, was not just revived but also reworked. For example, Converse's work (1964) on the role of ideology in public opinion brought back the old doubts about the idealized picture of democracy and democratic citizens (Lippmann 1954: 38–9) at the same time as it led to a view of society as composed of overlapping issue publics. The agenda-setting approach, while accepting the limited effects of mass media, proposed that the media's power to delineate issues and their public presence or absence goes deeper than direct effects. The 'spiral of silence' went even further, to claim that in addition to setting agendas the media perform a kind of social-control function by constraining individual courage, as it were, to express unpopular views. Finally there is cultivation analysis, which defines mass media as the source of the ubiquitous, manufactured discourse (see Beniger 1987).

In the 1980s a paradigmatic shift in mass communication, which had started in the mid-1970s, became apparent. It can be summarized as 'a change in dependent variables from attitudes to cognitions, as a shift in independent variables from persuasive communication to less directed media processes ranging from "framing" through "discourse" to the social construction of reality' (Beniger 1987: S52–S53). Like many previous research agendas and approaches this new paradigm utilized concepts which had been noted by classical writers or by its intellectual neighbours – for example Tolman's 'cognitive maps' or Lippmann's 'enlisted interest' (ibid.: S55). The logical, or rather methodological, consequence of the emergence of the new paradigm, referred to as the cognitive perspective, has been the widening of the range of data collection techniques to include content analysis, focus groups and quasi-experiments in addition to the traditional attitudinal survey. The change produced seven different strands of research: uses and gratifications, knowledge gap, co-orientation models, work on political cognition, various approaches to audience decoding, studies of media events, and hegemonic models (ibid.: S57).

PUBLIC OPINION RESEARCH AND PUBLIC RELATIONS

'Only fools, pure theorists, or apprentices fail to take public opinion into account,' wrote Necker, who served as the crown minister of finance to Louis XVI and who is described as one 'among the first to propose systematic governmental public relations' (Price 1992: 12). Many contemporary public relations practitioners can be described, like Necker, as placed within the classical approach as Lazarsfeld explained it: they realize that public opinion is an important factor and take it into account, but not on the basis of a scientific theory. In Necker's case, of course, no such scientific basis was available; for many contemporary practitioners it is a question of working on the basis of lay theories, not entirely without any link with or resemblance to the up-to-date body of knowledge, but at the same time more implicit and not entirely rigorous frameworks.

Herbst's (1993) research on lay theories of public opinion and their relation to political activity and ideology is worth further comment here. Although the design of the study did not permit generalizations, Herbst found some evidence indicating resistance to scientific definitions, and a conviction that public opinion is a fiction and that the Habermasian public sphere simply does not exist. Even more unexpected was the lack of any relationship between such beliefs and respondents' ideological positions uncovered by this exploratory study. It would be interesting to see what a similar research project might reveal about theories of public opinion on the basis of which public relations practitioners work. In the absence of such data, an indirect answer might be given on the basis of what public relations theory has to say about public opinion.

Cutlip et al. (1985, 1994) represent perhaps the most comprehensive source of information on public opinion for a public relations student. The authors' approach is fairly standard, acknowledging the problems in defining the term and providing a discussion of its constituent elements, 'public' and 'opinion'.[7] Public opinion is defined as '[representing] a *consensus*, which emerges over time, from all the expressed views that cluster around an issue in debate, and that this consensus exercises power' (Cutlip et al. 1985: 157) and as 'the aggregate result of individual opinion on public matters' (ibid.: 162).

In terms of Herbst's typology, the definitions fall clearly in the class of 'aggregation', which, as we have seen, underlies the empirical tradition of public opinion research. However, the definition changes in the latest edition to: '[public opinion] reflects a dynamic process in which ideas are "expressed, adjusted, and compromised en route to collective determination of a course of action"' (Cutlip at al. 1994: 243). The latest definition, with its focus on the public opinion formations process, is more comfortably placed in the discursive/consensual category.

It seems reasonable to explain the change as linked to the developments in public relations theory that emerged in the years between the two editions, namely the situational theory proposed by Grunig and Hunt in 1984 for identifying publics, and the augmentation of the position of the co-orientation model at the basis of the theory of excellence in public relations (Grunig 1992). Cutlip et al. devote a section to a discussion of situational theory (Cutlip et al. 1994: 245–7), which is followed by a discussion of the co-orientation model (ibid.: 247–54). As far as the definition itself is concerned, it seems to reflect the line of argument linking Grunig's original interest in co-orientation with his awareness of Habermas's concepts of communicative action and public sphere, as mediated by Pearson (1989a, 1989b; see also chapters 2 and 8); this provides not only a discursive definition of public opinion but also a justification for the (excellent) practice of public relations:

> communication system [as created by public relations] is based on two-way exchange of messages . . . It takes the form of . . . a dialogue and argument about politics and issues that goes beyond the revealing of private opinion to the forming of public opinion – the same sense in which Habermas referred to public opinion.
>
> (Ehling et al. 1992: 388)

Public relations, in this definition, seems to act as the enabling mechanism for public debate, therefore for public opinion and the public sphere. If this is how the practice appears, where then should the study of public relations as a discipline be located in the social sciences? In other words, which disciplines are the nearest intellectual neighbours? In chapter 1 the editors point out a range of answers to the question of the problem of academic location; on the basis of the present discussion it appears that the answer hinges on co-orientation, therefore mass communication and the process approach to communication. Grunig and Hunt (1984: 143) make this connection even more explicit in the situational theory which in conceptual terms is derived from Blumer – and originally from Dewey's *The Public and its Problems* (1927) – and which, in methodological terms, represents the instrumental approach dominating public opinion research.

Dewey's work has to be noted here for its contribution to interest group theory; it should also be remembered that group liberalism is cited as one of the presuppositions of symmetric models of public relations (see chapter 8). Somewhat indirectly, public relations seems to be positioning itself in relation to its unmentioned intellectual neighbour – political science. The view of society that seems to be assumed is that in which various interest groups (and publics) are unavoidably pitched one against another but where conflict can always be resolved by the process of negotiation, which breeds at least as much mutual understanding as is necessary for compromise. Government, not as a public or a client but as a social and political mechanism, seems to be conceptualized in traditional democratic terms as 'based on opinion' and, at least in principle, acting to safeguard public interest. Inherent in this vision, of course, is rationalism as the steering mechanism of social life. Reason, within this scheme of things, is not merely the instrumental intelligence needed to figure out the course of action leading to the fulfilment of self-interest, but rather the reason that guides the general will.

Public relations practice anchored in those wider social concerns as they appear in the above discussion is in a position to claim an ethical stance and at the same time to give an impression of neutrality, of being merely an enabling mechanism. Whether or not any ethical responsibility is claimed, public relations still works from a particular set of assumptions. The principles of the discursive/consensual model of the relationship between private actions and social outcomes are so deeply ingrained in our political culture that we accept them almost as common sense, but they still articulate a set of beliefs, a point of view: and what are these in the political sphere if not ideology?

5

CORPORATE IDENTITY AND CORPORATE IMAGE

Peter Meech

INTRODUCTION

The concepts 'identity' and 'image' have commanded the attention of thinkers and scholars across a range of disciplines from at least the time of the Ancient Greeks. Corporate identity, by contrast, has a relatively brief history. As a term it has established itself in common use, but, despite this, there is a lack of consensus over what it actually means. It can be regarded, on the one hand, as a modern label for an age-old phenomenon and, on the other, as a professional practice of comparatively recent standing. This chapter begins with an account of the likely origin of the term and of the factors which have determined the growth of corporate identity consultancy. The claimed benefits of a corporate identity exercise are considered, as is the controversy that the practice continues to attract. There follows a discussion of the use of the key terms in the field and of the process involved in such an exercise. Finally, a case study is presented to illustrate some of the points previously considered.

CORPORATE IDENTITY AS A PRACTICE

The likelihood is that the term 'corporate identity' was coined in the USA in the post-World War II era by Walter Margulies, whose New York consultancy, Lippincott and Margulies, had been founded in 1945. If so, his intention was probably to differentiate and 'add value' to the design work he was carrying out for major US companies in contrast to the simpler editorial styles being produced by his competitors. In the UK corporate identity work was already being undertaken by design consultants by the early 1960s, but Wolff Olins, established in 1965, claims to be the first company in the country to call itself a corporate identity consultancy. As a professional practice, corporate identity gained wider acceptance in the course of the following decade, a period characterized by a dramatic increase in acquisitions, mergers and divestitures. The commercial climate of the time made it necessary to heighten awareness on the part of the financial community of the merits of individual companies, both predators and those vulnerable to takeover bids. In addition, the problems of integration following the merging of previously distinct companies – each with its own culture and symbols – brought into sharp focus the need for corporate identity programmes, as did the increasingly global character of many concerns.

During the course of the 1980s successive Thatcher governments pushed through an extensive programme of privatizing the public utilities (e.g. gas, water and electricity), together with such publicly owned companies as British Aerospace and British Steel. The process initially involved raising the profile of each of these concerns, which in the case of the utilities had been largely taken for granted. A significant growth in corporate advertising came about, especially in the press and on television, and this rapidly became a lucrative source of revenue for media owners. The strategy was to generate both an awareness of and a positive attitude towards these new commercial institutions and, additionally, to prompt a readiness to invest in them. For much of this period the rise of advertising agencies and public relations consultancies, some of whom had also successfully promoted the Conservative Party, appeared inexorable. In the process a widespread view developed that the 'image business' had almost magical powers to influence perceptions and behaviour. During the same period graphic design also experienced a boom, becoming the most profitable part of the design industry, as companies queued up for corporate makeovers.

Ethical considerations have played a part too in the growth of corporate identity. Historically, philanthropic work has long been associated with Quaker companies like Cadbury's or Rowntree's, though by no means exclusively. Such activities, often local in scope, have recently been augmented by a more overt concern on the part of organizations about their role in society. 'Corporate social responsibility' has come to define attitudes and practices which distinguish those organizations which take heed of the wider consequences of their activities rather than being motivated by considerations of profit alone. The consumer awareness movement from the 1960s on played an important role in effecting this ethical change, but it is perhaps environmentalism which in recent years has intensified the pace and broadened the scope. The energy consumed and the environmental impact caused by a product's manufacture, distribution, use and disposal are factors that only a few years ago no one but specialists was likely to have bothered about. Nowadays more and more people are said to be taking such matters into account when making purchasing decisions, if only on the basis of secondhand, incomplete information. Hence the efforts made by companies to be identified by their various publics as 'green' and 'caring', not least by virtue of their explicit corporate identity programmes.

While the external environment in which organizations operate has been transformed in many ways, many have instituted internal changes too. The adoption of less hierarchical structures is one such example. Employees working in a more collaborative organization can be expected to have a more positive perception of that organization than those whose work is mechanistically organized. Likewise, there is increasing recognition of the contribution made by corporate culture. As Gareth Morgan notes, the culture metaphor focuses attention on the human side of organizations, in particular on the 'language, norms, folklore, ceremonies, and other social practices that communicate the key ideologies, values, and beliefs guiding action' (Morgan 1986: 135). Though management has a part to play in helping to produce patterns of shared meanings, this culture is to a large extent self-generating – that is, not imposed from above.

In order to survive and prosper, an organization needs to know what its *raison d'être* is and to ensure as far as possible that all groups with which it is strategically involved do too. Communicating this idea clearly and effectively both inside an organization and outside it is thus an activity of considerable importance. The means adopted will vary, but a common objective is to solicit goodwill, leading to such desired actions as purchasing, investing, donating, voting or joining. The identity of an organization, as of a person or country, is formed from many components.[1] Not all of these manifest themselves at any one time. But it is an assumption that managers and consultants alike proceed from that every organization has its own identity, however difficult that may be to define in practice. Furthermore, it is considered a potential asset in a competitive environment, since it functions simultaneously to distinguish the organization in question from others and to provide its own members with a collective sense.

More than anything else a chosen name is the key symbolic means of identification. Preserving the same name over many years is a priority for organizations concerned with reliability and tradition. Others, however, deliberately alter theirs to signal a change in corporate structure or strategy (Wathen 1987). For a small organization a simple design based on its name may be sufficient to help establish an initial presence and to function as an instrument to motivate staff. But as an organization matures and expands, it is almost inevitable that the earlier, intuitive identity will change and become more diffuse if left to itself. To guard against this and to protect a potentially valuable asset it is routine management practice to attempt to manage corporate identity by periodic reviews. In the case of a multinational conglomerate a full-scale corporate identity programme can last for many months, entail painstaking research, produce a significant change in internal and external perceptions and behaviour, cost a small fortune and still manage to provoke hostile media comment.

In attempting to meet these kinds of demands, the practice of corporate identity has become institutionalized and has developed significantly in recent years from its origins in design companies. It has been estimated, for instance, that during the 1980s corporate identity consultancy grew at an annual rate of about 40 per cent (Olins 1989: 214). This figure should be treated with caution, since work carried out also in public relations consultancies or corporate communications agencies makes it difficult to quantify the size of the industry with great accuracy. A small number of specialist companies did come to enjoy a high profile and maintained a settled existence, but the majority of those active in the area have been very small operations with a tendency to fragment and regroup. Nevertheless, the 40 per cent estimate indicates the burgeoning demand for specialists in the field during most of the Thatcher years. However, the recession at the end of the 1980s reduced promotional budgets and caused many companies either to shrink or to go bankrupt. With subsequent improvements in the economy the corporate identity business has started to grow again, though at a lower rate of growth than at its peak in the previous decade. The present competition is also much fiercer now than it was previously, and client companies are regarded as being better informed and more sophisticated.

It is not simply journalists who in recent years have expressed outrage at corporate identity exercises; ordinary members of the public have joined in too, as the practice has spread well beyond large corporations. The usual target is the logo, and the characteristic response one of incomprehension at the incommensurateness of the changes and costs involved. 'A million pounds for that?' began one otherwise informative business-section article, mimicking the standard complaint. 'The new BP logo, unveiled last week, had children playing spot-the-difference and adults marvelling at how so little could cost so much' (*The Sunday Times*, 5 February 1989). Naive and profligate managers, like the clothes-conscious emperor and his courtiers in the Hans Christian Andersen story, find themselves publicly pilloried for having been supposedly duped by clever but cynical advisers. Changes to the BP or ICI logos in the 1980s are cases in point, where the very subtlety of the alterations fuelled the moral indignation of many commentators in the press. In response, corporate identity practitioners will point out that little or no attention is usually paid to the 'invisible' benefits of such programmes. These might include an enhanced sense of belonging or the boost given to staff morale and pride after a painful process of restructuring.

Despite such negative reporting by the media, visual identity programmes have proliferated in recent years. The spread of market forces into areas which were previously exempt has played a crucial role in this as in other areas of social life. Nowadays it is not just companies which routinely invest large sums of money in this way, but government departments, political parties, media organizations, trade unions, hospital trusts, educational institutions, local councils and charities. Indeed, so widespread is the practice that it might be argued that not to undertake such a change periodically can today be interpreted as a sign that the organization concerned lacks the capacity to respond imaginatively to a changing environment. Consultants, not surprisingly, continue to be mostly involved with large-scale commercial operations, and the literature on the subject tends to reflect this.

ISSUES OF TERMINOLOGY

Corporate identity is of professional interest not simply to specialist practitioners, graphic designers, corporate communication advisers and public relations consultants, but also to academic observers in various disciplines. Given the range of practical concerns and theoretical perspectives involved, it is scarcely surprising that there is a degree of confusion regarding the relevant concepts. What follows is a consideration of the terms most frequently used by writers on the subject.

Corporate image

To begin not with the organization but with those with whom it has significant dealings may appear to be putting the cart before the horse. It certainly reverses the order in which it is traditional to approach the topic. But in doing this we are acknowledging the key role that publics or audiences play in the process. The term most widely used by practitioners to signify the impression these groups have of an organization is 'image', often qualified by such evaluative adjectives as good, poor, positive or negative. David Bernstein has no qualms about using 'image' in the title of his book on the subject, even referring to it as 'a "true reality"'(Bernstein 1984: 233). But a number of academic writers are more circumspect, not to say highly sceptical, because of the term's multifarious uses (Cutlip et al. 1985; Grunig 1992). In particular, the contrast with 'reality' suggests something illusory and hence dubious. This negative image of 'image' itself is due in large part to Daniel Boorstin's influential discussion of the creation by the US media and public relations of 'pseudo-events' (Boorstin 1961) and from the similarly caustic attitude taken by left-wing cultural theorists in the UK. Raymond Williams, for instance, comments:

> [Image] is in effect a jargon term of commercial advertising and public relations. Its relevance has been increased by the growing importance of visual media such as television . . . This technical sense in practice supports the commercial and manipulative processes of image as 'perceived' reputation or character.
>
> (Williams 1976: 130–1)

For the purposes of the present discussion 'image' will be used to signify the sum impression gained of an organization by an individual. This impression derives partly from the explicit, controlled ways in which an organization communicates with its various publics, through the visual design and verbal tone of its advertising and print materials, and, not least, through its choice of corporate logo. But communication in this sense is too narrowly conceived and takes no account of the messages conveyed, for example, by face-to-face dealings between employees and customers. Nor does this kind of communication exhaust the factors affecting an organization's image. Other sources of information which can play a decisive role include media coverage of activities and issues affecting an organization, the quality of its training, for instance, its rate of staff turnover or allegations of sleaze. Interpersonal communication, hearsay and gossip – activities beyond the immediate control of an organization – also have a potential impact to make. But corporate image is affected too by personal experience of a product or service and the resulting sense of satisfaction (or its lack) and value for money (or its opposite). As Grunig stresses, apropos of the interaction between organizations and their publics, 'Symbolic and behavioral relationships are intertwined like strands of a rope' (Grunig 1993b: 123).

It is a commonplace in the literature that different publics have different perceptions of an organization, each responding to it, as it were, *en bloc*. But while allowing for a degree of differentiation, this approach does not go far enough. Composed as it is of a multiplicity of elements, as noted above, an organization's image is better conceptualized as likely to vary from one individual to another. In one and the same person it may also be many-sided or even contradictory in character. Factual knowledge, for instance, may be at variance with emotional attitude. Nor is an image compelled to remain static, but rather it may undergo change over a period of time. Furthermore, it is not necessarily something an individual is fully conscious of or can adequately put into words when asked to. The point to note is that the individually specific circumstances of reception interact with the changing behaviours and communications of an organization to produce a plurality of corporate images. To assert, as for example Clive Chajet does, that identity management can secure a good image is thus to oversimplify (Chajet 1989:18). A single, unitary image and its management are both idealized accounts of a complex and ultimately unpredictable process. Empirical confirmation of some of the contingencies involved is provided by Mary Anne Moffitt in a recent case study of an Illinois insurance company's image (Moffitt 1994). Using a theoretical articulation model derived from work in British cultural studies on media audiences, she examines the personal, social, environmental and organizational factors that compete to determine corporate image and the circumstances under which shared meanings are possible.

If 'corporate image' is best conceptualized as the impressions – both cognitive and affective – produced within individuals in social settings, what of the other terms that are regularly encountered in the literature? How, in particular, are we to distinguish between 'corporate identity', 'visual identity' and 'corporate personality'? There is a measure of agreement here among writers on the subject, but sufficient differences also to warrant investigation. The main problem concerns the first term, for which there would appear to be four principal uses.

Corporate identity

In ordinary speech, and in some sections of the media, corporate identity typically comes to mean a company logo and little besides, something which we do no more than note at this stage. A second sense involves a broadening of the scope of the term, but still within the limits of planned communications. Thus, for Bernstein, 'Corporate identity . . . is the sum of the visual cues by which the public recognises the company and differentiates it from others' (Bernstein 1984: 156). Similarly Chajet remarks: 'Corporate identity is the most visible element of a corporate strategy' (Chajet 1989: 18). This use of the term is by far the most common in the specialist literature.

Before considering the third use, we should note that the term 'visual identity' has been coined in an attempt at conceptual clarification. Thus, when used of an organization, it signifies 'not just its logo, but the various other aspects of its physical presentation, such as its standard layouts, typography, colour schemes and interior design' (Keen and Warner 1989: 13). A major focus here is on publications such as annual reports, brochures, instruction manuals, letterheads, business cards, press releases, invoices and flyers; but equally important are the signs on buildings (Kinneir 1980), the buildings themselves, vehicles, uniforms and, of course, the product and its packaging, where relevant. Visual identity equates most closely with corporate identity in the second sense, although it has yet to establish itself as widely as a distinct concept. Understanding corporate identity in this way by concentrating on conventional visual aspects of communication is the approach traditionally taken by designers. (The addition of a musical phrase or jingle, while restricted in use, suggests the need for the related concept of 'acoustic identity'.)[2]

For most of the writers considered here, corporate identity embraces the visual elements of self-presentation but takes in also the numerous additional ways in which an organization communicates with people, both internally and externally. At one level this means considering, for instance, not just the uniform (style, colours, material, fit, etc.) of, say, airline flight attendants, but how they deal with passengers, their behaviour and manner of speech. At another level it comprises the speed and efficiency with which an organization copes with a crisis as well as the degree of openness it demonstrates towards the press, in good times and in bad. An organization's corporate identity, like its image, will inevitably vary according to circumstances. In the case of a company, the persona it desires to present to its shareholders is composed of its current profitability and future strategy at one level, its efficiency in running an annual general meeting and its well-designed annual report at another, and its social responsibility programme (if any) at yet another. However, this identity may be at odds with that which it presents to its own workforce, for whom low rates of pay, unsatisfactory working conditions and a company newsletter which is merely a management mouthpiece are the daily reality of the company. There again, the two versions may coincide. Clearly congruence is preferable, since a discrepancy could risk exposure by the media as corporate hypocrisy or be interpreted by potential recruits as a sign of a lack of cohesiveness.

Organizational reality has a primacy which corporate identity reflects, though changes in the latter may provide the impetus for changes in the former. Given the vital role played by the various elements that make up a corporate identity, it is not surprising that there is widespread agreement that the latter should be the subject of close and continuous attention by senior management, preferably by the chief executive. In the third sense, then, corporate identity includes everything from products or services (what you make or sell), environments (where you make or sell it – the place or physical context) and information (how you describe and publicize what you do) to behaviour (how people within the organization behave towards each other and towards outsiders) (Olins 1989: 29). In this all-encompassing sense corporate identity is the aggregate of an organization's activities and artefacts, everything it does and says, both deliberately and unintentionally, built up over a period of time.

Finally, there is a fourth sense in which 'corporate identity' occurs. Nicholas Ind, for example, refers to it as 'the term most commonly used to define the programme of communication and change that a company undertakes in conjunction with an external consultancy' (Ind 1990: 19). This sense differs from those previously discussed in focusing on corporate identity as a specific project, undertaken with professional assistance, rather than as an ongoing state of affairs. The typical stages involved in such a corporate identity exercise are discussed later.

Corporate personality

For analytical purposes, there is a case for recognizing 'corporate personality' as a distinct concept. Thus, whereas corporate identity can be equated with everything an organization does or says, its personality might be expressed as its own sense of self. Both corporate culture and corporate strategy are integral parts of this multifaceted entity. Mission statements are potentially of importance here as codified expressions of corporate aims. However, they are sometimes too idealistic to indicate the actual character of the organization and too platitudinous to assist in identifying features that make it distinctively different from others.

But can there really be such a thing as a stable, unitary corporate personality? Just as the concept of corporate image has been characterized as protean, so too corporate personality is perhaps better regarded as highly differentiated and dynamic yet capable of manifesting continuity (Gorb 1992). Members of an organization, differentially situated in terms of power, status, earnings, interests, not to speak of geography, will inevitably have different perspectives from which they form their perceptions. These are further affected by the filter provided by the personal experiences of the individual concerned within the organization. This is not to condemn a corporate personality audit as the pursuit of a will-o'-the-wisp. Both the findings of such an exercise and indeed the process itself may very well have practical benefits – the latter in so far as heightened self-awareness itself may lead to other kinds of beneficial change. But any attempt to determine corporate personality must take account of the plurality of views in an organization in as nuanced and objective a manner as possible, and recognize even then the partial and ephemeral nature of the picture gained.

This discussion of one set of concepts concludes with Bernstein's summary account of three of the terms treated: '[p]ersonality made manifest by identity is perceived as image' (Bernstein 1984: 60). For operational purposes this may be a useful aid to research, but as a description of the complex field of relationships involved it needs qualification. First, the changeable and ultimately indeterminate nature of corporate personality must be noted. Second, it has been argued above that there is merit in distinguishing the visual from other aspects of corporate identity for the purposes of analysis. And, as it stands, 'perceived as image' implies that the communication process between sender and receiver is straightforward and automatic, thereby downplaying the negotiation of meaning on the part of the latter.

At a more practical level there is a further set of terms which call for elucidation. The term 'logo' (from the Greek *logos*, speech, word, reason) is generally used to refer to the ways in which organizations represent themselves in graphic terms, whether or not verbal language as such is involved. The more specific 'logotype' applies to the use of the full name of an organization and 'monogram' to its initials, when these are designed for identification purposes. Traditionally many organizations have managed to survive by doing this simply through the use of either a logotype or a monogram version of their name. But some have always incorporated a pictorial element into their visual identity. These symbols may have an iconic resemblance to physical objects which are especially appropriate, e.g. the World Wide Fund for Nature's panda. Alternatively, they may be wholly abstract or seemingly arbitrary in their relationship with the organization, e.g. the hummingbird of the construction company Bovis. Either way, symbols are chosen both to aid recognition (their denotative function) and to evoke positive associations (their connotative function). As Keen and Warner demonstrate, the British university sector provides examples of each of these categories (Keen and Warner 1989: 14). Oxford Polytechnic (as it then was) used a logotype version of its name, whereas the University of East Anglia preferred the monogram 'UEA'. Through its shield symbol the Open University aligned itself with traditional universities, but at the same time a superimposed circle creating the plain blue and white 'OU' monogram suggested a more innovative institution. With the abolition of the binary line separating universities from polytechnics in the early 1990s, the latter undertook major corporate identity programmes to reposition themselves for competitive advantage. A common element in these was the design of new, distinctive visual symbols that boldly deviated from the norm of the traditional crest. The University of Greenwich's compass is a case in point, alluding as it does to the area's own maritime heritage, rather than to any generic similarity with other ancient institutions.

Organizations come in all shapes and sizes; many are commercial, others non-profit-making; most are geographically circumscribed, but some are global in their reach. The corporate identity issues that confront a large transnational conglomerate differ radically from those of a small-scale charity or a school, both in degree and scope. Yet at a fundamental level all organizations share a commonality of purpose. To assist an understanding of these differences and similarities two classificatory schemes devised by Olins may be found helpful. The first, touched on already, identifies the dominant mode of communication an organization has with what may be regarded as its main audience. Thus, the priority of a manufacturing company is the quality, reliability, design and price of a product, whereas for an up-market department store an atmosphere of exclusivity produced by decor is likely to be paramount. In contrast, for an institution such as the police the emphasis will be on behaviour towards the public (Olins 1989: 29). The second relates the structure of organizations to their corporate identity (ibid.: 78–129). Three broad categories are suggested, applicable to a wide range of concerns: the monolithic, the endorsed and the branded. Such a classification scheme runs the risk of oversimplifying a complex reality, of appearing too neat and tidy, as Olins himself readily admits. Nevertheless, it has been accepted by other writers as a useful working model. Ind, for one, adopts the same three basic types of structure, but employs different terms in two cases ('unitary' for 'monolithic', and 'diversified' for 'endorsed' (Ind 1990: 121).

The monolithic concern organizes itself, as the term implies, in a highly centralized way, with each section intended to perceive itself an integrated part of the larger whole. In the case of a manufacturer, the company's subsidiaries and their products all bear the same corporate name, as with Mitsubishi. At the other end of the spectrum, the branded approach is associated with greater decentralization and diversification and the use of a variety of product names, e.g. Procter and Gamble's range of washing powders and detergents. In between, the endorsed identity can be applied to those organizations where the two are synthesized: a degree of autonomy occurs in individual units but within an overarching framework. The regional operations of the UK-wide BBC provide an example from within the media; here sensitive local affiliations are given a degree of recognition (e.g. BBC Radio

Scotland). A prerequisite for undertaking a review of an existing corporate identity is to recognize the organization's dominant mode of communication and its basic structure. It follows from this analysis that any recommendations made in a corporate identity exercise should attempt to take these factors into account and be congruent with them.

THE CORPORATE IDENTITY EXERCISE

Let us assume an organization has resolved on a corporate identity exercise, has set a budget and has appointed a suitable consultancy to undertake the work. The following sketch of the process that follows is a necessarily simplified account, condensing it into four major stages: research, development, introduction and implementation. It is augmented by discussion of certain problematic aspects.

The first stage concentrates on determining as accurately as possible the status quo regarding the organization's corporate and visual identities, its personality and perceptions of it among the different groups with which it has dealings. Special attention focuses on any discrepancy between how an organization thinks it is perceived and how it actually is or would like to be perceived. All writers on the subject emphasize it is a stage that needs to be undertaken as thoroughly and dispassionately as possible. Because of the multiple aspects involved, present discussion of this stage is disproportionately long.

Empirical research conducted by consultants into the intangible areas of corporate personality and image is typically reliant on a mix of interviews, questionnaires and focus group discussions to elicit a cross-section of opinion. Inevitably, the more extensive and detailed the process of information and opinion gathering, the more labour-intensive and expensive the exercise becomes. The temptation for a client is to cut costs by settling for a consultation with a handful of senior managers and journalists, for example, or to forgo one altogether. At its best, an audit can provide valuable insights. However, many aspects of an organization's complex personality may still elude the standard techniques. By contrast, participant observation, a research instrument of anthropologists and sociologists, involves extensive immersion in a culture or institution. Theoretically informed fieldwork of this kind has a greater capacity to capture the unspoken values, the tacit assumptions – in short, the many taken-for-granted features – of an organization's culture. Such ethnographic work is time-consuming, its objectives are not usually instrumental and the findings are rarely framed for executive-style reading. It is a valuable alternative academic technique, providing rich insights that are unlikely to be registered otherwise. However, constraints of time and finance render it less attractive for routine commercial purposes.

The study of the visual statements made by an organization involves producing an inventory of every kind of printed material, signs, vehicle livery, uniforms, etc. This allows a check to be made of the degree of consistency with which the existing house style is being applied across the board. Such an audit is in principle a relatively unproblematic process, though in practice it can be lengthy, particularly in the case of a large, complex and geographically dispersed organization. With manufacturing companies the exercise will also extend to consideration of the packaging of the goods they produce. Existing typefaces, colours, layouts, logos and slogans may best be evaluated by comparing them with those of competitors, a process which can benefit from a semiotic analysis of each element and of the visual identity as a whole. Although largely ignored in the literature on the subject, semiotics provides a potentially valuable way of understanding how meanings are produced by the internal and external organization of individual elements. Each element, or sign, is held to acquire its meaning by way of its distinctive difference from other, similar signs. These are organized in informal codes which vary from culture to culture. It is clear, therefore, that a knowledge of these socially determined codes is vital for a full understanding of individual signs and their interaction with others in complete messages. Roland Barthes, in his essay 'Rhetoric of the Image', provides a semiotic analysis of how an advertisement by the food manufacturer Panzani is 'constructed' to evoke associations with Italianness, freshness, domesticity and even fine art (Barthes 1977: 32–51). But however perceptive and illuminating, such an analysis is likely to be criticized by the positivistically inclined for its lack of methodological rigour and reliability. Much depends on the interpretive skills of the individual analyst, and there is no guarantee that such meanings as are discerned will be shared by others.

Since visual identity is only a part of corporate identity, other factors require auditing too so as to determine what they reveal about the organization. Chief among these are the physical environment, the external appearance of buildings and surrounding grounds (if any), and the interior look of offices, reception areas, laboratories or wards. Here attention will be focused on colour schemes, lighting, furnishings, care and maintenance. An examination of these physical aspects can provide revealing insights into an organization's corporate identity. Ideally, they need to be supplemented by audits of how the organization communicates with its external and internal audiences and how it behaves towards both. These would typically include, on the one hand, an appraisal of everything from its advertising to its staff notice boards and, on the other, an assessment of its career development schemes and the civility of its telephonists and counter staff.

Returning to the standard course that a corporate identity exercise takes: after the data have been collected and analysed, the findings produced and recommendations made, a brief is agreed. On this basis the consultancy team starts its work of devising a new name or designing visual schemes for the new identity programme. This, the second stage of the exercise, inevitably involves a series of consultations with the client. Practical considerations, such as the range of surfaces involved or the suitability of the design for photocopying, must be taken into account. So too are questions of meaning. Will the logo be recognized as belonging to a generic set of logos yet avoid stylistic cliché and be sufficiently distinctive? Does the overall design connote sober tradition or forward-looking vitality? Do the colours or the shape of the symbol have unfortunate associations or are they likely to evoke only positive responses? Such questions, while not always articulated, must nonetheless be answered before the definitive design scheme is finally agreed. It may be noted in passing that a symbol can be entirely arbitrarily chosen, so long as its connotations are judged favourable. Thus, Yusaku Kamekura's remark concerning trademarks applies equally to logos: 'Ideally they do not illustrate, they indicate. They are not representational, but suggestive' (Kamekura 1966: 6).

The third stage, the introduction, may be phased in gradually over a period of time for economic reasons. In this way the cost of repainting vehicles or reprinting stationery can often be met out of normal maintenance or consumables budgets. Alternatively, a full-scale public relations launch may be used to solicit media attention and coverage, as in the case of the Prudential's new look (Traverso and White 1990). Whichever approach is taken, the need first to introduce the new visual identity to staff is a *sine qua non* for most writers on the subject. It is employees above all, they are surely right in arguing, who need convincing of the merits of such symbolic changes if the side benefits of improved morale and a renewed sense of collective endeavour are to be realized (Williams and Beaver 1990). Employees must also be convinced of the value of the exercise or their scepticism may undermine their capacity to act as corporate advocates in the community

The implementation stage offers the opportunity to symbolize not only a new corporate strategy but a (possibly new) cohesiveness within the various parts of an organization. In order for this cohesiveness to be expressed most effectively, a high degree of uniformity is required in the ways in which the design scheme is put into practice. A standard procedure is for a manual of implementation rules to be part of the package produced by the consultancy. These typically lay down precisely what is and is not permissible as regards colour schemes, typefaces, quality of paper and use of symbols, and as such are expressive of an understandable logic. However, there is a danger that these kinds of rules can also engender resentment on the part of those disposed to see in the exercise an expression of an authoritarian management style. For this reason, some consultants prefer to speak of guidelines, which may or may not permit greater flexibility.

Finally, although it is not usually treated as a stage as such, a nonetheless crucial element is the subsequent monitoring and evaluation of the visual identity exercise as part of a wider corporate identity change.

PETER MEECH

A SCOTTISH CASE STUDY

While most writers on corporate identity include an account of the process of researching, devising and implementing a programme, this is usually normative, detailing how the process *should* take place, often in checklist form, e.g. 'Ten Key Points to Remember' (Ind 1990: 198). And when actual case studies are included, they are typically exemplars of good practice (e.g. Williams and Beaver 1990; Traverso and White 1990). The use of exemplary case studies can clearly be justified from a pedagogical point of view, but the absence of discussion of failures or near-misses gives a somewhat unrealistic quality to these accounts. Practitioners such as Ind or Olins are understandably reluctant to publicize any projects that do not redound to their own credit, not least out of diplomatic consideration for their clients. The following discussion is a modest attempt to right the balance by looking at a less than successful corporate (= visual) identity exercise. The company concerned, having recognized its mistakes, subsequently undertook a second exercise, with a more satisfactory outcome.

Scottish Television plc has held the ITV licence for the Central Scotland region without interruption since 1957. During much of the intervening period it was content simply to fulfil its requirements to provide local programming to viewers and to sell airtime to advertisers wishing to communicate with most of the Scottish population, which has been its potential audience. The absence of an alternative vehicle for television commercials and the relative lack of competition for viewers for a quarter of a century were responsible for weaknesses in respect of corporate personality, identity and public image. The company was highly successful commercially, but the programmes it produced, with some notable exceptions, betokened a complacent attitude. One of the so-called five 'mini-majors', i.e. a second-division player, in the then ITV system, the company had long since settled for a quiet life, interrupted from time to time by complaints from Scottish intellectual and artistic circles about the poor quality of its output. Shareholders stayed loyal as the company maintained the highly profitable tradition already established by 1959, the year it was referred to by its then Chairman Roy (later Lord) Thomson as 'a licence to print money'.

The 1980s were a period in which Scotland underwent a profound renewal, at least in the cultural field. By mid-decade the company – driven by the Advertising Sales Department – decided to highlight its Scottish identity so as to enhance its positioning within the domestic and overseas television markets. The name by which the company was popularly known, STV, and its monogram logo were judged by management to lack distinctiveness and emotional appeal and to need replacing with something more arresting and meaningful. The process by which a replacement came about is instructive. It is no secret that the atmosphere within the company at this time was anything but cooperative, with much of the tension due to poor industrial relations between management and the unions. In this climate the company management commissioned the designer of Channel 4's innovative logos, Martin Lambie-Nairn, to produce a design that could be used both on-screen, in computer-animated form, and off-screen. At the same time the company name was introduced in its full form, with all the hoped-for benefits that would accrue from associations with the word 'Scottish'.

But four factors conspired to make the corporate identity programme less of a success than it might have been. First, no research was undertaken into the existing corporate identity and image. Second, the commission went ahead only as a design project and quasi-renaming exercise. Third, Robinson Lambie-Nairn as a company were relatively new to the field, were self-confessedly ignorant of the strategic implications and were 'only a few pages further forward' than STV's own in-house designer (personal interview with Martin Lambie-Nairn). Their lack of confidence in dealing with only their second client led, for example, to a reluctance to insist on a postponement of the launch, after Scottish Television changed its mind about the design just two weeks in advance of it. Finally, an uncooperative in-house design staff had not been adequately consulted, felt alienated from the new thistle motif and allegedly sabotaged its effective screening. The outcome was that the company started to use its full name but found itself stuck with an expensive logo featuring a stylized thistle (the national symbol) which was flawed in design terms. In the words of one senior executive of the company, 'I think it's an insult. It actually won a prize as the worst piece of graphic design.' Nor did the change achieve much in terms of boosting morale within the company. Externally, though, the change of name and the introduction of the thistle motif did at least help to emphasize the Scottishness of the broadcaster more than the previous corporate visual identity and the motif became indelibly associated with the company.

In contrast, Scottish Television adopted a more textbook approach in 1991–2 to coincide with major structural changes both within the company and in the industry as a whole. This time a specialist consultancy was brought in to research audience perceptions of the company's programming and its visual identity. On the basis of these findings a corporate programme strategy was produced for regaining the Central Scotland franchise. The findings also assisted in-house designers with the task of updating the corporate logo. Versions were tested on groups of viewers on this occasion, but little or no effort was made to sound out the opinions of employees, who were presented with a *fait accompli*.

CONCLUSION

At the start of *Corporate Identity*, the standard UK work on the subject, Olins reminds us that there is a long history to the symbolic display by institutions of their actual or would-be nature (Olins 1989). Visual symbols, in particular, have traditionally been used by dominant groups to communicate institutional distinctiveness, common goals and values, and a sense of belonging, both to subordinates and to outside groups. His nineteenth-century examples – the US Confederacy, the British Raj and successive French Republics – associate the phenomenon exclusively with Western political–military formations involved in the hegemonic struggle of nation-building. There is an apparent assumption here that corporate identity is socially progressive. Absent from the discussion, for instance, is the example of Nazi Germany (or that of other twentieth-century totalitarian regimes) as a more recent corporate identity programme of note.[3] In the case of the Third Reich striking symbols and a highly distinctive visual style helped to brand a whole nation. In this they played a significant part in the process of *Gleichschaltung*, the enforced coordination of beliefs, values, goals and practical activities for maximum internal and external effect. Citing the example of Hitler's Reich in this context is not to argue that a corporate identity programme which encourages a sense of purpose and belonging is inevitably repressive in intent or consequences. There are, after all, many benign examples to refute such a paranoid view. It serves merely as a reminder of Morgan's point that 'Most discussions of organization attempt to be ideologically neutral' (Morgan 1986: 316). This is of relevance here since the majority of the books on corporate identity have been written by practitioners in the field, employing a managerial rather than a social scientific perspective.

Though it has yet to achieve the same status as finance or human resource functions within organizations, corporate identity has clearly established itself as a professional practice. It is unthinkable, for instance, that a new company, healthcare organization or quango would take the risk of stinting on an identity programme. Similarly, existing organizations are more than ever likely to seek help in periodically updating the visual symbols through which they communicate to their various audiences. Ind cites an optimistic, pre-recession MORI survey indicating that as many as 77 per cent of leading industrialists believed in 1989 that the importance their company attached to developing and promoting its corporate image would increase in the medium term (Ind 1990: 13). And as many organizations become more globalized and introduce tele-working on a larger scale than at present, an increased use of corporate symbols can be anticipated to help obviate the loss of shared physical space and reduced human contact.

The process itself remains an expensive one, with a fee the standard means of remuneration for each discrete project. However, in future, if some practitioners are to be believed, a greater degree of continuity may be assured by the hiring of consultants on a retainer basis. These would act as permanent advisers on corporate identity matters, monitoring existing arrangements and perceptions, and making recommendations for change when appropriate. In short, there would be a shift towards a public relations orientation compared with that conventionally adopted by design agencies.

But for this to happen two things will be necessary. First, a change of attitude will need to be inculcated in the relevant sections of the design community, typically socialized to responding to problems with one-off solutions. Second, organizations will require convincing of the value of undertaking foundational research and of investing long term in an activity the cost-effectiveness of which is difficult to demonstrate. Whether or not such a trend establishes itself remains to be seen. Meanwhile, issues of corporate identity in the broad-based sense will continue to be important for organizations large and small, global and local, commercial and non-profit, since each unavoidably has its own identity and images, whether it attempts to manage them or not.

ACKNOWLEDGEMENT

The author would like to thank David Bernstein, Aird McInstrie, Wally Olins and Peter Townsend for their help in preparing this chapter.

6

CORPORATE RESPONSIBILITY AND PUBLIC RELATIONS ETHICS

Jacquie L'Etang

INTRODUCTION

This chapter explores the relationship between public relations and corporate responsibility. At the outset there is a review of the definitions employed in the chapter, and a discussion of the origins and development of the concept and practice of corporate responsibility and the relationship between business and society. The motivation behind, and the relationship between, corporate social responsibility, crisis management and issues management is debated to expose the essential tension that lies between the fight for organizational survival and concern for the public interest. The role of public relations both in managing community programmes and as a socially responsible occupation is debated and a number of problematic issues raised. There is also a review of the debate concerning issues of corporate responsibility and liability. Fundamental to this chapter is an approach which questions current practice and dominant perceptions of that practice.

The chapter is written from a moral philosophical perspective and thus is normative in approach. The approach taken in this chapter applies the classical philosophical moral frameworks of utilitarian and Kantian thought but does not relate these to the relativist and postmodern perspectives raised in some other chapters. The utilitarian and Kantian approaches are thought to be appropriate since the language and concepts are already employed by those in business and public relations, although, as will be shown, they do not always seem to be applied rigorously or in full comprehension of the implications of the positions adopted.

MORAL THEORIES

Moral[1] theories do two things: they give an account of what is 'good' and they judge 'right' actions. These frameworks of principles can be applied in a consistent fashion and used to evaluate situations or human behaviour. The frameworks used here define goodness differently and give different weightings to the importance of the motivation and the effects of actions in judging rightness of behaviour.

The utilitarian framework is probably the most familiar to non-philosophers and can be most simply described as 'the greatest happiness of the greatest number'. For a utilitarian, 'good' is defined as happiness and a 'right' action is that which increases happiness by at least as much as any other option open to the agent at the time. Utilitarianism is a type of consequentialism because it makes the rightness of actions solely dependent upon their consequences.

An alternative moral framework is a deontological (from the Greek *deon*, duty) approach, in which goodness is seen as being intrinsic to an act within the context of a relationship. This sort of approach is derived from Immanuel Kant, whose formulations about morality encompassed a number of key points of relevance to corporate social responsibility. Kant argued that a right act was one which was done out of duty and conformity to universal law and not out of inclination. He thus thought less highly of generous actions done through an impulse of sympathy or generosity and more highly of those motivated strictly out of duty. He attributed the action done out of duty with moral worth because the action arose from a rational process and included an understanding of obligation and duty. Kant argued that the moral worth of an act should be judged by asking whether one was willing for the act to become a universal law. An important aspect of this framework is that where self-interest plays a part in the motivation of the action, then that action is regarded as prudential[2] and cannot be regarded as a morally right action.

DEFINITION OF THE TERM 'RESPONSIBILITY'

The term 'responsibility' may be used in a number of different ways in the context of the moral responsibility of business, and perhaps it is this which leads to some confusion over the morality of both the practice of corporate social responsibility and the role of public relations in the field. When the adjective 'responsible' is used predicatively, as in 'XYZ Ltd was responsible for the pollution' or 'XYZ Ltd was responsible for the creation of new jobs', a statement is made about a causal link between the acts or omissions of the company and a subsequent state of affairs, which may be seen as either good or bad. There is no single negative equivalent of the adjective 'responsible' as used in this way: a company cannot be 'irresponsible' for pollution or job creation. When the adjective is used attributively, as in 'XYZ Ltd is a responsible company' a simple statement is made about the company's being answerable for its acts or omissions; however, a more important statement is also made in an evaluative and approving manner regarding the overall behaviour of the company. The negative equivalent can be used to show a lack of responsibility in this sense: 'through its irresponsible conduct, XYZ Ltd caused the pollution.' Thus, while the term 'corporate responsibility' can have many meanings, it is most widely used in an evaluative and laudatory manner, describing the conduct of business as a whole or of a corporation above and beyond its purely economic function. It is not that approval in itself is a bad thing but that approval needs to be based on a clear framework or rationale.

By exploring the philosophical principles behind corporate responsibility, together with a discussion of moral frameworks, we can begin to distinguish between corporate responsibility based on sound moral principles and that which is not. We need to analyse the justifications offered in favour of corporate social responsibility and the arguments which are presented against its practice. Below we shall be focusing on the idea of corporate social responsibility as a theory of obligation to society. It will be argued that the very term 'corporate responsibility' implies a contractual, rights-based approach because of the use of the term 'responsibility' and that therefore the most natural and coherent justification will be in terms of rights and duties.

CORPORATE RESPONSIBILITY: ORIGINS AND DEVELOPMENT

The concept of corporate responsibility is a broad one and includes a variety of ideas and practices. In terms of this discussion it will be useful to define the two main applications of corporate responsibility, the first of which is those actions taken by corporations in response to corporate disasters and the second those apparently voluntary and benevolent (though not necessarily beneficial) actions taken by corporations in society outside their primary economic function. In public relations these two areas present themselves directly in the fields of crisis management and community programmes.

Although corporate responsibility in the UK is presented as a modern concept and business practice it has its theoretical roots in philosophical debates and its practical roots in the activities of nineteenth-century philanthropists. These philanthropists were to an extent both paternalistic and self-interested. Providing housing benefited workers but also encouraged their loyalty. Currently, the terms 'philanthropy' and 'social responsibility' are sometimes used interchangeably in corporate literature, a practice which can and should be challenged. One challenge from a business perspective is given by Lord Sheppard of Didgemere, Chairman of Grand Metropolitan PLC:

> It *is* true that companies such as Cadbury and Rowntree were giving help to their local communities in Victorian times, but this help was the result of *individual* generosity. The activity was paternal and altruistic. *Today's* good corporate citizen believes that involvement in the

> community is not something separate from business but an integral part of it. The motive for it is not altruism, but vision and common sense . . . companies are discovering that their reputation as citizens influences both their ability to sell and their ability to attract investment.
>
> (*First Forum* 1995: 47)

From an academic perspective, philanthropy implies charitable and benevolent actions done beyond legal requirements or the call of duty. Philanthropic or charitable acts are voluntary, done out of beneficence, and the recipient of such acts has no right to expect or demand that such acts will take place. This is in contrast to the underlying implications of the term 'social responsibility' that there is a specific obligation and a relationship in which there are reciprocal rights and duties.

Corporate responsibility's twentieth-century incarnation originated as an American practice and was subsequently adopted in Britain and Europe. The practice was stimulated by the idea that affluent companies could well afford charitable donations to those less well off in society. The sense of obligation was nourished by social activists in the 1960s and 1970s, many of whom criticized the role of large corporations and power elites in society and argued that political and economic justice could only be achieved through a redistribution of goods and power. These sorts of arguments tend to promote an idea that increased power should bring with it increased responsibility and an obligation not to exploit or take advantage of individuals and small communities. In some literature the idea of obligation is encapsulated in the notion of contract, and this will be discussed later in the chapter.

Business writers and practitioners have not always been comfortable using ethical terminology implicit to the debate and some use a euphemism such as 'integrity' in preference to a standard moral philosophical term such as 'ethics' (see Nash 1990). An example of this sensitivity is given by White and Mazur, who cite Werner Baier, Henkel's Director of Corporate Communication, as saying, 'I think it is completely necessary to have values but I prefer not to talk about ethics but about our responsibilities. If you talk about ethics some people mentally shy away' (White and Mazur 1995: 8). In the 1980s executives were less inclined to try and define what they meant by corporate responsibility than is now the case: the growth of organizations such as Business in the Community, conferences and publications in the area of business ethics doubtless have made an impact.

The concept of corporate responsibility has become ever more closely associated with public relations as the function has extended its strategic scope. The emergence of issues management in America in the 1970s coincided with that of corporate responsibility. Issues management is linked to corporate social responsibility at a strategic level because it is seen as the way in which companies can predict emerging issues, often of a social nature, to which they can respond either through issues advocacy advertising, public relations campaigns or through programmes of corporate social responsibility. The danger is that corporations develop an incoherent, reactive approach to their social responsibility programmes, responding to external issues or trends rather than defining their moral responsibilities in a rational manner. Public relations became involved because of its representational role and responsibiity for managing relationships.

A good example of the overlap between corporate social responsibility and issues management which demonstrates the instrumentality of some corporate social responsibility practice is shown in a text of a letter published in the *Financial Times* in 1993 and written by senior industrialists representing the organization Business in the Community:

> by working in the wider community, business can help to build the social environment it needs for long-term wealth creation . . . Our view is simply that business has legitimate interests in public policy matters . . . This is not about business replacing government, but 'adding value' by bringing its own skills, attitudes and resources to the public policy table.
>
> (White and Mazur 1995: 225)

Grunig supports his view (Grunig 1992: 240) that corporate responsibility and excellent public relations 'balance . . . the private interests of the organization with the interests of publics and of society' with an argument presented by Steiner in favour of corporate social responsibilty:

> This is not solely a matter of defending the corporation but involves a deep interest in resolving major social problems, injecting more economic rationality into the political processes, helping to assure that our sociopolitical system works in the interests of everyone, and preserving political and economic freedom.
>
> (Steiner 1983: 29)

This quote clearly illustrates the way in which the organization may respond to social issues but also facilitate strategic interventions in public policy.

BUSINESS AND SOCIETY

Having established the strategic importance of corporate responsibility to business as part of issues management it will be useful to discuss arguments for and against the practice. If one were forced to identify an historical and historiographical 'turning point' in the debate about the role of business in society, the article written by the Nobel Prize winner Milton Friedman (1970) would provide the locus, and it has remained a critical piece cited in virtually all discussions of the subject. Friedman's ideas are pursued in some detail here partly because of their historical importance but also because they present the sharpest critique of corporate social responsibility. Friedman's view is that business is socially responsible in its profit-making function and he sees altruistic acts carried out on behalf of business as a violation of business's function and obligations (which are purely economic). This is part of a wider set of arguments about the role of morality in business which suggest that business does not have to be concerned with issues of morality. Friedman's ideal society maxmimizes individual freedom (which he sees as the greatest good) and limits regulation (by government) and the responsibilities of corporations. It is a strongly libertarian view and consequently portrays an individualistic and atomistic society, stressing individual not collective responsibilities. Friedman does not promote an amoral view as such; for him business is intrinsically ethical because it promotes free enterprise and freedom.

Yet economic activity is not separate from moral activity and, as has been pointed out elsewhere, the free market institution itself is a product of convictions about the nature of a good society and what constitutes a *fair* distribution of goods and services; economic goals *are* social and political goals (Hoffman and Moore 1990: 2).

Friedman is profoundly opposed to the concept of corporate responsibility, which he defines as corporations donating resources to charities or local communities. He thinks that the practice is inimical to democracy and freedom because it turns corporations into instruments of public policy though they are neither elected representatives of the people nor subject to them (as civil servants are). In fact, he argues, such an expansion is akin to the growth of government via the back door of corporate social responsibility: if corporations are not maximizing profit but embarking on other socially desirable ends, they are in effect imposing taxes on those to whom they are directly and primarily responsible – their shareholders. For Friedman, neither government nor business should contribute to the welfare of the needy in society; this activity should be left entirely to the actions of individual philanthropists.

The only way in which corporate social responsibility is acceptable for Friedman is if it is motivated entirely out of self-interest and justified on the grounds that such actions are being carried out to promote the company's interests. But he also argues that if it is in the long-term interest of companies to cover up their real intentions (of self-interest) by pretending to be motivated by some sense of duty or social obligation, then that is also acceptable. For Friedman, therefore, the only acceptable justification for corporate social responsibility is self-interest, and he is happy for the corporate representatives to deceive publics (consumers, media, shareholders) as to their real motivation.

If we reject the Friedman argument we must find some sound moral grounds for the justification of corporate social responsibility. Friedman's analysis is based in the right to freedom, and one route to justifying the practice is to argue that the right to freedom attracts complementary duties as part of a contract between business and society quite apart from the reciprocal rights and duties that arise from the relationship between business (as part of society) and government. Friedman himself did not believe that the concept of 'society' was viable, claiming that it did not exist, but contemporary business views are rather different, with chief executives working in ways to ensure that their companies can be described as 'good corporate citizens', as the following quotations illustrate:

> Good corporate citizenship provides tangible benefits in many ways. It provides strong links with the community in which we operate and community projects can often provide important training and experience to employees. The application of management skills to community projects and wider environmental initiatives is beneficial to the business and community alike.
>
> (David Davies, Chairman of Johnson Matthey PLC, *First Forum* 1995: 59)

> Debates about the relationship of the individual and the society . . . have been going on for more than 2000 years, but it's only in recent time we have begun to ask the same sort of questions about the relationship of business corporations to society. The realisation is growing that a *good* business is one which strikes the right balance between what it owes society and what it expects from it.
>
> (Lord Sheppard of Didgemere, Chairman of Grand Metropolitan PLC, *First Forum* 1995: 47)

A contractarian account of corporate social responsibility attempts to balance the conflicting rights and duties of citizens and business. In reality the debate which arises from this conflict focuses on large and influential businesses and their response to pluralist interest groups in society such as environmental groups and consumer lobbies. The nature of corporate obligation and the idea of corporate duties raise the question of the extent to which government has the right to regulate business. In the area of the environment, for example, legislation may be drafted to protect consumers, employees and the environment from risk. To avoid government restrictions business may choose to acknowledge responsibilities to society and, as part of its contract with government, self-regulate in return for being allowed to maintain a larger degree of freedom.

The concept of contract is identified by several writers (Baier 1984; Harrington 1978; Lodge 1986) as a significant component of capitalist ideology in relation to the exchange of money, goods and property, and as a method of avoiding conflict in society. Such writers find their sources of inspiration in Hobbes, Locke and Darwin. Contracts are seen by philosophical contractarians as a way of improving the lot of citizens, specifically by reducing conflict. For Hobbes, civil society is only arrived at through the implementation of contract, which creates the status of citizen. In politics the term 'social contract' is also seen as a way of ameliorating conditions or relationships between government and governed, such as the Labour government of 1974. Social contract is a way of mediating the claims of autonomous and free citizens and a centralized, powerful state to the mutual benefit of both (Turner 1986: 106).

While contract theory is a strong theme in business ethics literature, the concepts of contract theory in the corporate social responsibility sphere are by no means clear cut. A properly defined contract between business and society should make it clear what business can and ought to be responsible for. For corporate social responsibility, contract theory must be an ideal and not an historical contract. It is an implicit contract, but not one to which all businesses subscribed over time as a practice which is of intrinsic benefit to society, rather 'justice established itself by a kind of convention or agreement; that is, by a sense of interest, suppos'd to be common to all, and where every single act is performed in expectation that others are to perform the like' (Hume 1980: 498). This interpretation suggests that contract is a technique to achieve and formalize a particular type of relationship. The concept of fair dealing is implicit to contract, together with an understanding that the arrangement is a cooperative venture of benefit to both parties and that neither party should be coerced to contract. The practice of corporate social responsibility is potentially a way of redressing the balance and redistributing benefits and burdens in society on the grounds that business benefits from publicly funded infrastructures and considerable economic, social and political power and that this accumulation of power should lead to increased responsibility.

An analogy could be made between the concept of a government–society contract and a business–society contract; however, this cannot be sustained in its entirety because society is not given the option to vote for or against business leaders and policy-makers. The individuals who are promoted to run the companies and direct policy are subjected only to organizational hustings, often of a clandestine nature.

The idea that corporations have a requirement to redistribute further profit into the community is contentious and dependent on a society's arrangements for distributive justice and the extent to which arguments about sharing benefits and burdens predominate. It is important to maintain a clear distinction between corporate social responsibility activities which relate directly to a corporation's economic function linked to particular relationships (stakeholders) and those which do not; the latter should properly be described as philanthropy since they are supererogatory (above and beyond the call of duty). Clearly all corporate social responsibility activities are dependent upon the economic health of organizations, and this was demonstrated in the recession of the early 1990s. What becomes important, however, is that companies can justify particular donations in terms of the interests of their stakeholders, including the local community, and not simply in terms of corporate branding and as part of their promotional budget when times are good. A contractual relationship does not alter according to the economic climate.

PROGRAMMES OF CORPORATE SOCIAL RESPONSIBILITY: COMMUNITY PROGRAMMES

Corporate social responsibility programmes include a wide range of activities, often far removed from the corporation's economic function. Examples of such activities include sponsorship of sport or the arts, donations to charity and contributions in either cash or kind such as office facilities, equipment, professional advice, training, technology. Such gifts are normally given towards public- or voluntary-sector activities in the community in which the organization operates. The dominant view of corporate social responsibility is that it is a practice which benefits both society and business. It could be argued that public relations practitioners can potentially serve the public interest through programmes of social responsibility.

It may be argued that corporate social responsibility and public relations are two separate functions which should be evaluated independently. For example, one major financial institution separates the functions, in that it has charitable foundations to which it contributes but the work of these is not managed or publicized by the institution. However, this seems to be the exception rather than the rule. Corporate social responsibility is often managed by public relations practitioners for public relations ends, and therefore corporate social responsibility is seen as part of the public relations portfolio and as a technique to establish relations with particular groups (for example in the local community) and to signal messages to other groups in society. For example, one major oil company stated to the author that 'media coverage is not important – we prefer to make sure that the right people, i.e. those of influence in the community, know of our activities' (private correspondence, 1989). Another text promotes an explicitly prudential view: 'Behaving ethically makes increasingly good business sense' (White and Mazur 1995: 239).

Other companies set clear benchmarks for each project with regard to the target audience and objectives for media publicity. Consequently, public relations practitioners may be responsible for proposing corporate social responsibility activities and identifying relevant publics. In this way public relations practitioners are directly involved in policy formulation in which the starting point is the communication of a particular message to a particular group with a view to building a particular image in a specified audience. It is not therefore a question of senior management working out their organizational responsibilities and then the public relations practitioner communicating the policy or actions, but of public relations actively driving the programme and setting corporate objectives.

Corporate social responsibility has become important to public relations because such programmes offer the opportunity to build goodwill by promoting the benefits of the company to its stakeholders; corporate social responsibility delivers target audiences to those managing the corporate image. Corporate social responsibility falls within the public relations portfolio because it affects a company's image and reputation. It may well be seen as an investment against the day when a crisis occurs and the company needs all the goodwill it can muster. In addition to its strategic role in formulating policy and making recommendations as to the donation which will yield the most publicity, public relations also provides the necessary techniques to promote these activities among target publics, which may include not only the media but other individuals seen to be of influence and important to the corporation.

The rationale given in corporate publicity varies from the explicitly self-interested – 'our community affairs programme is based upon enlightened self-interest' (Sir Peter Walters, Chairman of BP, *BP in the Community*, 1989: 1) – to that which implies that corporations must recognize specific obligations to the community, that a community has rights and the corporation has duties: 'There rests on all companies, particularly large organizations like ours, a responsibility to assist through donations and help, the charities and agencies which exist in the community' (Lord Raynor, Chairman of Marks & Spencer, in a Marks & Spencer promotional brochure *In the Community*).

The justification that corporate social responsibility is enlightened self-interest of mutual benefit to both donor and beneficiary is questionable on a number of grounds. But there is clearly something wrong about claiming moral capital while at the same time being driven largely by self-interest. The term 'enlightened self-interest' seems to imply that the recipient's benefit is seen of being of equal value to the benefit which accrues to the company either through ensuring a healthier economic climate in which the company operates or in terms of improved image and competitive edge for the company. This is an unsatisfactory justification because the company stands to gain so much more in terms of long-term benefits and because the phrase seems to imply a far more equal relationship based on equal exchange than is usually the case in corporate social responsibility. For example, donors choose beneficiaries, activities and the amount of money, resources and the length of commitment so that the recipient has little, if any, autonomy in the decision-making process. Furthermore, some corporate donors not only specify that recipients must achieve a certain amount and type of media coverage in exchange for the donation, but may also require the recipients (which are often low-budget voluntary organizations or charities) to carry out all the media relations and monitoring work (private interview with recipient organization, 1993). In short, it appears that what may be important for the corporation is what the recipient can do for the corporation in terms of enhancing their reputation and not what the company can do for the recipient.

Some companies become involved in corporate social responsibility because of its perceived benefits. The motivation behind corporate responsibility may become explicitly self-interested. For example, 'Whatever its more altruistic role, proactive corporate social responsibility, and more particularly, the successful generation of public awareness and appreciation of it, is good for business' (Mannheim and Pratt 1989: 9). One book written for business audiences advises that

> Endowing a university chair is an expensive business, but can be valuable. Apart from the public relations benefits, it may mean that research can be directed into an area which interests you at less cost than establishing your own facilities.
>
> (Carmichael and Drummond 1989: 39)

The appeal to mutual benefit arising for donor and beneficiary appears to be based on some form of utilitarian approach. A utilitarian approach does not take account of concepts of rights and responsibilities or ideas about just relationships, which seem to be embedded in much of the language used in defining and discussing corporate social responsibility. If companies which adopt a utilitarian line of justification do not attempt to evaluate the effects of their corporate social responsibility programmes, not only in their own terms of media coverage but also by seeking the evaluation of beneficiaries, then they will not be in a position to claim that they have contributed to happiness. In short, corporate social responsibility justified on utilitarian grounds needs to demonstrate cost-benefit analysis from the perspectives of donor, recipient and society in general. If public relations is involved in identifying or choosing beneficiaries, then it would seem to be appropriate for the public relations practitioner to conduct a social audit based on sound research methodology in order to understand the different arguments and alternative perspectives of beneficiaries, stakeholders and 'public opinion'.

A Kantian approach to corporate social responsibility focuses on the motivation behind the programme and the nature of the relationship between donor and recipient. For Kant, a corporate social responsibility programme needs to demonstrate that it is motivated by duty, not self-interest. Self-interested or prudential motivation renders corporate social responsibility programmes immoral, not only because they are wrongly motivated but also because they treat beneficiaries as a means to an end. Kant argued that one was obliged to have regard for people's autonomy and to treat people with respect. On a Kantian account, corporate social responsibility is not a moral practice because it is wrongly motivated and because beneficiaries may be used as a means to the end of improving the company's image. If corporations took on board Kantian principles, then their programmes and accompanying publicity might look very different. A Kantian approach might exclude evaluation which focused on the benefits to the corporation and instead focus on the careful identification of corporate duties and responsibilities and on allowing the beneficiaries full scope in defining the relationship between the corporation and themselves.

This analysis shows that the terminology used in the area of corporate social responsibility has considerable implications in terms of moral discourse which are not normally taken into account. In many cases corporate literature is confusing because it appears to appeal to both utilitarian and Kantian principles yet apparently delivers on neither. This poses some difficult questions for the public relations practitioner, who can be seen to be contributing largely to the instrumental and self-interested approach while simultaneously claiming moral credit. The area of corporate social responsibility thus highlights a dilemma which arises generally in the role of public relations: the tension between organizational goals and declared responsibility for 'the public interest.'

CORPORATE SOCIAL RESPONSIBILITY IN PUBLIC RELATIONS LITERATURE

The issue of corporate social responsibility is presented as an unproblematic and praiseworthy concept in public relations literature,where it tends to arise in the context of discussion about community programmes and crisis management. For example, the textbook Cutlip, Center and Broom (1994) fails to define or distinguish between corporate social responsibility and philanthropy. Indeed, it is simply stated that 'Social responsibility based on "enlightened self-interest" links philanthropy to organizational goals' (Cutlip et al. 1994: 447). No connection is made between the terminology, the practice and the moral concepts other than the statement that 'As ethical standards change and commitments to corporate social responsibility grow, the role of public relations in business has become more clearly defined as helping corporations "do the right thing," as well as say the right thing' (ibid.: 438). There is no discussion about what 'the right thing' might be and why, or of the tension that arises for the public relations role between 'doing good' and merely 'looking good' let alone 'being good'. Indeed, corporate social responsibility is presented as a concept created to defuse criticism of business and which through strategic targeting can build (buy?) the goodwill of key publics.

The presentation in Grunig and Hunt (1984) is somewhat different but equally devoid of moral definitions, frameworks or debate. Here, social responsibility is presented as a prerequisite for obtaining freedom from government restraint; in other words, the practice is justified on the grounds that the organization will benefit. At the same time, it is suggested that social responsibility will automatically be exercised if an organization '*deals with* its public relations problems . . . public relations and public responsibility become synonymous' (Grunig and Hunt 1984: 55; italics mine).

While Grunig and Hunt clearly see corporate responsibility as central to the practice of public relations at a strategic level, they also identify a separate role for public relations in identifying organizational responsibilities.

> The organization must be responsible to maintain the freedom to behave in the way it wants, which it must do in order to be profitable or to achieve other goals. And it needs a communication link – a public relations function – to show what it has done to be responsible.
>
> (Grunig and Hunt 1984: 52)

Looking at these quotes together it seems that social responsibility is to be defined and implemented on the organization's terms, and it seems hard to reconcile this approach with the idealistic concept of 'symmetry' proposed elsewhere by Grunig and Hunt. It appears that the authors recommend a limited stakeholder-only model of corporate responsibility for primarily practical and self-interested purposes rather than normative and idealistic reasons. Social responsibility is also identified by Grunig (1992) as one of the characteristics of excellent organizations but this does not rule out the possibility that what is important about corporate responsibility is what it can do for the organization in terms of helping it meet organizational goals.

PUBLIC RELATIONS AS SOCIAL RESPONSIBILITY

The idea of public relations in itself as social responsibility has a long tradition in public relations literature. There are two main themes within this literature, one of which focuses on the relationship between the public relations function and society and which debates the contribution the role can make to the promotion of public welfare. The second pursues the idea of public relations performing the role of the conscience within the organization. Examples of these two strands in the literature will be critically reviewed and analysed as to their justification and validity. The presentation of these debates in student text books is given some emphasis.

Public relations and the public interest

The debate about public relations and its contribution to the public interest is bound up with rhetorical arguments designed to promote the idea of public relations as a profession. For example, 'Concern for the ethical behaviour in public relations addresses the emerging profession's efforts to qualify *morally*' (Cutlip et al. 1994: 135; emphasis in original); 'to qualify as a profession, practitioners – both individually and collectively – must operate as moral agents in society. This requirement *is the ethical basis for profession-*

al practice: placing public service and social responsibility over personal gains and private special interests' (ibid.: 134).

The interest that public relations has in ethics can thus be seen to be instrumental to its own status. There is little definition or discussion about concepts of ethics and how this might apply to public relations and its role in society. The text (and others such as Grunig 1984) does not explain fundamental concepts in moral philosophy, and where it goes so far as to make value judgements about the purpose of public relations the underlying source of these ideas are not revealed any more than sociological ideas about what constitutes a 'profession' are revealed. For example: 'The principle behind professional ethics is that one's actions are designed to create the greatest good for both the client and the community as a whole, rather than to enhance the position and power of the practitioner' (Cutlip et al. 1994: 130). This quotation is clearly based on utilitarian principles and public relations' benefits are identified as the end results of particular campaigns such as health campaigns, but nothing is said about the nature and context of communication events. The text appears to promote the view that there are stark choices to be made between 'information' and 'misinformation', clarity and obfuscation (see chapter 7 for some discussion of this issue in the context of persuasion).

Cutlip et al. acknowledge that 'public relations has impact well beyond the boundaries of client organizations' (Cutlip et al. 1994: 133). They identify 'major positives of socially responsible public relations' (ibid.) as being its contribution to making all points of view heard in society; its supply of 'information' to replace 'misinformation'; its replacement of 'discord' with 'rapport'; improving the conduct of organizations by emphasizing the requirement for public approval; and its promotion of human welfare 'by helping social systems adapt to changing needs and environments' (ibid.) Cutlip et al. also identify one of the positive aspects of socially responsible public relations as being its contribution to the professionalization of the practice by codifying ethical standards. The negative aspects of public relations are stated to be the promotion of special interests at the cost of public wellbeing (though no examples of this are given); the potential for cluttering communication channels and for 'cynicism and "credibility gaps"' (ibid.). It is, however, noticeable that whereas Cutlip et al. identify positive ends that public relations can achieve (business sponsorship of education, health campaigns, provision of goods and services, achieving profit for investors), they appear to shy away from identifying comparable examples demonstrating negative ends. One wonders whether the failure to do so is motivated by a worry that examples of negative effects implied by the 'promotion of special interests at the cost of public well-being' may be seen as propaganda. It is surely the fear of being associated with propaganda that partially fuels the drive to professionalization and the concern with ethics.

The ideal role of public relations is often presented as that of mediator between organizations and society without any sense of the possible tension that might result in this role. For example, Sharpe, a Professor at the School of Journalism at Ball State University, Indiana, in the USA, describes the purpose of the public relations role in society as being 'to harmonize an organization with the social environment' (Sharpe 1990: 23) by communicating honestly, consistently and continuously in order to achieve in return credibility, public confidence, fair treatment, mutual understanding and respect (ibid.: 32).

In another example, Matrat, styled as one of the 'grand old men' of public relations, argued that the role of public relations was to break down barriers between people, the cause of which he attributed to technological progress and specialization of functions in society: 'It is the purpose of public relations to re-establish communications and thus to improve human relations among groups and individuals. It does this by bringing into play the means to re-create such understanding' (Matrat 1990: 10). Matrat's analysis of the public relations role is to encourage good citizenship. He argues that an organization 'which regularly distributes information to give better knowledge of its structures, its role and the manner in which it carries out its functions, undoubtedly makes an important contribution to good citizenship *and to the functioning of democratic institutions*' (ibid.: 12; italics mine).

What these arguments do is present public relations as being intrinsically moral in its peace-making function as well as in its promotion and support of democracy. Arguments of this nature put emphasis on the 'public interest' and the promotion of 'dialogue'. The definition of 'public interest' is not always clear since in some cases (such as in Cutlip et al.) there is an assumption that the public interest is equated with some sort of utilitarian view. The link with democracy, however, enables public relations to act *against* the public interest on behalf of companies which produce, for example, cigarettes or weapons (Sorell 1991: 7). In some cases we do not have full knowledge of effects (for example of environmental pollution) and it could be argued that in such cases it is appropriate for activities to be tested in the court of public opinion (ibid.). But in other cases (cigarette manufacturers) we are in possession of evidence that demonstrates the effects of cigarette use in causing bronchitis, emphysema and lung cancer. In this case the freedom to choose to smoke or not and the freedom of cigarette companies to promote their products are regarded as being more beneficial to the public interest than preventative measures such as the banning of advertisements. It is this sort of example which Cutlip et al. do not consider when they cite the 'positives' of public relations.

There is, however, a problem in the attempt which some make to maintain the ideal of 'symmetry' alongside the role of public relations as advocate. Surely symmetry and advocacy are in opposition. The only way around this tension is to argue that public relations ensures that all views are held, i.e. that the playing field is level. Whether this sort of pandering to the liberal conscience is justifiable is a matter for debate: a debate which has yet to take place within public relations.

The appeal to democracy seems to arise as a way of protecting public relations from accusations of propaganda. It seems unthinkable to those that take this view that democracy might have its own propaganda. While there is not the space available here to review the debate about the relationship between public relations and propaganda it is worth noting that one could argue that some one-sided health campaigns could be defined as propaganda. Cutlip et al. clearly avoid any discussion of such issues since there is only one indexed reference to the term propaganda in their text. The reference arises only in the context of government communication. There is no indexed reference to propaganda at all in Grunig and Hunt (1984) or Grunig (1992).

The claim to promotion of the free flow of information and thus to democracy can be challenged simply because public relations services are only available to elite collectivities. Who, for example, will speak up for the unemployed? In the light of this example, claims that public relations helps democracy seem overblown. The alternative claim of supporting the public interest seems to imply neutrality and objectivity and to help the organization to change where it appears to infringe public interest, and this is especially true when such arguments are combined with ideas of harmonization in society. Such claims are surely as mythical as those of journalists to values of objectivity and truth-telling. Media sociologists have long since debunked these myths, yet they are still maintained in journalism academic and practitioner discourse (see *Journal of Mass Media Ethics*, vol. 4, no. 1, 1989). Some writers appear to assume that the media is an objective operation without any agenda-setting influence. For example:

> A social role of the professional persuader as advocate is to 'use' the media and other channels, to take advantage of a conduit function of mass communications to transmit messages that will reach the audience in as intact a form as possible.
>
> (Barney and Black 1994: 243)

Indeed, it is still the case that some debate about public relations ethics includes moral problems which arise for public relations because of its supposed origins in journalism (which, it is argued, espouses 'objectivity'), while public relations is more comfortable espousing advocacy (see McBride 1989: 5–20; Barney and Black 1994: 233–48).

Much of the literature about public relations ethics appears to be concerned with finding a justification for its practitioners. The emphasis appears to be on 'How they can gain – and deserve – the respect of a suspicious public while practicing the art and craft of persuasion, which entails creating and maintaining a favourable public image for their organization or client' (Barney and Black 1994: 234).

Such approaches seem so riddled with assumptions about the supposed potential benefits of public relations that it is quite hard to see them not simply as rhetoric, but as sophistry. Nelson recently wrote on behalf of the panellists featured in a special issue of *Public Relations Review* devoted to public relations ethics (vol. 20, no. 3) that public relations should re-evaluate its ethics to find an overall framework for ethical decision-taking. Nelson argues that what is needed is a 'more rigorous grounding in classical and contemporary theory rather than fallback to the expedient resort of journalistic wish-washyism and temporary ad hoc justifications. We need to anchor our personal and professional behaviour more firmly . . . in universal absolute principles' (Nelson 1994: 229). Nelson goes on to argue that knowledge of philosophers 'from Aristotle to Kant to Rawls' might have the effect of improving public relations 'rhetoric, performance and consistency – as well as peace of mind' (ibid.).

I would support this view in terms of the wider reading and understanding it implies, but would go further to suggest that it is not public relations 'performance' or 'peace of mind' that is of importance but that the implications of its social role are debated properly in society. Of fundamental importance in Nelson's position, however, is the implication that those involved in public relations, whether at a practical or academic level, should realize that their discipline is connected with long-standing philosophical and political debates. If public relations practitioners and academics do not like the way that they are portrayed, then they must master those philosophical and political ideas first before they come to the debating circle.

One way of conceptualizing the field in which organizational and other discourse takes place is that of the public sphere (see chapter 3). Habermas's ideas are important to public relations because of the presentation of the theoretical space for rational debate which is presented as the source for 'public opinion' to emerge from. Habermas's ideal conception of the public sphere of an arena for rational debate separate from economic and political considerations is threatened where certain interests have greater access and substantial resources with which to dominate.

Public relations increases the visibility and impact of large organizations, thus reducing available space for citizens. Far from liberating or facilitating public debate and dialogue or the expression of 'public opinion', public relations is profoundly instrumental, both intellectually and in terms of praxis. The use of largely positivist methodologies to 'measure' public opinion empowers clients, not publics. The use of the concepts of 'opinion leaders' or 'opinion formers' and 'networking' suggests that concepts of public opinion and democracy are as limited as they were in Habermas's coffee houses and as subject to elitism and class interests. Public relations facilitates the relationship between business and the media at the expense of others and thus contributes to the erosion of the public sphere. Public relations in itself is not accountable but is largely hidden in its contribution to predominating and deterministic 'market forces'. Individual campaigns may be criticized on various grounds but there is no route for criticizing the practice and its role in society as such.

Public relations as the conscience of the organization

Cutlip et al. suggest that one of the major positives of public relations is that 'Public relations improves the conduct of organizations by stressing the need for public approval' (Cutlip et al. 1994: 133).

Grunig makes a more modest claim for the public relations role in promoting organizational social responsibility in the context of the 'boundary-spanning role': 'public relations managers seldom have the power to make an organization publicly responsible. What they can do is communicate to organizational subsystems what publics believe to be irresponsible organizational behaviours' (Grunig and Hunt 1984: 56). Grunig goes on to say that the public relations role also encompasses communicating to publics what the organization has done that is responsible or irresponsible, and what it is doing to rectify the effects of any irresponsible actions.

These claims for the public relations role suggest that within the organization public relations is acting as the 'conscience' of the organization. For this reason it is sometimes suggested that public relations should be involved in setting up organizational codes of ethics and maintain a watching brief on organizational ethics. The scope of this brief could include monitoring the environment for publics' views on values; making company officials aware of prevailing ethical standards; helping companies refine their concepts of social responsibility; helping develop codes of ethics that are properly incorporated into planning, operating and appraisal procedures; developing strategies for explaining to publics how values shape company actions and decisions and helping senior managers to avoid crises that can damage reputation (Heath and Ryan 1989: 23-4).

The idea of public relations as the 'conscience' of the organization sounds moral and alluring perhaps because of its appeal to the idealistic concept of public relations acting as a peacemaker breaking down barriers between the organization and its publics. In practical terms, however, the 'conscience' concept seems to have specific implications which are rather less idealistic. It is quite clear that ultimately all the listening and soul-searching is directed towards organizational survival and that public relations is naturally only responsible to senior managers, not to employees or publics. Finally, a major implication for the sort of role outlined by Heath and Ryan is that the practitioner would need some knowledge of moral philosophy and applied ethics in order to manage discussion sensibly. Without this expertise it is hard to see how morality could avoid being subjected to organizational goals given the situation and role of the practitioner as outlined above.

JACQUIE L'ETANG

CORPORATE ACCIDENTS AND BLAME

Discussion of corporate responsibility often relates to specific incidents such as the well-documented cases of Bhopal,[3] *Challenger*,[4] *Exxon Valdez*,[5] the *Herald of Free Enterprise*[6] or the more recent *Estonia*[7] disaster. Such discussion often concerns the possibility of attaching blame to someone or something, i.e. the corporation itself, one of its principals or an agent acting on its behalf. Here I shall review debates in the field and draw out implications for the role of public relations.

The approach taken here follows Wells (1993) in discussing how a corporation may be regarded as criminally liable. The discussion relates to corporations because the concept of 'corporation' 'enables legal liability, whether criminal or civil, to attach to the enterprise itself rather than, or as well as, to any one person within it' (Wells 1993: 1). Most countries currently do not recognize criminal liability for corporations. The English common law system recognizes corporate liability to criminal prosecution but only where a senior official who personifies the corporation can also be prosecuted (Vidal and Cordahi 1995: 5). In Australia and Canada companies can be prosecuted even if no single person or collection of individuals can be identified for prosecution (ibid.). The rest of continental Europe uses civil law (which generally does not recognize corporate liability to criminal prosecution) and some countries such as Holland have specifically related environmental criminal law to corporate responsibility (ibid.).

The key issue is whether a corporation in itself could be held criminally liable or whether blame should be devolved to particular individuals held responsible for their actions. The argument rests on a particular conception of the nature of a corporation and its relationship to its constituent parts: its managers, shareholders and employees. Much of the legal discourse which has taken place on this issue is concerned with philosophical interpretations of legal concepts of organizations arrived at through a number of cases in legal history.

De George (1983) suggests that individuals and corporations may both be held culpable even though he accepts that the corporation in itself is not a moral agent, because the people within it are and actions done by them on behalf of corporations should be morally evaluated. He argues that

> People cannot be rid of their moral or legal responsibility simply by disclaiming it, or by seeking anonymity in corporate decisions, or by pretending decisions are impersonal or made by a corporation or organization that is not a moral being and so not morally accountable.
>
> (De George 1983: 164)

In practice, the legal conception of a corporation is an anthropomorphic legal fiction. On this account a corporation is an abstraction which possesses neither human mind nor human body and therefore is not capable of expressing intention. Intention is critical in criminal law as it applies to individuals, where judge and jury must determine whether a person was guilty because they had a 'guilty mind' (*mens rea*). Therefore, the corporation's

> active and directing will must consequently be sought in the person of somebody who for some purposes may be called an agent, but who is really the directing mind and will of the corporation, the very ego and centre of the personality of the corporation.
>
> (Viscount Haldane, cited by Lord Morris of Borth-y-Gest in *Lennard's Carrying Co. Ltd. v. Asiatic Petroleum Co. Ltd.* [1915] AC 713)

This makes it very difficult to hold corporations criminally responsible since the emphasis is on finding persons who can be identified as responsible and then deciding whether they work in the 'brain area' of the organization or whether they are simply the 'hands' or 'a cog in the machine'. If a corporation delegates full powers of responsibility to an individual, then he or she can be held responsible as part of the 'directing mind and will' or 'alter ego' of the corporation and the corporation may be held liable. If, however, an individual is deemed to have been 'directed' to perform certain functions and has failed to do so, then the individual is counted as 'another person' (not part of the corporate persona) and, provided the corporation can prove that it established adequate systems of line management and supervision, the corporation cannot be held responsible.

Some (Friedman 1970; Velasquez 1983) have argued that a corporation cannot be held responsible for actions because a corporation is not a human agent. Others (May 1986) argue that a corporation only acts in a vicarious way through the acts of those who are members of the corporation. Friedman (1970) argues that organizations cannot be moral agents with moral responsibilities because they are only 'artificial persons'. In his view, managers and employees are agents of the shareholders, directly responsible to them 'to conduct the business in accordance with their desires, which will generally be to make as much money as possible while conforming to the basic rules in society, both those embodied in law and those embodied in ethical custom' (Friedman 1970: 249).

For Friedman, employers are principal moral agents only when acting on their own behalf in their private lives. Friedman does not comment on the responsibilities of corporations in the event of corporate disasters; neither does he discuss the responsibilities of shareholders with regard to the corporations in which they invest. Velasquez (1983) focuses on the relationship between physical action and intention in order to argue that moral and criminal responsibility can only be attributed to an agent for actions which originated in the agent. Blaming the corporation is like blaming agents who were not involved in the action in question, which appears to infringe moral principle by effectively blaming the innocent. Velasquez argues that it is not correct to infer that the action of corporate members is the same as corporate action because the individual corporate members are autonomous and possessed of free will.

In contrast to Velasquez, French (1979) argues that corporate intentions may be inferred not only from individual actions but also from a corporation's official policies, decision-making procedures and lines of authority, which French refers to as 'CID' (Corporate Internal Decision structure). French's CID can be seen as a kind of group mind and is objected to because it encourages us to see and accept the corporation as a large-scale personality. Velasquez suggests that the danger here is that if the corporation is seen as an organic whole, then the interests and wellbeing of individuals both within and without the organization may be sacrificed to the organization's interests. As Wells points out:

> There is a public welfare in prevention of harm done to individuals by individuals as well as that done to individuals by collectivities and that done to the 'community' by collectivities. The state has a legitimate interest in all these.
>
> (Wells 1993: 7)

The suggestion that corporations should be more carefully restricted by legislation raises political issues and is likely to be strongly resisted by those who support free enterprise. In addition to these arguments one could also point out that companies do in fact deliberately promote themselves as personalities, developing expensive logos as symbols of their corporate identity (for further discussion of corporate identity, see chapter 5) in an attempt to cultivate a strong sense of corporate culture among their personnel. Public relations can be seen to be engaged in a process of symbolic management which helps both to define and then to capture, enhance and promote an identity or persona that stands for the organization, 'survival is understood as the maintenance of self-identity' (see chapter 8 for Pieczka's discussion of this organizational motivation in relation to the concept of autopoeisis). The scope of public relations in facilitating and promoting organizational totalitarianism in this context is considerable but currently quite outside both practitioner and academic public relations discourse.

As can be seen, there are a number of different positions on what constitutes corporate responsibility in the context of corporate accidents. While there are arguments for and against aggregating all individual actions, attributing responsibility to those in control or to those who were present when an accident occurred, there is considerable difficulty in identifying what might count as organizational as opposed to individual intent or recklessness. The central problem in dealing with a collectivity is that power and responsibility are almost always unevenly distributed within it. This problem becomes more apparent when one starts to consider what sort of punishment might be appropriate for an organization. While it seems just that in a hierarchical structure more blame should be attached to those responsible for conceiving and implementing policies, i.e. the 'mind' of the organization, the legal system is limited by the convention of criminal liability to attribute fault to individuals, not collectivities. The problem of attributing intention, mentioned at the outset, becomes an issue because 'Individual liability is . . . grounded in a theory of culpability based in mental states . . . not everyone is convinced that corporations can be said to possess a mental state' (Wells 1993: 95). The practical dilemma which arises from this is that 'the more diffuse the company structure, the more it devolves power to semi-autonomous managers, the easier it will be to avoid liability' (Feld and Jorg 1991: 150).

The process of individuation makes it difficult to prosecute corporations as entities and it also seems to inhibit discussion of another option: that of aggregating individual culpability and calculating the corporate responsibility from a quantitative as well as a qualitative evaluation. It certainly seems unjust that a corporation can escape criminal prosecution for manslaughter in cases where individual members have been allowed to carry out their duties in an irresponsible way. Wells suggests that if the 'concept of individual culpability is unsuitable for corporate conglomerates' (Wells 1989: 150), then an alternative standard and procedure may need to be developed. On the other side, Rafalko argues that 'the lesson of the Nuremberg trials is that guilt is individual; the notion of collective guilt has no place in American law' (Rafalko 1989: 923).

Rafalko goes on to argue that even the notion of individual guilt has its problems in a corporate setting because individuals may make a distinction between their private and work roles. He cites the Union Carbide/Bhopal case as an example where events highlighted this dilemma. Union Carbide's Chairman, Warren Anderson, initially pronounced personal moral responsibility and claimed that he would devote the rest of his life to helping people who had suffered during the tragedy, but a year later he said he had 'overreacted' when making this statement (Rafalko 1989: 923). The *New Yorker* magazine suggested that 'what Mr Anderson meant . . . perhaps, is that at first he reacted as a private man but in the intervening months he has remembered – or been reminded – that he is the head of a corporation' (quoted in Rafalko 1989: 923).

Even if one rejects the idea of a corporation possessing legal personhood, it has to be accepted that the corporation provides the context for moral action. Since a corporation has a certain amount of power and influence that derives from its position in society – for example power gained through the ability to attract media interest or conduct campaigns of public affairs and lobbying – it seems right that this should be balanced by a legal recognition of the corporation's moral responsibility. The appropriate punishment for organizations is also an area for debate. While at present erring companies may be fined, certain radical and imaginative writers have suggested that such companies should be 'beheaded' by wholesale sacking of top management or executed through compulsory nationalization (Rafalko 1989: 923).

What are the implications of the legal debate for the role of public relations? The role of public relations is likely to be extremely constrained by legal considerations and restricted to that of orator, dependent upon the advice of legal advisers: apologies and regrets must be carefully phrased. So public relations is here performing a subordinate role, not an advisory role. Second, in such a situation there is only room for advocacy of the managerial position, not of that of employees within the organization. External reputation may depend partly on success in attaching blame to one or two employees; public relations seems to be operating in an expedient way rather than on any considerations of ethics or justice. (This relates to the point made by Pieczka in chapter 8 about the attempt of public relations to join the dominant coalition for power-broking reasons while at the same time claiming values of 'decentralization, empowerment and trust' and the goal of symmetrical communication.) Finally, public relations acts on behalf of organizations to create corporate personae for marketing benefits. In this process it reinforces the sentimental and anthropomorphic conceptions of organizations which prevent us from seeing them for what they often are: autocratic and totalitarian. (Morgan's metaphors of political systems, social domination and psychic prisons are of relevance here; see Morgan 1989).

CONCLUSION

Corporate social responsibility as it is practised does not appear to conform to any theory of obligation (supported by contractual and deontological frameworks) as is implied by the language and concepts utilized by practitioners and corporate publicity. Corporate social responsibility seems largely dependent on some utilitarian concept of supererogatory action which benefits donor and recipient. However, the conceptualization of corporation appears to be somewhat different in the two distinct areas of corporate social responsibility that can be identified: those of crisis management and community programmes. In the field of crisis management, the process of conceptualization has been subject to much dispute and debate as corporate minds have been wonderfully concentrated by the potential threat of legal action; in this area it is in their interests to devolve responsibilities. However, in the field of community programmes, the corporation is very much presented as a moral person who can do good in society to the benefit of all. The notion of agency here is scarcely addressed, except in so far as it relates to the role of employees in such programmes. The contractual notions present in debates about crises are underdeveloped in terms of community relations since there is no sense in which the contract is negotiated or arbitrated: the corporation determines the playing field and referees the game. This is less true of community programmes which are focused on stakeholders or responsibilities arising from the economic role of the corporation, but there is no satisfactory justification for a deontological approach to non-stakeholders. The ability of corporations to determine the nature and scope of moral 'contracts' means that the only real bargaining occurs between state and business. This is where the conceptualization of the public sphere helps us to see the degree of domination present in our apparently democratic and open society. The role of public relations appears to be working to support that domination and thus working against, not for, democratic principles.

Corporate social responsibility is presented in public relations largely as a technique or tool for enhancing reputation. This chapter has shown that the field of corporate responsibility is a highly complex one involving ethical and political issues. Only if practitioners engage with such issues can they avoid the charges of superficiality and cynical exploitation of target audiences. The role of public relations itself is shown to be necessarily partisan and, furthermore, by operating on behalf of certain interests, intrinsically undemocratic.

One of the main conclusions which arises from this analysis is that public relations is implicated in a range of ethical and political issues of fundamental importance. Public relations can be seen to be intrinsically linked to power-broking initiatives in society and therefore a profoundly conservative force in society; the popular concept of public relations as 'neutral' seems to privilege the existing order over justice.

ACKNOWLEDGEMENT

The author would like to acknowledge the contribution made to the development of ideas in this work by the late Dr Murray MacBeath, who supervised her dissertation for the M.Phil. in Social Justice at the University of Stirling.

7

PUBLIC RELATIONS AND RHETORIC

Jacquie L'Etang

INTRODUCTION

This chapter explores the connections between rhetoric and public relations. Key terms such as persuasion, rhetoric and public relations are compared and contrasted. Ideas about public relations, persuasion, ethics and public opinion are explored partially through the description and analysis of key classical texts from which contemporary ethical and political implications are drawn out and discussed in the context of public relations theory. The debates which emerge from this analysis are related to the idea that the role of public relations is that of organizational rhetor.

The term 'rhetoric' is taken to mean persuasive strategies and argumentative discourse. However, the term has a long history and connotes a variety of meanings. The origins and development of rhetoric are discussed in relation to a variety of intellectual positions. It is argued that the study of rhetoric is of relevance to public relations in terms of its definition, its ethics and its epistemology. The chapter takes a broadly historical approach in that it tackles the classical concept of rhetoric prior to the review of contemporary developments in the field and a discussion of the relevance for public relations. The connections between classical and contemporary debates are enhanced by 'translating' some of the Greek ideas into modern concepts, following the practice of some of the sources used. This facilitates an understanding of the enduring nature of fundamental debates concerning communications practices in society. These are linked to discussion of the relationship between rhetoric and philosophy.

THE ORIGINS OF RHETORIC

The first formal usage of the term rhetoric (from the Greek *rhetorike*, public speaking) is thought to have been in one of Plato's dialogues, *Gorgias*, around 386 BC (Gagarin 1994: 46–8); the text is reviewed later in this chapter. The *Gorgias* was probably largely responsible both for the popularization of the term and for the development of ideas which condemned the practice: such condemnation resulted from Plato's unflattering representation of the practice and continues to the present day with the pejorative use of the term in phrases such as 'empty rhetoric'. For the Greeks, rhetoric was closely associated with logic and the development of persuasive speech. Rhetoric became a formal branch of learning in medieval Europe and was one of the seven liberal arts or sciences (the others being grammar, logic, arithmetic, geometry, astronomy and music) but did not survive as a subject after the Reformation (Hartley 1994: 264). The study of rhetoric gradually became absorbed into the study of literature and the philosophy of language.

There are different elements to the meaning and use of the term rhetoric which have strongly influenced the subsequent development of what is now recognized as a distinct yet interdisciplinary academic field. Especially important for an analysis which focuses on rhetorical aspects of public relations is the persuasive element: for Aristotle in particular, rhetoric was a technical skill which could be acquired to achieve persuasive effects. Persuasion is effected through the use of rhetoric, which is the application of techniques combining patterns of language and specific structures of argumentation, together with emotional appeals which can be expressed orally (oratory) or in written form. Aristotle's version of rhetoric emphasizes its 'social scientific' aspects, combining a type of behaviouristic psychology and logic in order to persuade, and could be seen as the precursor of Grunig and Hunt's (1984) 'asymmetric' public relations. The final and most controversial element is the ethical dimension: since Plato, writers have debated the ethics of persuasion. It appears that from at least the classical period, the concept of rhetoric encompassed analytical elements focused on the structure of language, the practical application of rhetoric in terms of persuasive effects, and debate regarding its social consequences. It is this broader approach which potentially links the debate about persuasion to that about propaganda and the latter's relationship with public relations.

Classical texts demonstrate the varying elements of rhetoric outlined above and clearly illustrate the conceptual difficulties involved in the definition of the boundaries of rhetoric, which are also reflected in the writing of recent and contemporary analysts. The roots of classical rhetoric began with a class of professional reciters who presented oral versions of Homeric texts known as *rhapsodes*, a word derived from the Greek *rhaptein*, which means 'to weave together' (Thomas and Webb 1994: 10). The skills thus developed were then applied by the Sophists and others for purely temporal ends. Even where the ethics and application of such a skill are doubted, as they were most clearly by Plato, the importance of good argument is recognized as a contribution to dialectical discourse. Thus, Socrates states in *Phaedrus* that speeches must be carefully constructed:

> any speech ought to have its own organic shape, like a living being; it must not be without either head or feet; it must have a middle and extremities so composed as to fit one another and the work as a whole.
> (Plato 1986: 79)

The techniques of rhetoric, however, developed in a specific social context which facilitated and encouraged men to acquire such skills.

THE CONTEXT OF CLASSICAL RHETORIC

The historical, cultural and political context of the texts of classical rhetoric demonstrate the original conceptions about the purpose of rhetoric and the role it played in society. Included in this review, which is largely based on Thomas and Webb (1994), is some discussion of various interpretations that can be made of the classical texts and their presentation of rhetoric. From the outset rhetoric has been associated with the development of varying forms of democracy. The standard interpretation is that rhetoric's origins were in Syracuse in the second quarter of the fifth century BC after the tyrant Thrasybulus had been deposed and a form of democracy established. Newly enfranchised citizens flooded the law courts with litigation to recover property that had been confiscated during the reign of the despot (Corbett 1965: 536). A Sicilian, Corax, assisted such citizens in pleading their claims in court and subsequently, with his compatriot Tisias, allegedly produced the first handbooks on effective speaking, which included 'examples of effective verbal argument' (Thomas and Webb 1994: 13). These handbooks, then, were the first steps towards an analytical and critical approach to oral language forms. This approach influenced those who became known as 'Sophists', the name derived from the Greek word for wisdom (*sophistes*, a wise man). The term 'Sophist' may be used in a variety of ways. It is sometimes used to describe travelling professional speakers who gave lectures on a range of philosophical topics, especially ethics, politics, epistemology and philosophy of language and of the mind (Lacey 1990: 227). Sometimes the term is used to specify pre-Socratic philosophers and on other occasions it is used in a pejorative sense to define later philosophers who made their living out of teaching argument that was effective but misleading. Later in this chapter we shall explore specific examples of this last type since they show how ethical issues became so bound up with questions of rhetoric.

In 427 BC, Gorgias, a Sicilian diplomat, brought the practice with him when he was posted to Athens, 'where democratic processes caused it to flourish' (Thomas and Webb 1994: 5). The Sophists advised others on the structure and style of speeches and on their dramatic presentation. They operated as 'consultants', charging fees for their advice, which was based on their research into the effectiveness of various speech styles and structures of argument (Lawson-Tancred in Aristotle 1991: 4). As writing technology developed so did the opportunities for creating permanent records and new applications and products for the Sophists to sell 'to ambitious young men from the Athenian upper classes for whom rhetorical training performed the same function as a modern university degree' (ibid.). In the context of Athenian democracy, the ability to present ideas and arguments in such a way as to sway an audience was a very important skill for citizens. Debates within the small citizen body determined policy and political appointments as well as legal cases, and, in the absence of professional barristers, a man's individual presentation skills and impression management might be required to help him defend his property, his position or even his life (Hamilton in Plato 1988: 7).

On one interpretation, the popularity of the Sophists owed as much to fears about democracy as to a rejoicing in it. It has been suggested that the institution of rhetorical training developed into a 'craze' and that 'The idea spread rapidly through the political elite that the worst consequences of opening up the constitution to mass accountability, in both the assembly and the law courts, could be mitigated by the mastery of new arts from abroad' (Lawson-Tancred in Aristotle 1991: 4). Consequently, the ability to persuade and influence public opinion was no longer assumed to be a gift but a transferable skill that could be taught by specialists who did not necessarily have any familiarity or expertise with the context or even the content of a given speech. There are clear similarities to be drawn here between the role of rhetoric in classical society and the role of public relations in contemporary pluralist societies. Indeed, since the 1970s critics have highlighted the importance of rhetoric in the modern practices of lobbying, mass media and advertising (Irwin in Plato 1979: 117, 131). In both public relations and rhetoric, practical emphasis on persuasive technique can distract from the political and philosophical implications of such a role, such as the correlation between social, economic and political power and the ability to have views represented and opinions taken account of within society. The power and influence of the rhetor is of paramount importance in gaining attention. The potential of organizational rhetors to dominate discourse is clearly greater than that of most individuals (royalty and leading politicians are potential exceptions), and a society structured around large organizations is likely to give more space for organizational rather than individual discourse.

However effective the Sophists may have been in their oral presentations and application of good argument, ultimately their reputation management was poor and their image in the literature arising from their contemporaries is not good. 'They were accused, especially by Plato, of logic-chopping and subversiveness, but also of pandering to popular tastes' (Lacey 1990: 227).

The Sophists were criticized in a number of texts, notably in Aristophanes' plays *The Wasps* and *The Clouds*. In *The Clouds* Strepsiades is

> driven by mounting debt to study with Socrates, who is pictured as a representative Sophist, so that he can learn how to escape from his

> creditors, whose cases against him are otherwise valid. Strepsiades' only reason for wanting to learn the tricks of the sophist is to cheat others.
>
> (Gagarin 1994: 47)

In *The Wasps* Aristophanes describes the typical Athenian juror as 'blinded by prejudice and utterly unconcerned with the truth of a litigant's case' (Gagarin 1994: 47).

The concerns regarding rhetoric in classical literature were largely focused on the lack of protection for society from evil men using rhetoric for their own ends. The 'essence' of rhetoric in terms of its definition, its moral content and its role in society was the subject of much debate by philosophers. In particular, the role of rhetoric in producing knowledge or truth was a major concern, as can be seen in the next section which summarizes criticisms made at the time.

GORGIAS AND THE CRITICISMS OF RHETORIC

One of the sharpest critiques of rhetoricians is that presented in *Gorgias* by Plato, through the character of Socrates, Plato's mentor and teacher. The character of Gorgias is loosely based upon the historical character described in the section above. A summary of the key aspects of the debate follows and this is later linked to contemporary concerns about the role of public relations. It is important to note that a traditional view of *Gorgias* is given here and that revisionist interpretations of the dialogue have highlighted a bias in Plato's presentation of the arguments.

The main approach which Plato takes in his critique in *Gorgias* is to raise questions about the ethics of the Sophists. Quite apart from his personal feelings and extreme bitterness about the fate of Socrates (who was coerced into taking poison by the Athenian people in 399 BC because he refused to recognize their gods and also because he was thought to be corrupting the younger generation), Plato was concerned with the implications for society of the role which the Sophists had begun to play and the influence which they appeared to be able to wield. The Sophists claimed that their practice was a distinctive skill or art which could be learned and applied to any body of knowledge to secure influence for those who could afford either to pay for such representation or to learn these skills themselves. Plato argued that the practice could lead to injustice being perpetrated in society even though the Sophists were presenting their craft as a neutral skill. Plato regarded the practice as potentially evil and also as an intellectual threat to his philosophical position, which sought to identify universal answers to the question 'How should a man live?' The Sophists' position, by contrast, appeared to be a relativist one. Some of the questions which Plato raised are useful in thinking about the role of public relations today and are reviewed in the following discussion of the dialogue *Gorgias*.

Gorgias expresses Plato's overall concern about the power and effects of oratory in society and his particular concern that a good orator may have the power to mislead his listeners. Through a dialogic medium the author explores the merits and demerits of the role of the persuasive communicator. Those taking part include a famous orator, Gorgias; a young man named Polus, who has written a thesis on oratory; a young and ambitious Athenian, Callicles; the host Chaerophon; and, of course, the philosopher Socrates.

The debate begins with Socrates questioning Gorgias about the nature and definition of oratory. Gorgias has some difficulty with this and Socrates teases him by suggesting that the power of oratory is almost supernatural. Eventually, Gorgias arrives at the following definition:

> GORGIAS: I mean the ability to convince by means of speech a jury in a court of justice, members of the Council in their Chamber, votes at a meeting of the Assembly, and other gathering of citizens whatever it may be. By the exercise of this ability you will have the doctor and the trainer as your slaves, and your man of business will turn out to be making money not for himself but for another; for you, in fact, who have the ability to speak and convince the masses.
>
> SOCRATES: Now, Gorgias, I think that you have defined with great precision what you take the art of oratory to be, and, if I understand you aright, you are saying that oratory is productive of conviction, and that this is the be-all and end-all of its whole activity.
>
> (Plato 1988: 28)

Gorgias clarifies his position, that 'Oratory serves . . . to produce the kind of conviction needed in courts of law and other large assemblies, and the subject of this conviction is right and wrong' (Plato 1988: 31). In response to this Socrates distinguishes between two kinds of conviction, that resulting in knowledge and that resulting in belief. The discussion ranges over the nature of conviction and the effect of orators on public opinion as Plato tries to show how certain questions about rhetoric raise some problematic ethical issues. Socrates suggests that it is always important to consult subject specialists rather than orators, so that if one was building a wall one would consult an architect, not an orator. Gorgias responds to this by citing an occasion where the siting of Athens' dockyards and harbour walls was decided not only by professional builders but as a result of the debate between Themistocles and Pericles: 'And you can see that when there is a choice to be made of the kind that you spoke of just now it is the orators who dictate policy and get their proposals adopted' (ibid.: 32).

Gorgias suggests in debate that a powerful orator does not need to be an expert in the subject he is speaking about. The example given is that on matters of health an orator could be more convincing than a doctor:

SOCRATES: The orator need have no knowledge about things: it is enough for him to have discovered the knack of convincing the ignorant that he knows more than the experts.

GORGIAS: And isn't it a great comfort, Socrates, to be able to meet specialists in all the other arts on equal terms without going to the trouble of acquiring more than this single one?

(Plato 1988: 38)

These same points can also be made about public relations. One could question the ethics of public relations officers representing the nuclear industry in cases where individuals have no specialist qualification in the relevant scientific field. On what basis might one believe such a person when he or she speaks about the safety of their installation or industry? In this case it appears that it is only their power to convince, not their knowledge, which has influence.

When pressed, Socrates himself defines oratory as a knack, a 'spurious counterfeit of a branch of the art of government' (Plato 1988: 44) and his criticisms focus on what he calls 'pandering', which he defines as the practice of giving the audience what they want (often in terms of entertainment) without regard to truth, justice or the general welfare. Socrates defines rhetoric as a skill which enables the orator to persuade others about matters of truth and justice while conveying neither knowledge nor understanding in listeners, only conviction. From this he argues that rhetoric is concerned only with appearances and is as far from justice as cooking is from medicine (Plato 1988: 8; Gagarin 1994: 47–8).

ARISTOTLE AND THE ART OF RHETORIC

Aristotle's *The Art of Rhetoric* is often presented as being the first formal attempt to define a science of persuasion. Then, as it sometimes is now, persuasion was usually seen as an intrinsic gift. While the early Sophists attempted to define practical advice based on the analysis of texts, they were not able to evolve clear principles from their research and so their contribution was limited, in the same way that some public relations teaching is limited by experienced practitioners adopting a 'how I did it' approach without reference to underlying principles (see the discussion about education versus training in chapter 1). Aristotle, however, sought to develop a methodical and rigorous approach to, and analysis of, the subject and it is really at this point that rhetoric shifts focus from a philosophical tradition based on essentialism and universal values to an approach akin to that of contemporary applied social science. Plato's criticism of the Sophists, while apparently focused on moral debate, is a strong critique of relativist ethics and an argument about epistemology.

The Art of Rhetoric is basically a manual of persuasion which explores the principles underlying various types of proof. It clearly anticipates contemporary communications, psychological and sociological research into persuasive communication, as well as the numerous practical guides on selling, advertising and public relations published in recent years. For example, its focus on the structure of argument is reflected in the contemporary application of social psychology (Bettinghaus and Cody 1994), and there are elements which imply and anticipate the use of psychological understanding about personality types and persuasibility and the effects of engendering different emotions to enhance persuasive effects. Aristotle's work specifies a much broader role for the rhetorician than that of mere orator, a role which encompasses that of an adviser or counsellor role in the devising and production of convincing arguments and proofs.

> It is this that justifies the definition of rhetoric not, as in earlier studies, as the artificer of persuasion, but as the technique of discovering the persuasive aspects of any given subject matter, and it is this too that justifies the close parallel frequently drawn with dialectic.
>
> (Lawson-Tancred in Aristotle 1991: 65)

Aristotle, therefore, clearly separated the act of communication (oratory) from preparatory research and the planning of logical argument structures.

Other writers discussing classical rhetoric make some shrewd points about the importance of trustworthiness and reputation in terms of contributing to the process of conviction. There is a familiar feel to the ideas expressed in terms of public relations practice; for example: 'Openness, manifested explicitly in a readiness to reveal things which one might be expected to conceal, or a promise to tell the whole story from the beginning helps to establish trust' (Carey 1994: 37). There is a clear similarity here with the guidance offered in crisis management texts in terms of media relations and in the management of corporate reputation.

RHETORIC AND PERSUASION

The relationship between rhetoric and persuasion is one of fundamental importance because a number of ethical and epistemological issues are contingent upon it. In rhetoric and persuasion there are examples of definitions which are more instrumental and others which highlight ethical considerations and fears of manipulation and coercion. The concept of free will is important in separating persuasion from negative connotations of manipulation, coercion, 'brainwashing' and propaganda. These terms raise a fundamental point about who is to define a piece of communication as persuasive, manipulative or coercive. A number of sociologists researching in this area (Barker 1984; M. Smith 1982) have argued that such definitions should be subjectively arrived at by the receiver of the communication. Perloff suggests that persuasion and coercion are not 'polar opposites' but part of a continuum:

> The differences are subtle; often they are not discernible to outside observers who use the term coercion to describe a social influence attempt [sic] that they disapprove of and employ terms like persuasion or information campaign to describe influence attempts that are consistent with their values.
>
> (Perloff 1993: 13)

Research into persuasion has focused strongly on the identification and measurement of the attitudes of those who have been the target of a particular persuasive communication in order to determine the effectiveness of different persuasion strategies. Such a scientific approach takes an 'objective' stance to the concept of persuasion, arguing that it is a neutral skill which can be applied for both good and evil ends and can be seen as descending from the Sophists. The argument about neutrality may be linked to that which proposes that public relations contributes to pluralist or liberal democracy because it helps the process of ensuring that all views get aired. There is an important tension here between the view that public relations is a neutral and technically driven operation which may be employed to promote the view of either party in a dispute and that which states that public relations is concerned with 'the truth'.

The concept of rhetoric has implications for criteria of knowledge and truth. If we accept the position that universal truths are achievable, then in a situation in which two parties take different positions we will believe that only one of them can be right. Alternatively, if we do not believe that there is only one right answer, we are accepting the (relativist) point that there may be different perspectives which can be derived only from analysing rhetor, rhetoric (the rhetor's product) and the audience of the rhetoric. As an example of the difficulty of finding 'universal truth' even in a specifically scientific context one can take the occasion in 1995 when the environmental group Greenpeace challenged the multinational company Shell over their plans to dump the disused oil storage platform the Brent Spar 120 miles north-east of the Shetland Islands. The ecological and scientific facts were subject to rhetorical strategies by both parties. Greenpeace claimed that the storage tanks contained more than 100 tonnes of toxic and radioactive material which would damage marine life if the platform were to be sunk, while Shell, admitting that the waste contained small amounts of heavy metals, claimed that any contaminants would be quickly diluted and that the decommissioning was the best option and was consistent with national law and international conventions. On 1 May 1995 British media reported that Greenpeace protestors had occupied the Brent Spar and these were removed by force. Greenpeace won the public relations campaign and public opinion in continental Europe forced a climb-down in Shell's policy.[1] In evaluating the event, news editors said that they thought they had been manipulated by Greenpeace: as David Lloyd of Channel 4 commented, 'The pictures provided to us [by the Greenpeace film crew] showed plucky helicopters riding into a fusillade of water cannons. Try writing the analytical science into that' (A. Cuff, 'Greenpeace used us, broadcasters admit', *The Guardian*, 28 August 1995). Subsequently, Greenpeace had to retract claims about Brent Spar's toxic cargo because their personnel had used the wrong methodology when testing materials on the platform.

Public relations construed as rhetoric argues for a particular perspective or version, i.e. 'the truth' is relative. On this account, then, the question of whether ethics is also relative must be considered. How is one to arrive at an acceptable ethic for public relations from a rhetorical perspective? This is a question I shall return to later but it should be noted that it is very difficult to make a case for ethics within the postmodern perspective (a concern in the contemporary field of rhetoric) which is implied by the rhetorical stance outlined above. For this reason, public relations scholars seeking ethical justification for the practice have based their arguments on modernist, rationalist constructs.

CONTEMPORARY DEVELOPMENTS IN RHETORIC

Rhetoric has had something of an intellectual renaissance due to the influence of structuralism, poststructuralism, semiotics and postmodernist thinking, streams of thought which move away from essentialist conceptions of society and knowledge towards relativist and phenomenological approaches: society and knowledge are explained as being the result of certain intellectual structures which arise partly from cultural experience and language. Debates which spring from structuralism and poststructuralism focus on the relationship between thought and language, and between the thinking, articulate subject and the object. Structuralism and semiotics explore the sources and signs of culture, and the ways in which our experiences and knowledge are influenced and structured by these. Structuralism abandoned the idea that there was an intrinsic 'essence' or meaning in a text or that the author's intention was either obvious or of paramount importance (Hartley 1994: 302). Work in the structuralist tradition tries to identify systems of structural patterns within a text which enable the reader to generate meaning. This philosophical position led to the form of analysis known as deconstruction, in which the critic or reader tries to extract that which is missing or suppressed, or regarded as deviant in the discourse(s) or power relations present in the text under review (ibid.: 304). A 'text' in this context has a very broad meaning and can refer to not only literary works but also dramatic performances, films, television and public or cultural events. Poststructuralism emphasized the reader rather than the text as a site of enquiry and therefore focused more on psychoanalytical influences on the interpretation of meaning and on external structures, such as ethnicity and gender, that facilitate meaning processes (ibid.: 304). Postmodernism presents an epistemology based on 'multiple and fragmentary worlds . . . that overlap, compete and transform themselves continuously' (Halloran 1993: 114).

These intellectual currents imply that the relationship between thought, language, signification, dialectics and knowledge is contested, dynamic and intrinsically rhetorical. Rhetoric focuses on the sign system, the devices and strategies that operate within texts and the sense-making function of specific discourses (Hartley 1994: 266). As Bizzell and Herzberg note, 'twentieth-century theories of rhetoric, in formulating the relationships between language and knowledge and in re-examining the powers of discourse, have extended the concerns of rhetoric to include nothing less than every instance of language use' (Bizzell and Herzberg, cited in Enos and Brown 1993: viii). Hartley also suggests that the forms of the cultural produce with which we are surrounded are 'highly rhetorical' and that 'Publicity, advertising, newspapers, television, academic books, government statements and so on, all exploit rhetorical figures to tempt us to see things their way' (Hartley 1994: 266).

Rhetorical thinking is thus connected to debate, argument (intentional communication) and persuasion (instrumental communication). The views of Sophists and ancient Sceptics anticipate relativism and postmodernism in their rejection of a universal standard in favour of a range of different perspectives. This is of importance to public relations for two reasons: first, because it suggests that there is no one overall standard with regard to those interests on behalf of which public relations operates, and, second, because it also suggests that there is no one overall standard for public relations practice itself. Much of the debate about the ethics of public relations has focused on its social role and conflict between client and public interest such as the promotion of causes thought to be unjustifiable (for example products or industrial processes which either are or have the potential to be injurious to the health of consumers or production workers, e.g. tobacco products or asbestos). Some have tried to get around this problem by arguing that public relations is intrinsically ethical because it promotes democracy and good citizenship (there is a detailed discussion of these claims and their supporting arguments in chapter 6). This move necessitates consideration of questions of power and access since these elements will influence ability to communicate as well as how a piece of communication is regarded. A discussion about the social role and ethics of public relations should at least acknowledge important linked debates about knowledge acquisition and communication ethics. The field of rhetoric is an important part of such a discussion, not only because of its historical link to public relations but also because currently it directly confronts questions of dialogue, debate and persuasion within a framework which takes account of ethics and postmodernist thought.

Contemporary developments in rhetoric have returned to explore the tension between philosophy (based on foundational and universalist principles) and rhetoric (seen as relativist) and thus to the problematic of the ethics of rhetoric. The renewed interest in the ancient concept of rhetoric began in the 1950s and the expansion and development of the field has been dubbed 'The New Rhetorics' (Enos and Brown 1993: vii–xiii). Work in this area connects with a wide range of analytical work in discourse analysis and postmodernism, as well as with more practical application of languages and argument in Departments of English or Schools of Communication and Writing. Thus it can be seen that the twin streams of analysis and practice, present in the classical tradition, are still represented today.

Cohen (1994: 69–82) identifies a number of separate perspectives in the New Rhetorics. These include an extension of the traditional understanding of rhetoric as a methodology for the study of argument; an attempt to overcome the traditional hostility between philosophy and rhetoric by using rhetoric itself as a way of explaining dialectical principles; the use of rhetoric as an analytical tool for fictional narrative; the attraction of rhetoric for postmodernists because of its rejection of philosophical conceptions of universals such as truth and knowledge. The New Rhetorics is marked by diversity, transformation and dialogue in order to achieve a broad understanding of what 'our contending viewpoints reveal about skilled human discourse' (Bazerman, cited in Enos and Brown 1993: x). These different approaches are reflected in a variety of contemporary definitions of 'rhetoric' reflecting different aspects of the historical, political and cultural baggage that the term encompasses. Bazerman suggests that the field can be approached in a variety of ways that reflect and 'characterize our approach to dividing up and studying the symbolic domain' (Bazerman 1993: 4). So, for example, one approach might look specifically at symbolic activity which seemed primarily motivated by persuasion, whereas an alternative approach might analyse the nature and focus of organizational rhetors and rhetoric. Bazerman argues from an instrumental perspective that most rhetorical study is concerned with its practical application and that our thinking about this matters because

> symbolic action is a major dynamic of society to be wielded for public and private ends. Prescriptions for traditional rhetorics, proscriptions for traditional rhetorics, proscriptions against stigmatized rhetorics, projections of new rhetorics – all advance social visions, perceived by their advocates to improve the human condition.
>
> (Bazerman 1993: 4)

The relevance of rhetoric to public relations lies not only in its communicative function but also in its symbolic and structural role managing meaning within and between organizations and publics and in the claim to be contributing to a better society by assisting the flow of information. Rhetoric, however it is defined, is important to public relations at both technical and theoretical levels and impacts upon both the practice and the interpretation of public relations.

PERSUASION AND PUBLIC RELATIONS

At this point it will be useful to review the role of persuasion in public relations and the way in which persuasion has been presented in the public relations literature. Practical 'how-to-do-it'-type manuals may equate public relations goals with persuasive goals: 'If you're a PR consultant you're in the persuasion business. By definition that means that your primary goal in life is to change the attitudes and subsequent behaviour of others to those viewpoints of your own (or your clients')' (Q. Bell 1991: 24).

This approach is common in practice but has been defined and critiqued as the asymmetrical model of public relations (Grunig and Hunt 1984; Grunig 1992). Grunig argues that the asymmetrical approach, defined as 'a way of getting what an organisation wants without changing its behaviour or without compromising' (Grunig 1992: 39), leads to actions which are unethical, socially irresponsible and ineffective. Grunig argues that 'Organisations get more of what they want when they give up some of what they want' (Grunig 1992: 39). While it is possible to imagine a continuum, at one end of which is coercion and manipulation and at the other end of which lies negotiation and cooperation, with persuasion somewhere in the middle, it is also possible to argue that if the organizational goal remains getting 'more of what they [organizations] want', 'symmetry' collapses into 'asymmetry'.

A rather different view is put forward by Miller (1989), who defines public relations as a process which attempts to manage symbolic control over the environment. He argues that effective persuasion and effective public relations are 'virtually synonymous because both are primarily concerned with exerting symbolic control over relevant aspects of the environment' (G. Miller 1989: 45). Miller proposes a model of persuasion which entails active participation by the persuadee, who in effect self-persuades. This is achieved through a process in which the persuadee is given the opportunity to become involved in the creation of the persuasive message through a dialogical process.

A consideration of the role of ethics in persuasion raises questions over the nature of evaluation methodology. Persuasion could be evaluated empirically in terms of effectiveness (an instrumental approach). In this case, questions arise as to what counts as effectiveness and the basis on which this should be decided. For example, in cases regarding public health it might be argued that decisions should be based on scientific and medical knowledge, which might be presented as a conception of 'the truth', and some concept of a majoritarian 'public interest', which may permit the infringement of the rights of a minority (to smoke, for example). Persuasion might be justified in such cases but there are clearly cases where 'hard' evidence is not forthcoming and so persuasion is based on a myriad of conceptions and opinions, shaped partly by argument but also by experience and knowledge. This is why arguments about concepts of 'truth' and the way in which knowledge is acquired and shaped are of such importance in public relations.

Alternatively, persuasive acts might be judged in terms of the relationship between the parties concerned and their views of each other (a co-orientation approach). This would raise issues of the nature of the communication between parties, such as the degree of 'openness', a concept which has received much attention in public relations theory.

The argument that can be presented on behalf of rhetoric is that it has the capability to publicize or make known 'truth' or 'facts', and for Aristotle this function served a justifiable and scientifically neutral purpose in society. On this account, rhetoric is simply a neutral conveyor of the truth which is apparently only available to the few. For Scott this

> suggests the dynamic of an elite, those who are . . . situationally fortunate, leading those who are not. One may call the process 'rhetoric' by which the elite govern, but, if so, one should realize the set of assumptions about people and knowledge in the world that accompanies the label.
>
> (Scott 1993: 122)

Public relations literature presents the function as a set of skills which can be used to promote a client's case. As suggested earlier, however, the role may effectively be promoting what Scott calls 'second-rate truth[s]' (Scott 1993: 124), i.e. ideas which are not amenable to the scientific method of research. But he points out that even 'scientific' evidence is within certain discourses which are subject themselves to rhetoric, so that scientific knowledge is to some degree socially constructed. The question of elitism arises again if one accepts that only certain qualified people have access to those truths. He goes on to argue that if there are no prior truths (because he suggests that these in themselves are subject to rhetorical creation and promotion), then rhetoric has a role in creating a concept of truth which is dynamic and evolutionary, ever subject to testing through dialectics. Porter argues that postmodernism shows that 'methods themselves are rhetorically invented entities. Dialectic is not prior to or free of rhetoric; it is itself subject to rhetoric' (Porter 1993: 212).

The public relations academic Pearson argues that

> The strongest claim about the epistemic role of rhetoric is that all epistemological endeavour is rhetorical . . . According to Leff (1978) this view collapses the empirical into the symbolic: We live in a symbolic world, and all knowledge is a function of how communities of knowers construe and manipulate symbols.
>
> (Pearson 1989b: 116)

It is this sort of approach which has led to a greater ethical focus on the *process* of communication rather than the specific content and is of value in discussing public relations.

THE RHETORICAL SCHOOL OF PUBLIC RELATIONS

A rhetorical approach to contemporary public relations studies views 'the organisation as speaker' (Toth 1992: 3) and gives emphasis to the impact of public relations in society. Such an approach may be instrumental, in evaluating 'the effectiveness of organisational messages in successfully advocating organisational stances' (ibid.: 6) but will also take account of and evaluate rhetorical messages in terms of their 'ethical value to the public interest' (ibid.: 6).

The approach promotes the concept of the organizational advocates who, through 'a dialectic process . . . use symbolic exchange to come to agreements about cultural structures, events and actions' (Toth 1992: 6). On this account, rhetoric is fundamental to the functioning of society and to communicative action. It acknowledges self-interest and argues that rhetoric facilitates the negotiation of relationships. As a research approach, rhetorical studies in public relations focus on identifying symbols and expressing and arguing opinions 'dialogically to search for truth' (Heath 1992: 19–20) Heath suggests that although rhetoric can imply manipulative one-way communication it can also be used to create a contested debate about issues and positions. Heath argues that while 'truth' is required as the basis for rhetoric if rhetoric is not to mislead, relativism is a necessary feature because of the necessity to interpret and debate issues: 'Indeed, "facts" demand interpretation as to their accuracy, relevance and meaning. Not only do people argue about facts, but they contest the accuracy of conclusions drawn from them' (ibid.).

The issue of relativism and its relevance for ethics and for public relations is addressed directly by Pearson (1989a). Pearson suggested that public relations was 'situated at precisely that point where competing interests collide' (Pearson 1989a: 67) and that public relations problems could be defined in terms of 'the collision, or potential collision, of these interests' (ibid.).

Following his identification of this crux, Pearson's argument has two threads: the first is that he suggests that empirically, public relations practitioners are relativists who see themselves as serving different interests (clients). Pearson proposes that in order to escape the difficulty of there being different views about the ethics of policies being advocated, efforts to reconcile difference should be refocused on to the 'type of communication system [that] can most likely mediate among these interests' (Pearson 1989: 70). Pearson states that the important structural elements in ethical communication are Grunig and Hunt's (1984) communication, negotiation and compromise. Pearson suggests that support for these ideas is to be found in Ehling's (1984, 1985) message exchange or communication-as-conversation, Ackerman's (1980) concept of neutral dialogue and Habermas's (1970, 1984) communication symmetry. Pearson uses Ackerman and Habermas to bolster Grunig's concept of 'symmetrical communication'.

Habermas's theory of communicative action (1984) proposes that all linguistic communication takes place on the assumption that certain communicative norms exist; these norms not only encompass the technical aspects of language (grammar) but also recognize that different types of intention lie behind different types of statement and that to common understanding reality comprises external objects, cultural norms and internal (private) intentions. Habermas's concept of conversation entails a constant probing and testing of claims made, and in an ideal speech communication either party should feel free to make such challenges, to introduce new concepts and to move from one level of abstraction to another. Habermas argued that the potential of communication to provide rational emancipation for all individuals was hindered by power relations. Habermas suggests that humans operate on the assumption and expectation of rationality in order to reach consensus and that this is necessarily reflected in the way in which communication takes place; any distortion in the process, such as an unequal distribution of power, is therefore irrational and inhibits the potential for 'the general symmetry requirement' or 'ideal speech communication' (Ray 1993: 26).

Pearson argues that Habermas's theory of the ideal speech communication act, which proposes a number of key rules which would promote the ideal speech communication situation, is 'couched in the language of symmetrical communication' (Pearson 1989a: 72).

The difficulty in applying these ideal concepts to public relations is that participants are clearly *not* equal. To take two examples: the power and resources of government will be greater than those of many organizations and the power and resources of many organizations will be greater than those of many publics. Furthermore, symmetrical communication and its associated concepts of negotiation and mutuality seem not to take account of the role of the media in mediating, reinterpreting or amplifying the 'conversation' between participants. The application of Habermas's framework and the concept of symmetry (which Pearson offers as a potentially practical and measurable framework when combined with a co-orientation communication model) oversimplifies the context within which public relations operates. Within the new rhetorical school in public relations there is the possibility of bringing organizational communication down to the individual level of spokespersons for the organization. This could obscure consideration of the collective responsibility for organizational rhetoric, policy-making and action, and inhibit comprehension and acknowledgement of the power which lies behind the organizational rhetor (see chapter 6 for further discussion of organizational responsibility). The framework's focus on spokespersons (orators) not only conceals the organizational dialectical dynamics which lead to the position adopted (a substantial rhetorical and political dimension) but also presumes an openness or transparency about all organizational communication which may not be justified, for example in the areas of public affairs and lobbying.

It also remains unclear whether a distinction between the concepts of symmetry and dialogue is to be made clear or is of importance in public relations. Both are presented as end-states which are desirable in themselves and partially achieved through debate and agreement (i.e. dialogue and symmetry) over communication rules which would facilitate those end-states. The argument thus appears to be circular: dialogue and symmetry can only be achieved through dialogue and symmetry. Pearson presents a choice between 'symmetry' (dialogue) and 'asymmetry' (monologue/persuasion) but does not explore the social or political contexts which allow certain interests an enhanced position in which they have more choice in the nature and type of communicative acts they carry out.

The development of rhetorical ideas in public relations is clearly a route through which the subject can be connected to important arguments in ethics and epistemology and seems likely to be a rich area for future debate. It should, however, be noted that to date self-proclaimed rhetorical scholars within public relations have not really presented an alternative paradigm, in that they still have sought to work within the systems framework. Heath, for example, argues that although the rhetorical paradigm acknowledges self-interest it 'is not antithetic to the symmetry paradigm . . . the assertion of self-interest can only go as far as others are willing to allow it to do so' (Heath 1992: 318).

CONCLUSION

Pearson's approach appears to site ethical value in the power of dialectic. There is disagreement by rhetorical scholars on the relationship between rhetoric and dialectic. For some (Rowland and Womack 1985: 13–31), dialectic is characterized by its truth-seeking function whereas rhetoric is simply a persuasive communicative technique. For such thinkers rhetoric in itself cannot be described as moral or immoral; it is as ethical as the ends to which it is put. As noted above, this argument is also employed in relation to public relations by those who think that the ethics of public relations are unproblematic or can be easily defined; for example:

> The purpose of public relations practice is to establish two-way communication seeking common ground or areas of mutual interest, and to establish understanding based on truth, knowledge and full information.
>
> (Black 1989: 1)

> There is no mystery about public relations. Practised, as it always should be, with integrity and with an honest presentation of the facts, to a great extent it is advocacy based on the intelligent use of the media of communication to promote mutual understanding and to enable the public to have an informed opinion.
>
> (Gillman 1976: v)

The expression of such 'motherhood' principles oversimplifies reality and tends to reinforce internal tensions within the subject. The challenge in addressing the ethical issue lies not so much in justifying the activity as a legitimate enterprise, but in untangling the nature of public relations and the assumptions which lie behind the concept. Such discussion requires careful definition and exploration of concepts, epistemology, methodology and ethics.

It is sometimes said that public relations is a recent phenomenon, but it is clear that its purpose and role in society and the type of communication entailed raise questions that have been asked of rhetoric 'for nearly two and a half millennia' (Scott 1993: 122). Since much of the relatively recent academic arm of public relations is located within instrumental or applied traditions, students and practitioners are often ill equipped to respond to (often superficial) criticism of their discipline. Consequently they may be tempted into making sweeping (and sometimes contradictory) statements which try to emphasize the positive aspects of the role of public relations. A theoretical approach to public relations and rhetoric may reveal the negative aspects of public relations as traditionally and originally publicized by Plato, but may also reveal understanding about and justifications for the discipline.

This chapter has tried to show that a discussion about public relations and its relationship with rhetoric has implications for ethical and normative theory in public relations. It is clear that developing ideas about public relations are related to fundamental issues in communication, ethics, politics and sociology. Consequently, it is proposed that basic theory-building in public relations should be informed by an understanding of debates in epistemology, linguistics, structuralism, poststructuralism, modernism and postmodernism. Approaches which take account of arguments from these traditions seem to have the potential to develop subtle and important theories about public relations which can improve our understanding of this major force in contemporary society.

ACKNOWLEDGEMENT

The author wishes to acknowledge that the original inspiration for this chapter came from the teaching of Sandra Marshall, Head of the Department of Philosophy, University of Stirling.

8

PARADIGMS, SYSTEMS THEORY AND PUBLIC RELATIONS

Magda Pieczka

INTRODUCTION

One of the presuppositions underpinning current public relations theorizing is the concept of a system; or, to be more precise, the belief that organizations behave in ways that can be conceptualized as closed or open systems (Grunig and Hunt 1984; Botan and Hazleton 1989a; Cutlip et al. 1985; Grunig 1992). This presupposition has far-reaching consequences in terms of attempts at building public relations theories per se, but also for the nature of emerging academic public relations discourse. This chapter attempts to address broader methodological questions by focusing on the way in which systems theory underpins current public relations theory. The aim is to fill a gap in public relations literature by showing the origins of fundamental presuppositions currently made by most academic writers in the field. The chapter thus presents both a critique and a source of references for those who wish to acquaint themselves with debates more fully.

Those who wish to tackle only the argumentative parts of the chapter as opposed to the careful mapping of the field may wish to proceed directly to the section 'Public relations discourse' (pp. 143–52), as it is from this point onwards that critical points about public relations theory are developed. The sections entitled 'Systems theory and public relations theory' (pp. 144–50) and 'Implications' (pp. 152–6) focus strongly on public relations theory and literature and critically analyse a number of key public relations texts for their treatment and use of systems theory.

In order to make its point, this chapter has to proceed in a particular manner: by introducing analytical tools and terminology, discussing relevant debates and, finally, presenting a set of concepts taken from public relations literature and analysing them within the framework provided by the first two sections. There is a fair amount of detail and referencing, which readers might find laborious but which is necessary for understanding the analytical approach and the structure of the argument. Briefly, the structure of this chapter can be compared to three different maps of the same intellectual area drawn from three different perspectives. The maps are imposed one upon another to achieve a more complete, three-dimensional picture. References and terminology provide the constants, the points with the help of which the maps can be fitted together.

The first map, 'Models of systems: an historical perspective' (pp. 126–34), discusses the concept of 'system' and its different incarnations in natural as well as social sciences over the last three hundred years or so. The purpose is to make it clear that 'system' was not discovered by the general system theory in the 1950s. In fact there had been a long tradition of explaining all kinds of phenomena as systems, however these might have been conceptualized. To appreciate the influence of this tradition on general systems theory a review of terminology connected with the concept is provided. As a result, 'system' emerges as an ambiguous concept that can be linked, for example in organization studies, to different theoretical positions.

The discussion then moves on to 'The battle of paradigms' (pp. 135–43), the second map, to show the relationship between organization theory, metatheoretical positions (paradigms) and systems theory. The vantage point chosen is that of Burrell and Morgan's (1979) work, which reviewed the field of organization theory using a four-paradigm framework constructed by the authors. The book made a strong impression, particularly with its argument about the functionalist dominance in the field. As the book was published in 1979 a further discussion was needed to show what happened to the debate about paradigms with the onslaught of postmodernism. The purpose of this section within the whole argument, then, is to introduce the metatheoretical dimension, necessary for any discussion of discourse(s).

Finally, our third map, 'Public relations discourse' (pp. 143–52), shows how systems thinking shapes the terrain of public relations theory. This aim can be achieved only by marshalling detailed evidence and analysing it using the framework constructed by earlier sections of the chapter. To manage the potentially massive amount of detail, the essay presents clusters of related concepts as 'units of analysis'. The analysis itself moves from terminology to discussion of the worldviews behind it in order to reflect on the public relations discourse revealed through such a discussion.

A similar interest was expressed by Pearson (1990), who also used Burrell and Morgan as his starting point. The main thrust of his discussion was a distinction between functionalism and a holistic approach emphasizing interdependence – each using a systems approach in rather different ways – to explore their implications for public relations. Pearson seems to have been influenced by Habermas in his approach to the role of communication activity in social life, and he developed this interest as a result of an exploration of ethics in public relations. To summarize crudely, Pearson believed that there was a choice for public relations between a narrow functionalist approach, i.e. an organization as a system driven by the need to attain its goals, and an ethical holistic approach as the basis for the practice. We shall refer to Pearson's argument in more detail later in the chapter, but, unlike Pearson, the author here is more interested in critiquing frameworks than in building them.

MODELS OF SYSTEMS: AN HISTORICAL PERSPECTIVE

The three models by which systems approach can be applied to understand human organizations (whether large organizations such as societies or smaller units such as commercial companies) are referred to in the literature as either mechanistic, organismic or social system models (Buckley 1967; Burrell and Morgan 1979; Morgan 1986; Gharajedaghi and Ackoff 1994). Buckley (1967) discusses the concept of the social system in the sociological tradition, and in so doing presents the following three models: equilibrium, homeostatic, and the process or adaptive system. These correspond to the mechanistic, organismic and 'social system' models of Gharajedaghi and Ackoff (1994). It has to be pointed out that the terminology used by Gharajedaghi and Ackoff can be rather confusing, as they see the 'social system' as a particular model of social systems within a more general understanding of the term. These terms are often used interchangeably in the literature and will be used so in this chapter, but we shall start with Buckley's terminology for the purposes of introduction and definitions. The equilibrium model describes systems 'which, in moving to an equilibrium point, typically lose organization, and then tend to hold that minimum level within relatively narrow conditions of disturbance' (Buckley 1967: 40). Homeostatic models 'apply to systems tending to maintain a given, relatively high, level of organization against ever-present tendencies to reduce it' (ibid.). And finally, there is the process or complex adaptive system model, which describes a system capable of elaboration or evolution of its organization and which 'depend[s] on "disturbances" and "variety" in the environment' (ibid.).

The equilibrium model

The roots of this model lie in the advances in physics, particularly mechanics (dealing with the motion of bodies: for example Kepler's laws of planetary motion or Newton's laws of motion), and in mathematics in the seventeenth and eighteenth centuries. These developments were so impressive in offering a rational deductive approach (in which true laws are developed from true assumptions through logical reasoning) that they came to be accepted as a paradigm for thinking about man and society.

Within this perspective, a universe is viewed as a clockwork mechanism, and a human being as a sophisticated machine whose actions can nevertheless be explained according to the same mechanistic principles that apply, for example, to planets.

> In 'social mechanics', society was seen as an 'astronomical system' whose elements were human beings bound together by mutual attraction or differentiated by repulsion; groups of societies or states were systems of balanced oppositions. Man, his groups, and their interrelations . . . constituted an unbroken continuity with the rest [of] the universe.
>
> (Buckley 1967: 8)

Terminology and concepts borrowed from mechanics, such as attraction, inertia, equilibrium (a state of perfect balance) or entropy (a measure of disorder), were thus applied to society by a number of sociologists, particularly from the end of the nineteenth century, producing concepts such as social entropy, fields of force, social equilibrium, and social coordinates. What this clearly demonstrates is that the influence of mechanics produced a mechanical model of society.

Vilfredo Pareto (1848–1923), an Italian economist and sociologist, is credited with developing this early, mechanistic view of society as a system consisting of 'interrelated parts with a boundary, and usually tending to maintain equilibrium' (Buckley 1967: 9). The implication of such a definition is that society is determined by forces acting upon it. The dynamics of such forces revolve around the pivotal point of equilibrium, so that any force directed away from equilibrium is counterbalanced by changes directed at restoring the balance. Pareto saw the concept of equilibrium as a useful analytical tool which could be applied in the social sciences; although for his followers there seemed to have been some ambiguity whether this was to be understood purely as an abstract, analytical concept or rather as a description of social reality (Burrell and Morgan 1979: 47).

Pareto's main work, *Trattato di sociologia generale*, originally published in 1916, strongly influenced the Harvard School of Sociology in the 1930s, as can be seen in the work of a number of sociologists such as Mayo (1933), Homans (1950) and, perhaps most significantly, Parsons (1951).

The homeostatic model

If the above mechanistic model offers one paradigm, the advances in biology epitomized by the Darwinian revolution – the theory of the evolution of the species – established a different approach, often referred to as the organic or organismic approach. The analogy between a living organism and society has an ancient lineage, yet it reappeared in a new shape in the early nineteenth century in the work of Auguste Comte, recognized as the founder of both positivism and sociology; and in the late nineteenth century in the work of Herbert Spencer, representing Social Darwinism.

It was Comte's view that the science of society should adopt the model of the natural sciences with their positive methods whereby the observation of empirical facts and reasoning leads to the discovery of universal laws governing the phenomena under study. In his own writing society is, for purposes of analysis, compared to an organism. Spencer took from Comte both the methodological interest in applying natural sciences methods to sociology and also the organismic analogy. The enormous impact of the theory of evolution – which by that time was well established, even if seen as strongly controversial – made the analogy a persuasive one.

In very broad terms, in Spencer and his followers we find a school of thought which sees society as consisting of a number of parts performing specific functions and in this way contributing to the existence of the whole organism/society. This perspective assumes a fundamental 'unity, interdependence, and ordered nature of constituent relationships' (Burrell and Morgan 1979: 43); the focus on evolutionary change is linked to the interest in functional differentiation and specialization. However, as Buckley points out (Buckley 1967: 12–13; Burrell and Morgan 1979: 43), the unitary perspective resulting from the application of evolutionary principles at the microscopic level of organism is in contradiction to the Darwinian principles of the struggle for survival and the process of natural selection.

If we follow the history of the organismic analogy beyond Spencer, we find a line of thinkers who are grouped together as the functionalist school in sociology. Durkheim, although critical of Comte and more sympathetic to Spencer, did accept both the principle of a social reality which can be investigated scientifically and the 'integrationist' framework (Burrell and Morgan 1979: 13) which resulted from a belief in the holistic nature of society, in which the concept of functional differentiation is linked to that of the interdependence of parts; in other words, society is held together by 'organic solidarity' (ibid.: 41–6).

Structural functionalism, although originally articulated theoretically by two anthropologists, Malinowski and Radcliffe-Brown, became the predominant mode of sociological analysis until the rise, in the 1970s, of Marxism, ethnomethodology, poststructuralism, and symbolic and cultural analysis (Reed 1993: 163). Both Malinowski and Radcliffe-Brown, in their studies of 'primitive' societies, employed the concept of function as the basis for explanation: anthropological facts could be understood in terms of the functions they performed in the system of culture under study. Radcliffe-Brown, in his theoretical work, consciously referred to the organismic analogy, placing a strong emphasis on the distinction between structure and process, which in his work appears as a distinction between social morphology and social physiology (Radcliffe-Brown 1952; Burrell and Morgan 1979: 51–4). Talcott Parsons, one of the most influential functionalist sociologists, preoccupied himself with the study of the latter, i.e. the explanation of how social structures function. Such an explanation needs to address four 'functional imperatives' (Parsons 1959; Rocher 1974; Burrell and Morgan 1979): adaptation, goal attainment, integration, and latency or pattern maintenance, across all of which a system's equilibrium is to be maintained.

This brings us to an interesting point, namely the continued reference to the concept of equilibrium – derived originally from the mechanistic analogy, but now found in a framework clearly built on the organismic model. Burrell and Morgan (1979: 57–63) point out that this theoretical inconsistency was made apparent by von Bertalanffy's work on general systems theory and open systems theory (von Bertalanffy 1950, 1956), in which equilibrium is, according to the second law of thermodynamics, a state inevitably attained in a closed system isolated from its environment, i.e. the type of system that is described by conventional physics. Open systems, on the other hand, are engaged in a constant exchange with environment (input, output) and may, though this is not a necessary condition, achieve a state of holistic balance within this flux (homeostasis). Von Bertalanffy's work can therefore be seen as establishing the widely accepted distinction between mechanistic, closed systems and homeostatic, organismic, open systems.

Pursuing the connection between sociology and organization theory, we have already mentioned Pareto, Homans and Mayo as followers of the first model; we have also mentioned Parsons's work as combining elements of both. Classical management is linked with the closed systems model (Morgan 1986: 45); whereas the open systems perspective can be found in the work of Katz and Kahn (1966), the Tavistock group – in the concept of a socio-technical system (Emery and Trist 1946) – and as the basis for contingency theory (Lawrence and Lorsch 1967). This organismic, open systems approach typically operates a number of concepts, such as boundary, process, input, output, feedback, homeostasis, systems behaviour, subsystems, and boundary transactions (Burrell and Morgan 1979: 63; Morgan 1986: 46–7).

Gharajedaghi and Ackoff (1994), in their review of the three models, establish clear links between the models as theoretical tools and the empirical reality of organizations that fit these categories. The mechanistic organization is reductionist, inflexible, preoccupied with control and coordination and, consequently, centrally controlled and hierarchically structured. Organismic organizations are preoccupied with survival and its necessary condition, growth; individual parts possess a certain degree of self-control; the structure is less formal and supported by direct communication between parts; there is also more two-way communication. Finally, introducing the social systems model, the focus of their discussion, holism and synergy seem to be the main features. These three models are also linked to types of system behaviour as identified by Ackoff and Emery (1972: 30–1): 'most systems display some combination of these types of behaviour. Nevertheless, it should be noted that mechanistically conceptualized systems are modelled as predominantly reactive; organismically conceptualized systems as predominantly responsive [goal-seeking]; and socially conceptualized systems as predominantly active [purposeful]' (Gharajedaghi and Ackoff 1994: 34).

The process or adaptive system model

This model was proposed by Buckley (1967) as a critique of the traditional mechanistic and organismic models. His interest lay in explaining the process of structure elaboration (morphogenesis) and in doing so he addressed issues such as conflict, deviance and social control, which traditional models are unable to deal with. Theoretically, he attempts to 'synthesize the whole range of functionalist paradigm – from interactionist [Mead, Simmel and Blumer] to the social systems theory [Homans and Parsons] – and makes passing references to . . . Marx' (Burrell and Morgan 1979: 99).

The process model uses cybernetics as its analogy to avoid any teleological bias in explanations of goal-seeking behaviour, often inseparable from organismic analogies. This model also helps to focus on the role of information in the system's dynamics. The socio-cultural system thus 'emerges from a network of interaction among individuals in which information is selectively perceived and interpreted in accordance with the meaning it holds for the actors involved' (Burrell and Morgan 1979: 100).

Gharajedaghi and Ackoff (1994) conclude their review of these three system models and their practical implications by equating mechanistic management with its prime interest in efficiency; organismic management with a focus on growth and survival; and social-system management with the overriding interest in development, defined as 'the process in which individuals increase their abilities and desires to satisfy their own needs and legitimate desires, and those of others' (Gharajedaghi and Ackoff 1994: 36). Organizations operating on these principles are said to serve

> the purposes of the system, its parts, and its containing systems. There may be conflict between these levels or within them. Therefore, resolution or dissolution of conflict is one of management's principal responsibilities. A social system should be viewed as an instrument of those it affects. Its principal function is to encourage and facilitate their development. For management of social systems, planning should consist of designing a desirable future and inventing or finding ways of approximating it . . . Such management should attempt to maximize the freedom of choice of those it affects. Only from experience of choice can one learn, hence develop.
>
> (Gharajedaghi and Ackoff 1994: 39)

Ironically, this interpretation of Buckley, originally published in 1984, seems to bring us back to our starting point, and we could draw out a number of familiar characteristics from this extract. It is functionalist in its acceptance that not only an organization but, it seems, the whole social world is a system of interdependent, cooperating parts. Although the existence of conflict is acknowledged, the whole emphasis of the social system is on maintaining unity. This, interestingly, is achieved through the intervention of management, which apparently possesses both the knowledge and the ability to devise and implement rationally ways in which conflict can, and should, be worked out of the system. We find, then, a clear normative approach demonstrated, and linked to a rational view of human nature, which under favourable conditions (freedom) tends towards 'socially responsible' action. So, social systems are designed to provide freedom, which allows individuals to satisfy their needs and which also produces social harmony.

Autopoiesis and social systems

When general systems theory emerged in the 1950s, it was greeted with a considerable degree of excitement:

> Under the banner of systems research . . . we have witnessed a convergence of many specialized contemporary scientific developments . . . These research pursuits and many others are being interwoven into a co-operative research effort . . . We are participating in . . . the most comprehensive effort to attain a synthesis of scientific knowledge yet made.
>
> (Ackoff 1959: 145)

The ambitious final statement here may have echoed von Bertalanffy's aim of achieving 'a unity of science', made possible since general systems theory started uncovering the 'isomorphy of laws in different fields' (von Bertalanffy 1956: 8; quoted in Burrell and Morgan 1979: 58). Rapoport referred to general systems theory as 'a direction in the contemporary philosophy of science' (Rapoport 1968: 452); and Buckley seemed to have views similar to those already quoted above, defining general systems theory as

- A common vocabulary unifying the several 'behavioural' disciplines;
- A technique for treating large, complex organizations;
- An operationally definable, objective, non-anthropomorphic study of purposiveness, goal-seeking systems behaviour, symbolic cognitive process, consciousness and self-awareness, and sociocultural emergence and dynamics in general.

(Buckley 1967: 39)

By the end of the 1960s, functionalism and systems theory were going out of fashion. 'The problematic of order' by the late 1970s had been displaced by 'the problematic of domination'; and the 1980s, in turn, saw the emergence of 'the problematic in which the construction of organizational reality, through the skilled utilization of largely arbitrary linguistic and cultural representation or "language games" has become the central concern' (Reed 1992: 10–11; see also Ackroyd 1992). Put differently, systems-based contingency approaches focusing on 'the adaptability of organizational designs to environmental imperatives' came to be criticized for relying on 'devalued theoretical capital' (Reed 1992: 2–3). This explains a shift in the 1970s away from the static view of organizations – units constrained by the environment – to an interest in organizational reproduction and transformation through a cultural and political process, which could not be explained by the systems approach with its 'logic of effectiveness'. Hence alternative approaches to the study of organizations started emerging, such as action frame of reference (Silverman 1970), negotiated order (Strauss 1978), ethnomethodology (Cicourel 1968) and political theories of organizational decision-making (Pettigrew 1973; Pfeffer 1981; see Reed 1992: 2–3). Finally, from the late 1970s and throughout the 1980s the range of interests and approaches was widened still further:

> First, then, there was an increasingly potent emphasis on the cultural and symbolic processes through which organizations were socially constructed and organizational analysis academically structured (Turner 1990). Second, the macro-level power relations and ideological systems through which organizational forms were shaped became a central theme for analysis (McNeil 1978). Third, the retreat from natural science conceptions of organizational analysis seems to make an intellectual and institutional space available for approaches focused on the complete interaction between theoretical innovation and social context (Morgan 1990).
>
> (Reed 1992: 4)

The above discussion is, as is every generalization, a broad and probably simplified account of changes in organization studies. There is, however, one specific strand of theorizing that emerged in the social sciences in the mid-1980s which requires more attention from our point of view – the concept of autopoiesis and its applications. Originally, autopoiesis, or the autopoietic model of systems, was proposed in 1974 by two Chilean biologists, Varela and Maturana, in cooperation with the systems theorist Uribe. It was taken up in social science following Luhmann's pioneering work (1984, 1986; see Kickert 1993: 263).

The originality of autopoiesis lies in its presenting a fundamentally different model of the relationship between the system and its environment. Instead of the traditional view that systems adapt to the environment, the new model sees systems as self-referential and closed. The system is driven by its need to survive, but survival is understood as the maintenance of self-identity. Environment exists for the system only as a projection of its self-identity – or, to simplify, it is constructed by the system.

The original, biological, model focused on redefining the nature of 'living' and in the process redefined the concept of the system. But for Varela and Maturana, a living system is primarily a 'network of interactions of components' and

> Instead of looking at what makes a living system reproduce the parts of the system . . . [Varela and Maturana] looked at the organization of the living system that is reproduced . . . not reproduction as such, but rather the reproduction of the organization of the living system . . . which makes it 'living'.
>
> (Kickert 1993: 263)

The autonomy of such a system lies in its unity, which 'consists of a network of component-producing processes such that the interactive components recursively generate the same network of processes' (Kickert 1993: 264).

This proved an intriguing new idea which received a lot of attention from systems theorists. As Burrell and Morgan observed, following von Bertalanffy's conceptualization of the closed system as being isolated from the environment, social scientists had decided that it was an inadequate model to apply to social phenomena. It became fashionable to criticize Weber and classical management theory as examples of outmoded, closed-system thinking. In fact, the very notion of the closed system tended to be avoided like 'a dreaded disease' by the social sciences (Burrell and Morgan 1979: 60). Varela and Maturana's ideas about autonomy and closure as the way in which systems survive seemed to turn this traditional concept of the closed system on its head, and promised a new lease of life for systems theory.

Although Varela and Maturana themselves argued very strongly against autopoiesis being applied outside biology, Kickert (1993: 265–6) lists a number of elaborations and applications of the model 'outside the realm of living': notably Jantsch (1981), who related it to notions of chaos and order; and Ben-Eli (1981), who linked autopoiesis and self-referentiality with evolution. Following its career among systems theorists, autopoiesis eventually found its way to the social sciences when Luhmann applied it to the social system, and also introduced the idea of 'a paradigmatic shift in systems theory from the holistic notion of parts and whole, via the distinction of system and environment, towards a theory of self-referential systems'(Kickert 1993: 267).

In the light of our discussion so far, Luhmann's paradigmatic shift could be seen as focusing on the differences between the mechanistic, organismic and process models of systems discussed earlier in this chapter, although such a comparison has to be conducted rather cautiously.

So by 1984 (that is, in about a decade) autopoiesis had not only become well established in the social sciences, but also undergone some important changes in the process. First, the requirement of closure was considerably relaxed, or even dropped; second, from the original concept of self-reproduction, we seem, via self-organization, to have arrived at a much broader concept of self-referentiality, as employed by Luhmann (Kickert 1993: 267).

Autopoiesis comes into our orbit of interest in Morgan's metaphor of flux and transformation (Morgan 1986: 235-40), where he explains an autopoietic system as producing 'images of reality as expressions or descriptions of its own organization' (ibid.: 238) and interacting with these images, the way, for example, a human brain does. Interestingly, Morgan links Weick's concept of enactment with autopoiesis:

> The ideas on autopoiesis add to our understanding of . . . enactment, in that they encourage us to view organizational enactments as part of the self-referential process through which an organization attempts to tie down and reproduce its identity. For in enacting the environment an organization is attempting to achieve the kind of closure that is necessary for it to reproduce itself in its own image.
>
> (Morgan 1986: 241)

Pearson, in his discussion of systems theory in public relations, argues that the prevalent approach is that 'which emphasized processes and uses terms like *input*, *throughput*, and *output*' and is attentive to the concept of interdependency, taking a holistic view of a system; while simultaneously referring to management by objectives, viewing a system as goal-seeking (Pearson 1990: 222). In terms of the models identified above, this is perhaps closest to the homeostatic, or organic, model. This approach, Pearson claims, lies clearly within the functionalist tradition; and his interest, therefore, focuses on examining the implications of this 'metatheoretical perspective, or paradigm'(ibid.: 220) for the discipline of public relations.

Although Pearson refers to Burrell and Morgan, his assumption about systems theory constituting a paradigm seems to be incompatible with their definition of a paradigm. This explains perhaps why Pearson can see as meaningful the question of when systems theory is not functionalist. He argues that taking the idea of holism to its logical conclusion one arrives inevitably at a completely different framework – an ethical rather than a goal-directed view of behaviour. Similarly, if one considers the differences between the three system models presented so far, the adaptive system – close in many respects to the self-referentiality of autopoiesis – poses a serious question about the metatheoretical assumptions behind it: is it or is it not functionalism? In order to explore this problem, however, it is necessary to understand what a paradigm is and how theories are related to paradigms.

PARADIGMS, SYSTEMS THEORY AND PUBLIC RELATIONS

THE BATTLE OF PARADIGMS: ORGANIZATION STUDIES AND PUBLIC RELATIONS

> The word 'paradigm' is just about the most over-used in the philosophical lexicon. In fact, professional philosophers tend to avoid it like the plague, and today it is much more commonly used by sociologists, scientists, and journalists . . . Part of the problem is that the word 'paradigm' is as slippery as the word 'God'. Everyone who uses it means something slightly different. Too frequently the term is used as a propaganda tool, bolstering the pretensions of some supposed major breakthrough: paradigm founder today, Nobel prize winner tomorrow, burial in Westminster Abbey the day after that.
>
> (Ruse 1993: 118)

This discussion of the debate about paradigms in organizational studies is introduced, quite consciously, by questioning the meaning and usage of the term itself. It seems that the following discussion can be enlightening in many respects and useful to public relations, and my intention is to reflect on how public relations as a discipline 'thinks', or at least on some aspects of this question. As a new discipline, public relations seems to be rather sensitive about its academic status; but this position is neither unique, nor can it be solved by bolstering false pretensions. The term 'paradigm' has therefore been avoided as far as possible so far, but will be used, without any apologies, in the context where it seems legitimate, i.e. the debate about philosophical positions underlying theories in sociology and organization studies, which I shall attempt to extend to public relations.

The debate about paradigms has already begun in public relations (Botan 1993; Everett 1993; Hallahan 1993). It is seen as a sign of the discipline maturing and developing a range of different approaches; at the same time the process is not seen as advanced enough for a full-blown paradigm struggle, or debate, to be able to take place (Botan 1993: 108). Although the term paradigm is used, and although it is a notoriously ambiguous term, the meaning with which it has appeared so far in public relations is rather narrow – a model with a group of followers seems to be sufficient to merit the term. The difficulty with this interpretation is that it leads to unnecessary fragmentation and confusion, precisely the problem which Burrell and Morgan tried to get away from by suggesting their four-paradigm scheme for discussing organizational theory (Burrell and Morgan 1979: x–xiv).

There are two slightly different accounts of how and when the debate started in organization studies. Reed (1993) traces the beginning back to Silverman (1970); Ackroyd (1992) looks to Burrell and Morgan (1979), who, in turn, seem to be in agreement with Reed about the pivotal role played by Silverman in opening the floodgates for alternative approaches to organization and challenging the systems orthodoxy. It seems that the point of disagreement between Ackroyd and Reed is over whether Silverman organized his work on the principle of Kuhnian paradigmatic shift – Ackroyd's point (1992: 171) – or according to a 'serial' approach, in which theories follow one another and constitute series, admittedly sometimes very short ones (Reed 1993: 110). Avoiding taking sides on this point, I shall take Burrell and Morgan as central to this debate in view of their later contributions.

Before we step into the thick of the debate itself, a number of other introductory comments must be made. First, Burrell and Morgan's work should be seen against the background of, on the one hand, dissatisfaction with functionalism and the contingency approach dominating at the threat of stopping other developments and, on the other hand, the lack of debate, if not hostility, between theorists representing various approaches. Burrell and Morgan's response was to create an 'effective synthesis of diverse approaches to theory' by mapping these approaches within a single 'general frame [which] denied exclusive authority to one approach to organization' (Ackroyd 1992: 111). They consequently dealt with the apparent differences as being attributable to simpler expositions. However, there was a danger inherent in the design of their 'general framework': in suggesting the desirability of paradigm closure, and therefore the necessity to choose between them, Burrell and Morgan reinforced inadvertently the imminent 'fragmentation of organizational studies into querulous and squabbling factions' (Reed 1993: 172).

Second, as hinted before, there are other ways of categorizing or grouping theories of organizations. Aldrich provides an interesting discussion of ecological, institutional and interpretative approaches differentiated on the basis of 'their products rather than the process of their construction' (Aldrich 1992: 18). Gergen (1992) proposes an approach that follows the process of theory construction, i.e. he uncovers the influence of romanticism, modernism and postmodernism. Thus, romantic dimensions can be found in the work of the Tavistock Institute; theories drawing on psychoanalysis (Zeleznick); theories drawing on Jungian archetypes (Denhardt, Mitroff); research presuming fundamental human needs (Mayo, Maslow, McGregor); approaches to leadership based on personal resources (Fiedler, Hollander); and Japanese management theory (Ouchi). Modernist conceptions include time and motion studies; general systems and their extensions (Lawrence and Lorsch); exchange theories (Homans); cybernetic theories; trait methodology presuming the stability of individual patterns of behaviour (Fiedler); cognitive theories; and theories of industrial societies based on the rational laws of economic organizations. Finally, there are postmodern approaches inspired by the work of Wittgenstein, Quine, Kuhn, Garfinkel, Goodman, Foucault, and feminist critiques; Morgan's metaphorical approach to organizations is one of only a few examples identified in organizational studies.

Burrell and Morgan start by considering a variety of assumptions about the nature of science (nominalism–realism in ontology; anti-positivism–

positivism in epistemology; voluntarism–determinism in debates about human nature; ideographic–nomothetic theory in methodology); and assumptions about the nature of society (the order–conflict debate). This discussion allows them to produce four paradigms placed along the horizontal axis of 'subjective–objective'; and the vertical axis of 'regulation–radical change'. The four paradigms are: the functionalist paradigm (containing objectivism, social system theory, pluralism, theories of bureaucratic dysfunction; action frame of reference); the interpretative paradigm (containing hermeneutics; phenomenological sociology, phenomenology, and solipsism); the radical humanist paradigm (containing solipsism, French existentialism, anarchic individualism and critical theory); and finally, the radical structuralist paradigm (containing contemporary radical Marxism, conflict theory and Russian social theory).

Each paradigm is then discussed in terms of its main assumptions and thinkers, and then again in connection with theories of organization, providing a way of both grouping various theories and tracing their origins in terms of metatheory. Functionalism, for example, is primarily objectivist and concerned with the sociology of regulation:

> It is characterised by a concern for providing explanations of the *status quo*, *social order*, *consensus*, *social integration*, *solidarity*, *need satisfaction* and *actuality*. It approaches these general sociological concerns from a standpoint which tends to be *realist*, *positivist*, *determinist* and *nomothetic*.
>
> (Burrell and Morgan 1979:26)

The roots of this paradigm are traced to Comte, Spencer, Durkheim, and Pareto; but also to Weber, Simmel and Mead, whose work, seen as incorporating elements of German idealism, found its place in the least objective region of functionalism. Burrell and Morgan's extensive discussion of the functionalist paradigm has already been referred to, but in order to summarize and to facilitate making links with the discussion of public relations, I shall identify those writers and works in organizational studies which are seen as operating within this paradigm.

As we have seen, there are clear groups of approaches within this paradigm: social systems theory and objectivism, under which we find classical management theorists and industrial psychologists (Taylor, Fayol, Mooney, Urwick; Mayo, Roethlisberger and Dickson); and, separately, post-Hawthorn objectivist studies of job satisfaction and human relations (Likert, Maslow, Herzberg). Burrell and Morgan continue their discussion with socio-technical systems (Trist), grouped together with the work of Argyris; equilibrium theories of Bernard and Simon; the structural functionalism of Selznick, and the open systems perspective (again invoking the Tavistock researchers Trist and Emery, but also Katz and Kahn); finally we find empirical studies of the Aston group; and similar work in the USA carried out by

Hall; Hage, Aitken and Blau. The latest of the discussed approaches which was inspired by the open systems theory is Lawrence and Lorsch's contingency theory.

The action frame of reference is represented by Silverman – a position with which Reed (1993: 172) takes issue, seeing it as an illustration of the futility of the whole paradigm debate; other important writers mentioned are Goffman and Turner. Theories of bureaucratic dysfunction, influenced by Mertonian theory of cultural and social structure, are represented by Selznick, Gouldner and Blau. The last approach within the paradigm is pluralist theory. The tack Burrell and Morgan adopt in this section is to refer to the pluralist strand within the work of writers already classified elsewhere (Selznick, Gouldner, Goffman, Silverman, Blau). In doing so the authors emphasize the point made earlier about various traditions feeding into individual theories and approaches, often across the paradigmatic divisions.

None of the three remaining paradigms produced discussions as extensive as functionalism, or, for that matter, as many examples of their application in organizational studies. This quantitative imbalance was not a matter of design and led to the conclusion that the bulk of theory and research is located within a narrow range of theoretical possibilities.

> This concentration of effort in a relatively narrow area defines what is usually regarded as the dominant orthodoxy within the subject. Because this orthodoxy is so dominant and strong, its adherents take it for granted as right and self-evident.
>
> (Burrell and Morgan 1979: xi)

Let us briefly summarize Burrell and Morgan's views on the three alternative paradigms. The interpretative paradigm is traced back mostly to the work of early German idealists (and beyond that to Kant), with the more recent influence of Dilthey (hermeneutics), Husserl (phenomenology) and Weber. Within organizational studies in this paradigm the authors distinguish ethnomethodological approaches to the study of organizational activities to be found in Bittner, and to a certain extent in Zimmerman, and Silverman; and phenomenology in the work of symbolic interactionists (Sundow, Emerson).

Radical humanism derives its main origins from the work of Hegel and 'Young Hegelians' like Feuerbach and the young Marx. The separate strands of thought within the paradigm are critical theory (The Frankfurt School), anarchistic individualism (Max Stirner) and French existentialism (Jean-Paul Sartre). This framework, applied to organizational studies, produced anti-organization theory (Clegg 1975; Silverman and Jones 1976; Beynon 1973). The problem with which these theories are preoccupied is alienation, and the seemingly objective forces impinging on human consciousness. Burrell and Morgan (1979: 323) break these problems down into a list of more specific factors in which anti-organization studies are interested: the concept of purposive rationality; rule and controls within which the purposive rationality is exercised; roles as limiting human activity; language and the Habermasian concept of communicative distortion; ideological mechanisms within the workplace which support roles; the worship of technology as a liberating force; and reification as applied to concepts of work, leisure, profitability and scarcity.

Radical structuralism originated from Marx's later work and in some respects from Weber's concern with the 'iron cage', i.e. bureaucracy as social domination: Burrell and Morgan describe it as 'a fusion of plurality of philosophical, political and social traditions' (Burrell and Morgan 1979: 333). There are three broad approaches distinguished within the paradigm: Russian social theory (Plekhanov, Bukharin) and, connected with it, anarchistic communism (Kropotkin); contemporary Mediterranean Marxism (Althusser, Colletti); and conflict theory (Rex, Dahrendorf). In organizational studies these approaches can be seen as either a radical Weberian position or a Marxian structuralist approach. The former is interested in problems such as the role of the State and the general process of bureaucratization, corporatism and power relationships; writers discussed in this context are Miliband (1973); Eldridge and Crombie (1974); McCulloch and Shannon (1977). The latter is to be found in Baran and Sweezy (1968); Braverman (1974); Allen (1975).

The above summary is too brief to do justice to Burrell and Morgan's discussion; it should be taken more as a rough map of the vast intellectual territory traversed, or as an early skirmish in the paradigm battle before it became further complicated by the arrival of postmodernism on the field of organizational studies. There have been many voices in this most recent phase of the debate: there are writers whose work has explored organizations in a postmodern world; there have also been those writing 'on a more self-consciously theoretical level' (for discussion of postmodernity as an epoch and postmodernity as a philosophical position, see M. Parker 1992). It seems easier for the purposes of this review to focus on the latter and in doing so give examples of the first group of writers.

In 1988 *Organization Studies* started publishing a series of papers discussing the relevance of 'postmodernist concerns for the study of organizations' (M. Parker 1992: 4). Cooper and Burrell's (1988) was the introductory article, which approached the debate via 'a return to Weber's concerns about the "iron cage" of rational bureaucracy' (M. Parker 1992: 4). Taking this as their focal point, Cooper and Burrell examine the concept of rationality as underlying the modernist discourse, and contrast this with the postmodernist discourse seen as a critique of rationality.

Modernism is supported by the well-established rationalist tradition in philosophy, starting from Kant (critical modernism), and in sociology, right at its source in the work of Saint-Simon and Comte (systemic modernism). The common area for both forms of modernism is their belief in Reason as the foundation for the world, which is, therefore, intrinsically logical and meaningful.

> This takes two forms: (1) that discourse mirrors the reason and order already 'out there' in the world, and (2) that there is a thinking agent, a subject, which can make itself conscious of this external order.
>
> (Cooper and Burrell 1988: 97)

In the case of systemic modernism, system is the agent. Since it works according to 'cybernetic discourse', its logic is accessible through the application of scientific methods of enquiry; and the logic resides within the system, rather than its parts. For critical modernism, the thinking subject is the network of interacting individuals who 'through the commonsense of ordinary discourse, can reach a "universal consensus" of human experience'(Cooper and Burrell 1988: 97).

Searching for the expression of modernist discourse in organization studies, it appears that systemic modernism expressed as instrumental rationality is the dominant type. The authors cite as an example D. Bell's (1974) interpretation of the post-industrial society as organized through theoretical knowledge for control and innovation, thus offering a way of managing the complex, large-scale systems characteristic of the modern world. Apart from the large-scale unitary system, Bell also points out another characteristic feature – the economizing mode, operationalized as productivity and performance. Similar ideas are developed further by Luhmann, where society becomes a gigantic organization, like a corporation, governed by performativity, or 'the optimization of the global relationship between input and output' (Lyotard 1984: 11; quoted in Cooper and Burrell 1988: 96).

Critical modernism occupies a somewhat ambiguous position in this debate: although criticized implicitly for being modernist in the first place, it seems to have some redeeming features – its interest in language and, more generally, its opposition to the 'cybernetic-like monolith of systemic modernism' (Cooper and Burrell 1988: 97). Critical modernism is discussed briefly by exposition of Habermas's interest in language as the medium of reason, and in the process of 'the colonization of the life-world by systemic reason' (ibid.), i.e. rationalization rather than rationality.

It is impossible to present any comprehensive discussion of postmodernism in two paragraphs, and it is virtually impossible to summarize Cooper and Burrell's discussion of it in such a brief way either. I shall, therefore, resort to focusing on those elements of their paper that are of interest in this context, while trying not to lose their original sense.

For Cooper and Burrell 'difference' is perhaps the key concept around which they build their discussion of postmodernism. It allows them to draw together the work of Derrida (1973), Foucault (1977a, 1977b, 1980) and Lyotard (1984), and to contrast it with the modernist position (Habermas 1984). Difference is defined as

> a form of self-reference in which terms contain their own opposites and thus refuse any singular grasp of their meanings. Difference is . . . a unity . . . divided from itself, and . . . it is that which actually constitutes human discourse. . . . the human agent is faced with a condition of irreductible indeterminacy.
>
> (Cooper and Burrell 1988: 98)

These ideas produce two irreconcilable positions. The modernist discourse is referential, it legitimizes itself by reference to 'some grand narrative such as the dialectics of Spirit, the hermeneutics of meaning, the emancipation of the rational or working subject, or the creations of wealth' (Lyotard 1984: xxiii; quoted in Cooper and Burrell 1988: 94). Postmodern discourse, however, sees systems as self-referential; thus any attempt to analyse them in terms of purpose and meaning is purely an interpretative position. What postmodernist discourse attempts to do is 'to show that the world of commonsense structures is the active product of a process that continually privileges unity, identity and immediacy over the differential properties of absence and separation' (Cooper and Burrell 1988: 100). Postmodernist effort, then, can be seen as focused on deconstructing concepts of unity and identity.

Cooper and Burrell's article provoked other writers to respond and take positions on different sides of the question about whether or not the modern and postmodern paradigms can be reconciled. Cooper, Burrell and Gergen believe they cannot, and suggest that a way forward for organizational studies is to pursue the postmodern critique (Cooper and Burrell 1988; Gergen 1992). M. Parker (1992), while believing that the paradigms are ultimately irreconcilable, advocates a need for 'cross fertilization' between these two positions. Tsoukas talks about 'soft' postmodernism, which is ontologically close to reflexive rationalism (critical modernism), while challenging 'the cognitive monopoly of an allegedly omniscient subject-centred rationality' and thus investigating the postmodern concepts of instability and discontinuity (Tsoukas 1992: 648). Reed (1992) rejects the paradigm mentality altogether as unhelpful, fostering a 'camp' mentality, and Ackroyd seems to share his view when he writes about the 'silliness' that such forms of thinking may produce (Ackroyd 1992: 172).

An obvious question to ask at this point is whether any postmodern work has actually been produced by organizational researchers, or whether the debate is a purely 'academic' event, in the worst sense. Hassard (1993: 16–17), in his discussion of postmodernism and organizational analysis, points to Clegg (1990) and his identification of de-differentiated postmodern organizational structures consistent with theories of flexible specialization and post-Fordism (see Piore and Sabel 1984; Pollert 1988; C. Smith 1989; Hirst and Zeitlin 1991). Postmodernism – not as an epoch (post-modernism), but an epistemological position – is more problematic for organizational analysis. First of all, there is the problem with theory construction as being essentially dependent on the belief in 'the factual nature of a knowable universe' (Hassard 1993: 18), which cannot be easily reconciled with the postmodern belief in the unconquerable ambiguity of the universe, which is both constructed and at the same time obscured by language. However, if one persists, examples can be found: Gergen's relational theory of power (Gergen 1992), which operates somewhere in the 'middle ground between the "strong" epoch and epistemology traditions' (Hassard 1993: 20); or ethnographic research, known as the organizational culture and symbolism movement (for further discussion, see Hassard and Parker 1993).

Thompson (1993), in his outspoken criticism of postmodernism in organizational studies, points out that the characteristics of a postmodern organization as defined by Clegg (1990) appear at the centre of contemporary pop-management. The broad themes running through the work of writers such as Handy (1987, 1989), Naisbett (1982), Peters (1987), Peters and Waterman (1982), and Deal and Kennedy (1982) are broadly those of flexibility and disorganization. More specifically, postmodern interests are conceptualized by Clegg (1990: 203) as diffusion, democracy, trust and empowerment; and he juxtaposes them with the modernist focus on specialization, bureaucracy, mistrust and disempowerment.

What conclusions, then, can be drawn from this debate about paradigms, and how can it be relevant to public relations? The debate represents a period in the development of organization studies characterized by intensive methodological introspection. As late as 1979, Burrell and Morgan wrote about the functionalist dominance in the field (although many would dispute their definition of the functionalist paradigm), and in their review they chose to highlight not particular theoretical solutions to particular practical problems, but the big ontological and epistemological questions underlying such solutions. The subsequent explorations of postmodern concepts and their application to the study of organizations intensified the introspective process. Having grappled with the idea of paradigm closure and the effects of the postmodernist onslaught, organization studies began to re-form in 'the renewed quest for a sustained dialogue which has direction and gives the field an identifiable coherence' (Reed 1993: 174). Although the tendency of this introspective debate to encourage polarized positions cannot be dismissed, the methodological awareness it brings with it can be used constructively, in the

> making and re-making of intelligible narratives concerning organization theory's historical development and its significance for present-day concerns . . . [This] will extricate organizational studies from the intellectual paralysis and 'collective amnesia' which came to pervade as a result of the 'triumphalism' of systems orthodoxy or the 'forgetfulness' of postmodernist thinking.
>
> (Reed 1993: 174–5)

What seems to be emerging out of this period of strife is a more mature discipline, at ease with the idea of its own identity as being continually remade, a discipline that is open to issues beyond its own limits at any particular time and capable of accommodating theoretical and methodological variety without disintegrating. Armed with this knowledge, let us take a critical look at the emerging discourse of public relations within academia.

PUBLIC RELATIONS DISCOURSE

The first part of this paper has presented a review of the systems approach in sociology and organizational studies. Three models, or strands, of thinking about social systems have been identified, in order to supply the analytical framework for discussing the application of systems theory in public relations. These three models, as we shall see, have indeed been recognized and used in public relations. My aim is to sketch a critique of that awareness, and its broader implications.

The data for analysis consists of a selection of examples of particular uses or applications of systems theory in a number of public relations academic texts. The books chosen for consideration are:

- Grunig, J. and Hunt, T. (1984) *Managing Public Relations*;
- Cutlip, S.M., Center, A.H. and Broom, G. (1985, 1994) *Effective Public Relations*, 6th and 7th edns;
- Botan, C. and Hazleton, V. (eds) (1989) *Public Relations Theory*;
- Grunig, J. (ed.) (1992) *Excellence in Public Relations and Communications Management*.

There are a number of reasons for this particular selection. First, there seems to be a general consensus, arising from the documentation of historical developments and the educational tradition in the field of public relations, that American scholars lead in the field. Second, American academic textbooks in the field of public relations seem to dominate the market, at least in the UK, which offers further support for the claim of the strong position of American scholars. Third, within the field the more practice-oriented textbooks make only a cursory reference to systems theory, if any, and have therefore been disregarded. Finally, the choice of textbooks rather than other texts has been decided on the assumption that within the category of 'published work' in the academic context, a textbook is firmly associated with the establishment, in the sense of representing the views central to the field and containing an up-to-date body of knowledge. In other words, a textbook serves as a medium through which the direction of the development in a field is reaffirmed, and also functions as a mechanism for self-perpetuation. The following analysis assumes that the application of systems theory to public relations as observed in the texts considered is representative of this academic field in English-speaking countries.

Another point that should be clarified here is the fact that despite citing a number of textbooks as the data, I focus mainly on the work of James Grunig and a group of researchers contributing to the 'Excellence' study in public relations. There are four reasons for this focus: first, James Grunig's position as a researcher who has been active for about twenty years; second, the enormous influence of his views and his achievements in providing a theoretical basis for public relations, claiming for it the status of an academic discipline (see Botan 1993); third, his leading position as the director of the research team for the 'Excellence' study, which itself is a unique project within public relations. The 'Excellence' study is a project funded by the International Association of Business Communicators (IABC) and initiated in 1985. *Excellence in Public Relations and Communications Management* was published after seven years and represents the first stage of the project, theory building, which is to be followed by empirical research. A project of this length and size would constitute a serious research effort in any discipline and, to date, is outstanding in public relations. Fourth, and finally, the core of the theoretical effort represented in *Excellence*, such as the definition of public relations, and its presuppositions of a public relations theory can be traced to Grunig's earlier work (see Grunig and Hunt 1984; Botan and Hazleton 1989).

Systems theory and public relations theory

Systems theory appears in public relations directly as systems theory in chapters bearing the appropriate headings – 'A "system" focus' (in Grunig and Hunt 1984), 'The systems approach' (in Cutlip et al. 1985); or applied as a framework to particular problems: 'The systems concept of management' (in Grunig and Hunt 1984), 'The systems perspective of effectiveness' (in Grunig 1992).

There is also a more indirect route whereby systems theory is applied to a problem, but the acknowledgement or clarification is not found directly in the title of the appropriate section or chapter, though it can be traced through the book's index: 'What are the community publics', indexed under 'Systems theory, in community relations', and 'The concept of linkages', indexed under 'Systems theory, interpenetrating systems related to linkages' (both in Grunig and Hunt 1984).

Finally, there is the indirect route, whereby concepts derived from systems theory enter public relations via a different source, often under a different term. These are more difficult to identify, but are also more pervasive in Grunig (1992) than in any other of the texts, given the nature of this particular book: a combination of extensive literature review and theorizing, more useful for the purposes of academic research than as support for straightforward instruction. Perhaps the most useful way of identifying such influences is by clusters of concepts.

I examine these concepts in the four, numbered sections that follow, showing in each of them the sources referenced by the authors in their discussion. This signposting technique should help relate the two parts of the discussion presented in this chapter. In other words, I shall attempt to superimpose our rough map sketched out in 'The battle of paradigms' on to the mainstream public relations writing and see what happens. As noted previously, the following discussion can only provide a rough sketch, in view of the amount of material available even within the limits of my selection.

(1) I shall begin with concepts of autonomy, interdependence and relationships in a chapter dealing with organizational effectiveness, 'What is an effective organization?' (Grunig 1992: ch. 3). The way in which this chapter speaks systems language is by focusing on concepts such as goal-attainment as a measure of organizational effectiveness (Pfeffer and Salancik 1978). The concept of autonomy, defined as independence from environmental intrusion, is juxtaposed with that of interdependence, traced back in a more or less direct way to the work of a number of writers (Katz and Kahn 1966; Parsons 1960; Gouldner 1959; Perrow 1961; Blau and Scott 1962; Etzioni 1964; Price 1968). The need for an organization to be open to its environment is also linked to the concepts of cooperation (Hage 1980; Quinn and Hall 1983) and interaction (Buccholz 1989).

Interdependence is based in relationships which the organization has with groups, internal and external, that compete for power. Following Mintzberg (1983), the authors of this chapter - Grunig, Grunig and Ehling - accept that competition for power can lead to a high degree of 'politicization'. This, however, is ultimately a positive factor, as it 'kills organizations that are not well-suited to their environments' (Grunig 1992: 69), a view reminiscent of Darwinian survival of the fittest and the ecological perspective in organizational studies. Other important sources in the discussion of relationships seem to be Aldrich (1975) and Zeitz (1975).

Finally, requisite variety and enactment (Weick 1979) are invoked: the argument seems to be that the more variety the more effective the process of enactment. The conclusion to the chapter is a proposition linking the various elements discussed with the practice of public relations: its contribution to organizational effectiveness lies in building relationships with strategic constituencies (which are quantifiable in monetary terms). The work of a public relations practitioner can be effective only if public relations is part of the dominant coalition, i.e. if it participates in strategic decisions of goal-setting and identifying strategic constituencies (Grunig 1992: 86).

(2) In his discussion of management decision-making, in 'Public relations and management decision making' (Grunig 1992: ch. 4), the key concept is that of boundary-spanning, which is necessary for organizations which are open to environment. Environment, as such, is defined as a 'construction built from the flow of information into the organization' (Grunig 1992: 92). The construction itself is a process of selecting some of that information for

further analysis; in other words, the process of enactment.

This constitutes an introduction, which is followed by a review of literature on decision-making with references to, for example, Mintzberg et al. (1976) and Pfeffer (1981). Boundary-spanning is also strongly linked with the concept of meaning as a 'cultural artifact' (Grunig 1992: 99). Strangely, the authors, White and Dozier, do not offer any references here to literature on culture or symbolism. In fact, rather uncharacteristically they do not offer any references in this particular section.

The concept of requisite variety reappears as 'requisite scenarios' (Grunig 1992: 100). Decision-making is thus seen as an iterative process fully dependent on managers' ability to produce scenarios ('simplified models of possible future') – that is, their imagination – 'and the perceptions/meaning they bring to the decision-making process'.

The discussion is summarized in a number of propositions, which warrant a longer comment:

- Proposition 1: The more environmental scanning that practitioners conduct, the greater their participation in management decision making.
- Proposition 2: The more turbulent and uncertain the organisational environment, the more environmental scanning practitioners will be expected to conduct.
- Proposition 3: The more turbulent and uncertain the organizational environment, the greater the participation of practitioners in management decision making.
- Proposition 4: The greater the conflict between practitioner provided input and existing language/codes/frameworks, the greater the mistrust of practitioner loyalty to the organization.
- Proposition 5: The greater the conflict between practitioner-provided input and existing language/codes/frameworks, the better the quality of the decision provided.

(Grunig 1992: 106)

These propositions seem to be based on a number of unrevealed metatheoretical assumptions. Environment is external to the organization and constructed from information brought into the organization. The more information is available, the clearer the picture, and thus we are faced with the positivist belief in the objectively existing world, which organizations reconstruct from information. On the other hand, this objectivist belief is moderated by the realization that it is the human being that acts as the information-processing unit, and therefore the whole process has to take account of human sense-making strategies. Thus on the one hand we are presented with the picture of the organization as separate but dependent on the environment, and on the other hand we seem to be moving towards a more interpretative framework with the human being, rather than a system, in the centre.

Finally, conflict seems to play an important role within this scheme. There is an implicit acknowledgement that conflict between the organization and its environment, if not inevitable, is likely to arise. Indeed, the more extreme it appears, as revealed through the work of the public relations practitioner, the better for the decision-making within the organization. It seems fair to interpret this proposition as saying that the more divorced the organization is from its environment, the more imperative the process of adaptation or alignment. Public relations, then, appears as an element in the negative feedback loop. The worldview in which such an explanation makes sense is that of systemic modernism, ruled by performativity.

(3) 'What is excellence in management?' (Grunig 1992: ch. 9) is of interest for this discussion for two reasons. First, it takes the excellence framework as proposed by Peters and Waterman (1982), but also by other writers interested in distinguishing between good and poor organizations on other than purely financial factors (Grunig 1992: 222–3). Second, there is a clear attempt to link the distinction between mechanistic and organic structures with a discussion of how organizational structure influences organizational effectiveness.

The chapter attempts to bring together two different models of systems, factors linked to ideas of excellence, and Grunig's models of public relations. In a section devoted to organic structure (Grunig 1992: 225–9), Grunig makes an explicit distinction between 'centralized, formalized, stratified and less complex' organizations, referred to as mechanical; and organic ones characterized by a lesser degree of centralization, formalization and stratification, and a larger degree of complexity. The key to this distinction is autonomy (understood as the extent of discretion employees have in their jobs). This provides a good vantage point for reviewing various ideas on what constitutes excellence and linking these ideas to a systemic approach. The chapter goes on to discuss intrapreneurship, i.e. 'an innovative, entrepreneurial spirit', and claims a clear link between human resources, organic structure and intrapreneurship, which are likely to occur together and, from the public relations perspective, to be facilitated by excellent public relations (Grunig 1992: 248).

Other elements of excellence are identified as strong cultures, symmetrical communication systems, empowering leadership, decentralization of strategic planning, and social responsibility. The implication drawn out for the public relations function is that 'excellent public relations probably cannot exist within mechanical structures' (Grunig 1992: 229).

If we follow the theme of synthesizing various models of systems, models of public relations and a deterministic view of relationships between organizational structure and environment, we find it explored further in Dozier and Grunig's chapter 'Organization of public relations function', which draws on Hage and Hull's typology linking 'overall organizational structure to the environmental niche in which the organization fits' (Grunig 1992: 403). The press agentry/publicity and the public information models are seen as reflecting the closed-system orientation; two-way asymmetric and symmetric models are based on an open systems view of organizations. In terms of Hage and Hall's typology organized around concepts of scale and complexity, press agentry is associated with craft organizations; mechanical organizations are linked with the public information model; the organic organization tends to practise two-way symmetric public relations and the mixed organization practises both two-way models. (Grunig 1992: 403–4).

(4) 'Public relations management and operational research' (Grunig 1992: ch. 10) starts by locating the source of operational research firmly within the development of cybernetics. The function of operational research is to help managers make decisions; it is 'the approach to problem-solving that examines the system (a set of interacting entities) in which the decision problem is contained' (Richmond 1968; quoted in Grunig 1992: 258). In conclusions to this chapter, Ehling and Dozier write:

> The point of this chapter is not to suggest that every strategic communication of public relations decision must be made fully operationalized as a mathematically designed decision-making model; it is the kind of thinking that is more rigorous, more demanding, and more benefit oriented than the questionable 'by-guess-and by-gosh' methods so frequently employed by those who manage 'by the seat of their pants'.
>
> (Grunig 1992: 281)

'In contrast, operations research thinking calls for careful planning and designing of public relations and communication programs of action and constant evaluation of program performance' (Grunig 1992: 281). Operations research thinking requires that a manager be mindful that the goals and end-states of public relations and communications activities must be

- socially warranted
- ethically acceptable
- conceptually well-specified
- organizationally relevant
- structurally distinguishable
- administratively feasible
- operationally attainable
- empirically measurable
- economically optimal.

(Grunig 1992: 281)

There are, again, a number of interesting points that invite more comment. Although there is a clear insistence that not every decision has to be worked out in a mathematical model, the requirement that it has to be empirically measurable does imply that public relations should aspire to using quantitative methods of research as the final proof of its effectiveness.

Organizational goal-states are clearly linked to economic factors, but also to moral considerations, apparently on the assumption that what is socially warranted is also ethically acceptable. Perhaps more interestingly, the manager appears to be in a position to decide what is in the public interest and what is ethically acceptable. This claim can only be sustained if one accepts a unitary view of society with an unambiguous and generally accepted normative system.

So how is systems theory used in public relations as it emerges from *Excellence*? In broad terms it seems to be consistent with the Parsonian four imperatives (adaptation, goal attainment, integration and latency). More specifically, in terms of system models, there is a very consciously argued preference for organic (open) systems. Yet, if we look back to Buckley's adaptive model, or even more interestingly to Gharajedaghi and Ackoff, we cannot fail to notice that the inclusion of the ethical dimension of social responsibility implies a shift closer to the adaptive (purposeful) system. It seems that there is some degree of ambiguity about which model is being applied, or why more than one. If we look back to the discussion of the connection between models and paradigms (see also Pearson 1990), it becomes clear that the difference is not merely between different analogies used, but possibly also between different metatheoretical presuppositions. Yet again, the focus of the project on the question of effectiveness pulls us back into the organic model with its logic of goal-attainment and environmental fit. This is not necessarily an inconsistency, if we accept the argument that most systems exhibit a combination of various types of behaviour.

This particular point, however, draws our attention to another characteristic: the ease of moving across different approaches. For example, the sources revealed in the chapter on effectiveness – Hall, Hage, Perrow, Lawrence and Lorsch, Pfeffer, Blau and Scott, Etzioni, Gouldner – represent a whole spectrum of functionalist approaches as defined by Burrell and Morgan (1979), which seems to be consistent with the hybrid nature of many of these approaches but at the same time does not seem to pay any attention to debates and difference within the paradigm. The choice of the paradigm, or worldview, itself is not surprising, given the focus of the study; but it is more problematic when one looks at the sources in the discussion of a concept such as power (Grunig 1992: 483–501). True, it has been explored within the functionalist paradigm; nevertheless, the apparent lack of other points of view (critical theory, Marxism, postmodernism) has to be noticed. This is not to say that there is any obligation to explore all possible perspectives, but not doing so becomes then a choice with reasons behind it. In this case, the choice might be explained by, on the one hand, the problem-solving approach and, on the other, the theory-building agenda and therefore the need for internal consistency.

In fact, the drive for internal consistency, the need to translate into systems language, may produce some curious effects, such as using the argument of requisite variety to support the entrance to the profession for minorities; no doubt well intentioned, and by no means the full extent of the argument, it creates an apparently irreconcilable tension. Is there not some degree of confusion between an organization's instrumental reason for a particular action and a moral principle of a different order?

One could also speculate whether it is the need for internal consistency which is responsible for 'Excellence' not exploring the concept of self-referentiality and organizational identity. Morgan (1986) makes the connection from autopoiesis to enactment; and there is also, as we have seen, a connection from autopoiesis to concepts of evolution and chaos. The perspective adopted for the study of effectiveness has the organizational fit as the focus; self-referentiality does not, which perhaps explains why this particular line is of no interest to the study.

Models of public relations

This brings our discussion directly to questions about paradigms, or worldviews, a term preferred by Grunig in 'Symmetrical presuppositions as a framework for public relations theory' (Botan and Hazleton 1989) and in 'The effect of worldviews on public relations theory' (Grunig 1992), a chapter co-written with White. There is a considerable degree of overlap between these two chapters, although the later version seems to present a more extended discussion not just of Grunig's own approach, but also of alternative approaches as far as the social role of public relations is concerned.

The asymmetrical model is supported by seven presuppositions (Grunig 1989: 32–3; Grunig 1992: 43): internal orientation (inability to see the organizations as outsiders do), a closed system (information flows out but not in), efficiency (control of cost more important than innovation), elitism (leader of the organization knows best), conservatism (resistance to change) tradition (as culture-generating, thus providing the organizational glue) and central authority (autocratic organizations, no autonomy for employees).

On closer examination these characteristics seem to collapse one into another. For example, a closed (mechanistic) system is defined by its inward orientation. The idea that information flows out of but not into the organization is rather difficult to reconcile with any model of systems thinking, though again the mechanistic one is perhaps the most feasible (see earlier discussion of von Bertalanffy's work). Efficiency, conservatism and tradition, as defined by Grunig, may refer to the same trait – inability to sustain organizational change. Central authority and elitism seem to describe the concentration of authority and organizational wisdom at the top of the hierarchical structure. Thus it appears that the asymmetrical model is a closed system model and therefore corresponds to mechanistic organization.

The symmetrical view of organization, on the other hand, presupposes (Grunig 1989: 38; Grunig 1992: 43–4) holism, interdependence (with other systems in the environment), an open system (free exchange of information across the boundary) and moving equilibrium (this is not within the organization but with other organizations). In addition to presuppositions specifically derived from open systems approach, there are eight more presuppositions. The first of these, in fact the first on the list, is 'communication leads to understanding', derived from symmetrical models of communication (Newcomb 1953; Chaffee and McLeod 1968). An effort is made to distinguish symmetrical communication from persuasion, as the latter is regarded as less desirable.

The remaining presuppositions are equity (equal opportunities and respect for members of the organization), autonomy (seen as the degree of individuals' discretion over their tasks and linked to job satisfaction), innovation (new ideas privileged over tradition and efficiency), decentralization of management (decentralized and collective; increasing autonomy, employee satisfaction and innovation), responsibility (i.e. social responsibility), conflict resolution (through negotiation, communication and compromise) and interest-group liberalism.

The concept of open system, interdependence and moving equilibrium can in fact be summarized as some of the basic features of an organismic model. Autonomy, innovation and decentralization are elements of the open system, but also almost exact opposites of elitism, efficiency and central authority; this points to a conscious juxtaposition of mechanistic and organismic models of social systems. Reinterpreted in this way, concepts of systemic closure and openness seem to be used almost symbolically, in a way which seems to be very conscious of 'the dreaded disease' symptom pointed out by Burrell and Morgan (1979). 'Closed' (and for Grunig press agency/public information and two-way asymmetrical models) connotes 'bad', 'old-fashioned'; 'open' (two-way symmetrical model) connotes 'good', in fact more than that, 'excellent'.

The last three characteristics of the excellent model of public relations are responsibility, conflict resolution and interest-group liberalism. These are not derived from systems theory and originate from a consciously taken theoretical and ethical position. An excellent public relations theory, argue Grunig and White (Grunig 1992: 38) must fulfil internal criteria (logical, coherent, unified and orderly); external criteria ('effective in solving organizational problems as judged by relatively neutral research or history'); and ethical (concerned with building 'caring – even loving – relationships'). These criteria in turn lead to the view that excellent public relations is 'symmetrical, idealistic or critical, and managerial'.

The first characteristic, symmetry, is derived from a number of sources: theories of symmetrical communication; game theory and negotiation; and Gouldner's (1960) norm of reciprocity, which solves the problem of unequal power in social relationships and thus serves 'to inhibit the emergence of exploitative relations which would undermine the social system and the very power arrangements which had made exploitation possible' (Gouldner 1960: 174; quoted in Grunig 1992: 47). The idealistic stance seems to refer both to the social role of public relations and the normative character of the proposed theory. It means that 'public relations serves the public interest, develops mutual understanding between organizations and their publics, contributes to informed debate about issues in society, and facilitates a dialogue between organizations and their publics' (Grunig 1992: 53). Idealistic also means 'exemplary' and thus supports public relations ethics. If public relations takes a critical position, it contributes by revealing the areas of practice or theorizing that are at odds with the normative view. A further possible source for the idealistic position can be interest-group liberalism, which champions the interests of citizens against the government; or which is, to quote another of Grunig's sources, the kind of liberalism which

> possesses a strong faith that what is good government is good for society . . . sees as both necessary and good a policy agenda that is accessible to all organized interests and makes no independent judgement of their claims . . . it defines the public interest as . . . the amalgamation of various claims.
>
> (Grunig 1989: 39)

The managerial characteristics of public relations come from research into roles (Grunig 1992: ch. 12) which makes a basic distinction between public relations technician and manager. For public relations to be effective, the practitioner must participate in strategic decision-making. In other words, if public relations is to serve as an effective adaptive subsystem, it must have a say in the highest level of decision-making, concerned with relating the system to its environment.

On the face of it, the theory is seamless – it is carefully constructed, and offers coherent explanations of a range of problems and a promise of empirical evidence. There is a clear awareness of the metatheoretical basis for the position taken, and there is also a discussion of alternatives, with reasons why they have been rejected. In addition to these, the sheer size of the project and the range of literature searched suggest a definitive theory. Not only does Grunig not make any such claims, but he even states that the theory may well be reworked following the empirical stage of the project (Grunig 1992: 2); yet, the above characteristics of the work have already made it immensely influential. If this is the case, it is even more important to scrutinize both the basis of this theory and its implications.

IMPLICATIONS

As we have seen, the research on which the theory seems to be based is predominantly functionalist, in the broad sense given to the term by Burrell and Morgan. At the same time, however, there are other sources cited, notably

Weick and Peters and Waterman, which could just as easily be seen as coming from beyond the modernist framework. This kind of discussion or comment does not seem to be necessary and one could ask how methodologically conscious, therefore, the theory-construction process really has been. One could, however, also ask what it matters which paradigm the ideas come from, especially since the whole debate about paradigms has been abandoned in organization studies as unhelpful.

In presenting the debate about paradigms, I have tried to show the importance of methodological introspection and the knowledge it brings with it: paradigms rest on different ontological and epistemological bases which cannot simply be ignored. True, intense paradigm battles might be seen as disruptive, but that does not mean that metatheoretical presuppositions can be freely mixed. It is also worth remembering that our knowledge of paradigm struggle here is derived from organizational studies; yet in terms of history and volume of academic research, organizational studies and public relations are in rather different positions and, if anything, more theoretical variety might be healthy for public relations development.

Let us start with the nature of the excellence study: it is a project funded by a professional body and with research questions very specifically defined from the outset:

1 When and why are the efforts of communication practitioners effective?
2 How do organizations benefit from effective public relations?
3 Why do organizations practice public relations in different ways?

(Grunig 1992: 1)

One could argue that such an approach puts answers before questions, in the sense of limiting the possibilities of what the answers might be. This process of limitation stems from the original assumptions present in the questions (the bottom-line imperative which implies systems theory rather than other approaches), which in turn influence, in this case, the selection of literature relevant to the problem. Methodologically, the project seems to be designed as a deductive process, so the original selection of literature comes in turn to be translated into hypotheses to be tested empirically at a later stage. If the sources are too restricted, or used without due consideration being given to their broader context, all the subsequent research steps might be affected.

To complicate matters further, we are dealing with an attempt not only to answer the research questions but also to propose a normative theory of excellent public relations. What such a position means is that vast areas of activity (three of the four of Grunig's models) can be seen as public relations that is not quite right, dysfunctional. Although there may be objective causes, such as the structure of the organization, which do not allow the excellent model to be practised, there nevertheless is an implication of failure.

But what exactly is wrong with believing in improvement, in the call for progress implicit in such a theory? What is wrong with a normative theory? Well, what is wrong with the Ten Commandments? Only that they make perfect and profound sense to the converted, but appear problematic to those who operate outside them. To carry on with this religious metaphor, one finds a somewhat proselytizing approach emanating from the theory of excellent public relations: if public relations practitioners resist or do not understand the excellence ideas, it is because they do not know any better, even if through no fault of their own.

> Practitioners often do not understand or accept theories like ours because they work from a pragmatic or conservative worldview. We argue that practitioners with a pragmatic worldview have a set of asymmetrical presuppositions even though they do not realize it. They take an asymmetrical view, usually a conservative one, because their clients hold that view.
>
> (Grunig 1992: 10)

This is rather reminiscent of Victorian missionaries explaining savages' habits of walking about naked or praying to rain by their lack of civilization. It is not a bad explanation; but it is a good one only from a particular point of view.

The all-inclusive approach to the sources at an early stage can also lead to internal tensions within the resultant theory. For example, how can it be possible to talk about decentralization, empowerment and trust, and at the same time claim that to be effective public relations needs to be in the dominant coalition. In other words, no matter how strongly one believes that organizations should be diffused and autonomous in relation to their employees, there is still a centre of power and to make a difference one has to be in this centre.

Let us look at the ethical dimension of the theory. On the one hand, we see that ethics in this context is defined as 'a process of public relations rather than an outcome' (Grunig 1992: 308). So the outcome, which could be a compromise not consistent with the views of any of the parties involved, is ethical if arrived at through two-way symmetrical communication. On the other hand, at the core of public relations ethics is the concept of public interest. Ultimately, it seems, we can arrive at a paradoxical situation whereby what is good for the whole society/system is not good for any of the groups it consists of. How is it possible to arrive at such a position?

Lippmann (1954), in 'The image of democracy', presented an interesting argument about the historical circumstances surrounding the crystallization of Jefferson's ideas about democracy and their subsequent career which could be helpful in addressing the problem at hand. Jefferson, he claimed, conceived his ideas in a specific historical context, when communities were small and fairly isolated. In such conditions, a community has a very real and clear set of rules derived from the same education received, the same religious beliefs shared, and a real participation of citizens in the matters of government which were to do with their families, properties, security, and the provision of communal services for themselves and others in the community. If differences of opinion arose, these were likely to stem from a misunderstanding of some of the shared norms or their application. A free debate could, therefore, reveal the misinterpretation and resolve the conflict. Although the specific conditions have disappeared, people seem to operate explanations about the mechanisms of social life as if modern society were still such a rural township. Ironically, systems theory can be seen as providing a modern way of recreating the rural township.

It is ineffective, even practically impossible, as a public relations practitioner, to be concerned with everyone, since not everyone has an impact on the organization, or vice versa. A way of selecting who the organization should be concerned with is by segmenting the environment into publics. In public relations literature this constitutes a preliminary step to building relationships. The outcome of such a process is an approximation of the rural township. Logically, then, communication should lead to conflict resolution, if conflicts arise. Unfortunately, what holds this recreated township together is likely to be issues, not shared norms.

If one cannot be sure that a failure in reasoning is the only cause of misunderstanding, the focus shifts from the substance of the debate on to the process of debate itself, and we seem to be left with the form only – dialogue. The moral imperative for public relations seems to be about rule clarification (Grunig 1992: 60); in other words, creating conditions for dialogue. But who does the organization's talking? Who writes newsletters, scripts, speeches, briefing documents, letters to customers? Who advises on community relations? The process of talking involves saying; that is, taking positions, making judgements, stating opinions – even facts are not unequivocal, objective entities. Can the distinction between form and substance be made so easily? The tension within the theory that can be gleaned from this example is that it seems to advocate the inseparability of moral involvement from the practice of public relations, yet avoids dealing with the implications of this position by claiming that moral values for public relations practitioners reside in the formal rather than the substantive element of their activities. In other words, if the game is played by the rules, the outcome must be satisfactory.

This chapter has attempted to provide support for the argument that the theory of public relations presented in 'Excellence' is in fact more than just a theory; it has grown into a discourse – not just a tentative proposition about relationships between phenomena, but a way of thinking. If, however, we stop and think about how the theory so far has been constructed, we realize that it is, and should be treated as, a particular point of view; a view that is firmly based in the belief that society exists around the equilibrium of consensus. It is not a dramatic saga of a heroic stance in a society pulled apart by antagonistic forces, but a story of a well-ordered household proving to itself how civilized it is.

There is nothing wrong with choosing one of these views over another, as long as it is clear that as a result of the choice certain questions do not get asked. These might be questions about power and knowledge or power and language; or they might be questions about the position of the public relations practitioners, and researchers, within the scheme of things: is knowledge independent of the one who knows? Could one not see society as organized not around consensus, but struggle?

The lesson that can be drawn from the debate about paradigms is that ignoring such broad philosophical considerations leads to privileging one point of view over another. Public relations research revealing potential for other approaches has already been published (see Botan and Hazleton 1989; Toth and Heath 1992), and hopefully we shall see the range of research interests and perspectives extended even further.

To summarize, this chapter has endeavoured to show the origins, development, scope and limitations of systems theory and the way in which it has been adapted in public relations. It is argued that the process of adoption has so far not been clearly charted and that this creates the possibility of contradictory assumptions being built into the model created. The lack of critical work in public relations compounds the problem, as the lack of challenge leads to the development of a somewhat confused or hybrid form of systems theory achieving the status of ideology within the public relations canon.

NOTES

1 PUBLIC RELATIONS EDUCATION

1 The 1995 Public Relations Education Trust (PRET) Report both exemplifies this and acknowledges the problem. PRET notes that there has been a poor response to the Trust's attempts to stimulate a research programme in the UK and contrasts the situation with that in the United States. PRET suggests that 'perhaps . . . we have to accept that the academic contribution to the development of public relations theory and practice has taken many years there to build up and we must have the patience to persevere with funding to build into the general fabric of the profession the notion of research based studies, even if the early results are not particularly encouraging'.

2 PUBLIC RELATIONS AS DIPLOMACY

1 Since this book went to press I have found another useful and interesting source: Gryspeerdt, Axel (1994) 'L'entreprise comme embassade ou la métaphore de l'ambassadeur dans la communication institutionnelle', *Recherches en communication* 1. This article contrasts the role of the business communicator with that of diplomat, paying particular attention to the language, signs and images employed by such practitioners, the social significance of the commercial entreprise and its implications for the role of journalism. Attention is drawn to the rhetoric employed by the two occupations to describe their activities: Gryspeerdt contrasts the practice which has been called 'honourable espionage' when performed by diplomats with the strategic function of environmental monitoring in public relations, and he implies that terminology in public relations presents such activities as more neutral and less self-interested than is really the case.

2 The term 'intermestic' is used to describe international communication targeted at the domestic publics of other nations.

3 It seems as though in the recent past writers within the Grunig school (such as Pearson 1992) have suggested that Grunig's position is supported by Jürgen Habermas's Theory of Communicative Action (see chapter 7).

4 I owe this question to Jim Wyllie, Senior Lecturer in Strategic Studies, University of Aberdeen.

3 PERFORMANCE IN POLITICS AND THE POLITICS OF PERFORMANCE

1 An example of a recent articulation of this view was *Why I Hate PR*, written and presented by former Conservative MP Matthew Parris as part of Channel 4's *Without Walls* series.

2 The issues discussed in this essay are developed at greater length in McNair 1995.
3 See, for example, the ITV documentary *To Sell a War*, broadcast on 6 February 1992.
4 Examples of outlets on British television and radio where politicians may gain publicity and exposure for their views.

4 PUBLIC OPINION AND PUBLIC RELATIONS

1 See also Katz et al. 1954: 50.
2 For a discussion of Habermas, see also Calhoun 1993.
3 See also Noelle-Neumann (1979: 147), who gives the date as 1744 rather than 1750.
4 See Price 1992: 12–14.
5 See also Berelson 1956.
6 See also Converse 1987.
7 See Allport 1954; Young 1954; Blumer 1954; Price 1992.

5 CORPORATE IDENTITY AND CORPORATE IMAGE

1 The concept of identity in relation to brands, as distinct from brand image, is discussed by Kapferer (1992).
2 See G. McCusker (1995) *Public Relations and the Audio Logo: A Case Study of Radio Scotland's On Air Identity*, unpublished master's dissertation for the MSc in Public Relations, University of Stirling, which explores this concept in depth.
3 Olins, to be fair, deals briefly with the Third Reich's corporate identity in his earlier book (Olins 1978: 22–5).

6 CORPORATE RESPONSIBILITY AND PUBLIC RELATIONS ETHICS

1 It should be noted that the terms 'moral' and 'ethical' may be used interchangeably.
2 An action characterized by care and caution with regard to one's own interests.
3 In 1984 Union Carbide's pesticide plant at Bhopal in India leaked a cloud of toxic gas, killing thousands of men, women and children. Union Carbide successfully 'Indianized' the situation, becoming famous for their skill in crisis management.
4 In 1986 the space shuttle *Challenger* was launched against the objections of some designers and engineers and exploded shortly after take-off.
5 In 1989 the Exxon oil tanker *Exxon Valdez*, under the authority of a captain absent from the bridge, ran aground on Bligh Reef in Prince William Sound, Alaska, and leaked 11 million gallons of crude oil, killing thousands of sea birds, sea otters, seal pups and other wildlife. The community was radically affected by Exxon's subsequent clean-up since the arrival of numbers of highly paid workers required a new infrastructure.
6 In 1987 the cross-channel ferry *Herald of Free Enterprise* capsized with the loss of nearly 200 lives because the bow doors had been left open on departure from Zeebrugge.
7 In 1994 the Swedish ferry *Estonia* capsized with the loss of 500 lives.

7 PUBLIC RELATIONS AND RHETORIC

1 I am grateful to Magda Pieczka for the supply of material in relation to the Brent Spar case.

BIBLIOGRAPHY

Ackerman, B. (1980) *Social Justice in the Liberal State*, New Haven, CT: Yale University Press.

Ackoff, R.L. (1959) 'Games, decisions, and organizations', *General Systems* 4: 145–50.

Ackoff, R.L. and Emery, F.E. (1972) *On Purposeful Systems*, London: Tavistock Publications.

Ackroyd, S. (1992) 'Paradigms lost: paradise regained?', in M. Reed and M. Hughes (eds) *Rethinking Organization*, London: Sage.

Aldrich, H.E. (1975) 'An organization–environment perspective on cooperation and conflict between organizations in the Manpower training system', in A.R. Negandhi (ed.) *Interorganizational Theory*, Kent, OH: Kent State University Press.

Aldrich, H.E. (1992) 'Incommensurable paradigms? Vital signs in three perspectives', in M. Reed and M. Hughes (eds) *Rethinking Organization*, London: Sage.

Allen, V. (1975) *Sociological Analysis: A Marxist Critique and Alternative*, London: Longman.

Allport, F. (1954) 'Toward a science of public opinion', in D. Katz, D.Cartwright, S. Eldersveld and A. McClung Lee (eds) *Public Opinion and Propaganda*, New York: Holt, Rinehart & Winston (originally published 1937, *Public Opinion Quarterly* 1: 7–23).

Andrewes, A. (1986) *Greek Society*, London: Penguin.

Argyris, C. (1964) *Integrating the Individual and the Organization*, New York: Wiley.

Aristophanes (1972) *The Wasps*, London/Harmondsworth: Penguin.

Aristotle (1991) *The Art of Rhetoric*, London/Harmondsworth: Penguin.

Asante, M.K. and Gudykunst, W.B. (eds) (1989) *Handbook of International and Intercultural Communication*, London: Sage.

Baier, K. (1984) 'Duties to one's employer', in T. Regan (ed.) *Just Business: New Introductory Essays in Business Ethics*, New York: Random House.

Baker, K. (1990a) 'Fixing the French constitution', *Inventing the French Revolution*, Cambridge: Cambridge University Press.

Baker, K. (1990b) 'Public opinion as political invention', *Inventing the French Revolution*, Cambridge: Cambridge University Press.

Baran, P. and Sweezy, P. (1968) *Monopoly Capital*, Harmondsworth: Penguin.

Barker, Sir Ernest (ed.) (1966) *Social Contract*, London: Oxford University Press.

Barker, E. (1984) *The Making of a Moonie: Choice or Brainwashing?*, Oxford: Blackwell.

Barney, R.D. and Black, J. (1994) 'Ethics and professional persuasive communications', *Public Relations Review* 20(3): 233–48.

Barthes, R. (1977) *Image-Music-Text*, London: Fontana.

Baudrillard, J. (1983) *In the Shadow of the Silent Majorities*, New York: Semiotext.

Bazerman, C. (1993) 'A contention over the term "rhetoric"', in T. Enos and S.C. Brown (eds) *Defining the New Rhetorics*, London: Sage.

Beauchamp, T.L. and Bowie, N.E. (eds) (1988) *Ethical Theory and Business*, Englewood Cliffs, NJ: Prentice-Hall.

Bell, D. (1974) *The Coming of Post-industrial Society*, London: Heinemann.

Bell, Q. (1991) *The PR Business*, London: Kogan Page.

Ben-Eli, M.U. (1981) 'Self-organization, autopoiesis and evolution', in M. Zeleny (ed.) *Autopoiesis: A Theory of Living Organization*, New York: North Holland Publishers.

Beniger, J. (1987) 'Toward an old new paradigm: half century flirtation with mass-communication', *Public Opinion Quarterly* 51: S46–S66.

Berelson, B. (1956) in L. White (ed.) *The Study of the Social Sciences*, Chicago: Chicago University Press.

Berelson, B. and Janovitz, M. (eds) (1966) *Reader in Public Opinion and Communication*, 2nd edn, New York: Free Press; London: Collier Macmillan.

Bernays, E. (1923) *Crystallizing Public Opinion*, New York: Boni & Liveright.

Bernays, E. (1955) *The Engineering of Consent*, Norman: University of Oklahoma Press.

Bernstein, D. (1984) *Company Image and Reality*, Eastbourne: Holt, Rinehart & Winston/Advertising Association.

Bettinghaus, E.P. and Cody, M.J. (1994) *Persuasive Communication*, Orlando, FL: Harcourt Brace.

Beynon, H. (1973) *Working for Ford*, Harmondsworth: Penguin/Allen Lane.

Bizzell, P. and Herzberg, B. (1990) *The Rhetorical Tradition: Readings from Classical Times to the Present*, Boston: Bedford.

Black, S. (1989) *Introduction to Public Relations*, London: Modino Press.

Black, S. and Sharpe, M. (1983) *Practical Public Relations*, Englewood Cliffs, NJ: Prentice-Hall.

Blau, P. and Scott, W.R. (1962) *Formal Organizations*, San Francisco: Chandler.

Blumer, H. (1954) 'Public opinion and public opinion polls', in D. Katz, D. Cartwright, S. Eldersveld and A. McClung Lee (eds) *Public Opinion and Propaganda*, New York: Holt, Rinehart & Winston (originally published 1948, *American Sociological Review* 13: 542–54).

Boggs, C. (1978) *Gramsci's Marxism*, London: Pluto Press.

Boorstin, D. (1961) *The Image*, London: Weidenfeld & Nicolson.

Boorstin, D. (1962) *The Image*, London: Weidenfeld & Nicolson.

Botan, C.H. and Hazleton, V. (eds) (1989a) *Public Relations Theory*, Hillsdale, NJ: Lawrence Erlbaum.

Botan, C.H. and Hazleton, V. (1989b) 'The role of theory in public relations', in C.H. Botan and V. Hazleton (eds) *Public Relations Theory*, Hillsdale, NJ: Lawrence Erlbaum.

Botan, C.H. (1989c) 'Theory development in public relations', in C.H. Botan and V. Hazleton (eds) *Public Relations Theory*, Hillsdale, NJ: Lawrence Erlbaum.

Botan, C.H. (1993) 'Introduction to the paradigm struggle in public relations', *Public Relations Review* 19(2): 107–10.

Bourdieu, P. (1979) 'Public opinion does not exist', in A. Mattelart and S. Siegelaub (eds) *Communication and Class Struggle*, New York: International General.

Braverman, H. (1974) *Labor and Monopoly Capital*, New York: Monthly Preview Press.

Broom, G., Cox, M.S., Krueger, E.A. and Liebler, C.M. (1989) 'The gap between professional and research agendas in public relations journals', in J.E. Grunig and L.A. Grunig (eds) *Public Relations Research Annual*, vol. 1, Hillsdale, NJ: Lawrence Erlbaum.

Buccholz, R.A. (1989) *Business Environment and Public Policy*, 3rd edn, Englewood Cliffs, NJ: Prentice-Hall.

Buckley, W. (1967) *Sociology and Modern Systems Theory*, Englewood Cliffs, NJ: Prentice-Hall.

Bull, H. and Watson, A. (1984) *The Expansion of International Society*, Oxford: Oxford University Press.

Burrell, G. and Morgan, G. (1979) *Sociological Paradigms and Organisational Analysis*, London: Heinemann.

Calhoun, C. (ed.) (1993) *Habermas and the Public Sphere*, Boston, MA: Massachusetts Institute of Technology.

Carey, C. (1994) 'Rhetorical means of persuasion', in I. Worthington (ed.) *Persuasion: Greek Rhetoric in Action*, London: Routledge.

Carlson, R. (ed.) (1975) *Communications and Public Opinion*, New York: Praeger.

Carmichael, S. and Drummond, J. (1989) *Good Business: A Guide to Corporate Responsibility and Business Ethics*, London: Business Books, Century Hutchinson.

Cerny, P.(1990) *The Changing Architecture of Politics: Structure, Agency, and the Future of the State*, London: Sage.

Chaffee, S. and McLeod, J. (1968) 'Sensitization in panel design: a coorientation experiment', *Journalism Quarterly* 45: 61–669.

Chajet, C. (1989) 'The making of a new corporate image', *Journal of Business Strategy* (May/June): 18–20.

Cheney, G. and Dioniopsoulos, G.N. (1989) 'Public relations? No, relations with publics: a rhetorical-organizational approach to contemporary corporate communications', in C.H. Botan and V. Hazleton (eds) *Public Relations Theory*, Hillsdale, NJ: Lawrence Erlbaum.

Cheney, G. and Vibbert, S. (1987) 'Corporate discourse: public relations and issue management', in F. Jablin, L. Putnam, K. Roberts and L. Porter (eds) *Handbook of Organisational Communication: An Interdisciplinary Perspective*, London: Sage.

Chisman, F. (1976) *Attitude Psychology and the Study of Public Opinion*, University Park, PN: Pennsylvania State University Press.

Cicourel, A. (1968) *The Social Organization of Juvenile Justice*, New York: Free Press.

Clegg, S. (1975) *Power, Rule and Domination*, London: Routledge & Kegan Paul.

Clegg, S. (1990) *Modern Organizations: Organization Studies in the Postmodern World*, London: Sage.

Cockerell, M. (1988) *Live from Number 10*, London: Faber.

Cockerell, M., Hennessey, P. and Walker, D. (1984) *Sources Close to the Prime Minister*, London: Macmillan.

Cohen, D. (1994) 'Classical rhetoric and modern theories of discourse', in I. Worthington (ed.) *Persuasion: Greek Rhetoric in Action*, London: Routledge.

Converse, P. (1964) 'The nature of belief systems in mass publics', in D. Apter (ed.) *Ideology and Discontent*, New York: Free Press.

Converse, P. (1987) 'Changing conceptions of public opinion in the political process', *Public Opinion Quarterly* 51: S12–S24.

Cooper, R. and Burrell, G. (1988) 'Modernism, postmodernism and organizational analysis: an introduction', *Organization Studies* 9(1): 91–112.

Corbett, E.P.J. (1965) *Classical Rhetoric for the Modern Student*, New York: Oxford University Press.

Cottone, L.P. (1993) 'The perturbing worldview of chaos: implications for public relations', *Public Relations Review* 19(2): 167–77.

Craib, I. (1992) *Modern Social Theory From Parsons to Habermas*, Hemel Hempstead: Harvester Wheatsheaf.

Culbertson, H.M. and Jeffers, D.W. (1992) 'Social, political, and economic contexts: keys in educating the true public relations professionals', *Public Relations Review* 18(1): 53–67.

Cutlip, S.M., Center, A.H. and Broom, G.M. (1994) *Effective Public Relations*, 7th edn, London: Prentice-Hall.

Cutlip, S., Center, A. and Broom, G. (1985) *Effective Public Relations*, 6th edn, Englewood Cliffs, NJ: Prentice-Hall.

Dalton, R. (1988) *Citizen Politics in Western Democracies*, Chatham, NJ: Chatham House Publishers.

Davison, W.P. (1987) 'A story of the POQ's fifty-year odyssey', *Public Opinion Quarterly* 51: S4–S11.

De George, R.T. (ed.) (1978) *Ethics, Free Enterprise and Public Policy: Original Essays on Moral Issues in Business*, New York: Oxford University Press.

De George, R.T. (1983) 'The social business of business', in W.L. Robison, M.S. Pritchard and J. Ellin (eds) *Profits and Professions*, Clifton, NJ: Humana Press.

Deal, T. and Kennedy, A. (1982) *Corporate Cultures*, Reading, MA: Addison-Wesley.

Der Derian, J. (1987) *On Diplomacy: A Genealogy of Western Estrangement*, Oxford: Blackwell.

Derrida, J. (1973) *Speech and Phenomena*, Evanston, IL: Northwestern University Press.

Dewey, J. (1927) *The Public and Its Problems*, Denver: Swallow.

Dickie, R. and Rouner, L. (1986) *Corporations and the Common Good*, Notre Dame: University of Notre Dame Press.

Donelan, M. (1992) *Elements of International Political Theory*, Oxford: Oxford University Press Clarendon Paperbacks.

Ehling, W.P. (1984) 'Application of decision theory in the construction of a theory of public relations I', *Public Relations Research and Education* 1(2): 25–39.

Ehling, W.P. (1985) 'Application of decision theory in the construction of a theory of public relations II', *Public Relations Research and Education* 2(1): 4–22.

Ehling, W. (1992) 'Public relations education and professionalism', in J. Grunig (ed.) *Excellence in Public Relations and Communications Management*, Hillsdale, NJ: Lawrence Erlbaum.

Ehling, W., Grunig, J. and White, J. (1992) 'Public relations and marketing practices', in J. Grunig (ed.) *Excellence in Public Relations and Communications Management*, Hillsdale, NJ: Lawrence Erlbaum.

Eldridge, J. and Crombic, A. (1974) *A Sociology of Organisations*, London: George Allen & Unwin.

Emery, F. and Trist, E. (1946) 'Socio-technical systems', in C. Churchman and Verhulst (eds) *Management Science, Models and Techniques*, vol. 2, London: Pergamon.

Enos, T. and Brown, S. (eds) (1993) *Defining the New Rhetorics*, London: Sage.

Etzioni, A. (1964) *Modern Organizations*, Englewood Cliffs, NJ: Prentice-Hall.

Everett, J. 'The ecological paradigm in public relations theory and practice', *Public Relations Review* 19(2): 177–85.

Ewing, R.P. (1990) 'Moving from micro to macro issues management', *Public Relations Review* (Spring): 19–24.

Falb, R. (1992) 'The place of public relations education in higher education: another opinion', *Public Relations Review* 18(1): 91–7.

Fedler, F. and Smith, R. (1992) 'Faculty members in ad/PR perceive discrimination in academia', *Public Relations Review* 18(1): 79–91.

Feld, S. and Jorg, N. (1991) 'Corporate liability and manslaughter: should we be going Dutch?', *Criminal Law Review* (March): 50.

First Forum 8(4) (1995) special issue on corporate social responsibility.

Fisher, G. (1989) 'Diplomacy', in M. Asante and W. Gudykunst, *Handbook of International and Intercultural Communication*, London: Sage.

Fiske, J. (1993) *Introduction to Communication Studies*, London: Routledge.

Foucault, M. (1977a) *Language, Counter-memory, Practice*, Ithaca, NY: Cornell University Press.

Foucault, M. (1977b) *Discipline and Punish: The Birth of the Prison*, London: Allen Lane.

Foucault, M. (1980) *Power/Knowledge*, Brighton: Harvester Press.

French, P.A. (1979) 'The corporation as a moral person', *American Philosophical Quarterly* 16(3).

Friedman, M. (1970) 'The social responsibility of business is to increase its profits', *New York Times Magazine* (13 September).

Friedman, M. (1993) 'The social responsibility of business is to increase its profits', in G.D. Chryssides and J.H. Kaler (eds) *An Introduction to Business Ethics*, London/Glasgow: Chapman & Hall.

Gagarin, M. (1994) 'Probability and persuasion: Plato and early Greek rhetoric', in I. Worthington (ed.) *Persuasion: Greek Rhetoric in Action*, London: Routledge.

Gandy, O. (1982) *Beyond Agenda Setting: Information Subsidies and Public Policy*, NJ: Ablex Publishing Corporation.

Garnham, N. (1986) 'The media and the public sphere', in P. Golding, G. Murdock and P. Schlesinger (eds) *Communicating Politics: Mass Communications and the Political Process*, Leicester: Leicester University Press.

Gergen, K.J. (1992) 'Organization theory in the postmodern era', in M. Reed and M. Hughes (eds) *Rethinking Organization*, London: Sage.

Gharajedaghi, J. and Ackoff, R. (1994) 'Mechanisms, organisms and social systems', in H. Tsoukas (ed.) *New Thinking in Organizational Behaviour*, Oxford: Butterworth-Heinemann.

Gillman, F.C. (1978) 'Public relations in the United Kingdom prior to 1948', *International Public Relations Review* (April): 43–50.

Glover, J. (1970) *Responsibility*, London: Routledge & Kegan Paul.

Golding, P., Murdock, G. and Schlesinger, P. (eds) (1986) *Communicating Politics: Mass Communications and the Political Process*, Leicester: Leicester University Press.

Gorb, P. (1992) 'The psychology of corporate identity', *European Management Journal* 103: 310–14.

Gore-Booth, L. (1978) *Satow's Guide to Diplomatic Practice*, 5th edn, London: Longman.

Gouldner, A. (1959) 'Organizational analysis', in R.K. Merton, L. Broom and L.S. Cottrell (eds) *Sociology Today*, New York: Basic Books.

Gouldner, A. (1960) 'The norm of reciprocity: a preliminary statement', *American Sociological Review* 25: 161–78.

Grant, C. (1991) 'Friedman fallacies', *Journal of Business Ethics* 10. 907–17.

Groom, A. and Light, M. (eds) (1994) *Contemporary International Relations: A Guide to Theory*, London: Pinter.

Grunig, J. (1989) 'Symmetrical presuppositions as a framework for public relations theory', in C. Botan and V. Hazleton (eds) *Public Relations Theory*, Hillsdale, NJ: Lawrence Erlbaum.

Grunig, J. (ed.) (1992) *Excellence in Public Relations and Communications Management*, Hillsdale, NJ: Lawrence Erlbaum.

Grunig, J. (1993a) 'Public relations and international affairs: effects, ethics and responsibility', *Journal of International Affairs* 47(1): 137–62.

Grunig, J. (1993b) 'Image and substance: from symbolic to behavioral relationships', *Public Relations Review* 19(2): 121–39.

Grunig, J. and Grunig, L. (1989) (eds) *Public Relations Research Annual*, vol. 1, Hillsdale, NJ: Lawrence Erlbaum.

Grunig, J. and Grunig, L. (1990) 'Models of public relations: a review and reconceptualization', Association of Education in Journalism and Mass Communication (AEJMC).

Grunig, J. and Hunt, T. (1984) *Managing Public Relations*, New York: Holt, Rinehart & Winston.

Habermas, J. (1984) *The Theory of Communicative Action I: Reason and the Rationalization of Society*, Boston, MA: Beacon Press.

Habermas, J. (1989) *The Structural Transformation of the Public Sphere: An Inquiry into a Category of Bourgeois Society*, translated by T. Burger with the assistance of

F. Lawrence, Cambridge: Polity Press.
Hage, J. (1980) *Theories of Organizations: Form, Process, and Transformation*, New York: Wiley.
Hainsworth, B.E. (1990) 'The distribution of advantages and disadvantages', *Public Relations Review* (Spring): 33–9.
Hall, S., Crichter, C., Jefferson, T., Clarke, J. and Roberts, B. (1978) *Policing the Crisis*, London: Macmillan.
Hallahan, K. (1993) 'The paradigm struggle and public relations practice', *Public Relations Review* 19(2): 197–205.
Hallin, D. (1986) *The Uncensored War*, Oxford: Oxford University Press.
Halloran, S.M. (1993) 'Further thoughts on the end of rhetoric', in T. Enos and S.C. Brown (eds) *Defining the New Rhetorics*, London: Sage.
Hamel, J., Dufour, S. and Fortin D. (1993) *Case Study Methods*, Newbury Park: Sage.
Hamilton, K. and Langhorne R. (1995) *The Practice of Diplomacy: Its Evolution, Theory and Administration*, London: Routledge.
Handy, C. (1987) *The Future of Work*, Oxford: Blackwell.
Handy, C. (1989) *The Age of Unreason*, London: Business Books.
Harlow, R. (1976) 'Building a public relations definition', *Public Relations Review* 2(4): 34–42.
Harrington, M. (1978) 'Corporate collectivism: a system of social justice', in R.T. De George and J.A. Pilcher (eds) *Ethics, Free Enterprise and Public Policy: Original Essays and Moral Issues in Business*, New York: Oxford University Press.
Harris, R. (1991) *Good and Faithful Servant*, London: Faber.
Hart, R. (1987) *The Sound of Leadership: Presidential Communication in the Modern Age*, Chicago: University of Chicago Press.
Hartley, J. (1994), in T. O'Sullivan, J. Hartley, D. Saunders, M. Montgomery and J. Fiske *Key Concepts in Communication and Cultural Studies*, 2nd edn, New York: Routledge.
Hassard, J. (1993) 'Postmodernism and organizational analysis', in J. Hassard and M. Parker (eds) *Postmodernism and Organizations*, Newbury Park: Sage.
Hassard, J. and Parker, M. (eds) (1993) *Postmodernism and Organizations*, London/Newbury Park/New Delhi: Sage.
Hatfield, C.R. (1994) 'Public relations education in the United Kingdom', *Public Relations Review* 20(2):189–99.
Hayward, R. (1990) *All About Public Relations*, 2nd edn, London: McGraw-Hill.
Hazleton, V. and Cutbirth, C. (1993) 'Public relations in Europe: an alternative educational program', *Public Relations Review* 19(2): 187–97.
Heath, R. (1992) 'The wrangle in the marketplace: a rhetorical perspective of public relations', in E. Toth and R. Heath (eds) *Rhetorical and Critical Approaches to Public Relations*, Hillsdale, NJ: Lawrence Erlbaum.
Heath, R. (1993) 'A rhetorical approach to zones of meaning and organizational prerogatives', *Public Relations Review* 19(3): 141–57.
Heath, R. and Cousino, K. (1990) 'Issues management: end of first decade progress report', *Public Relations Review* (Spring): 6–18.
Heath, R. and Nelson, R. (1986) *Issues Management: Corporate Public Policymaking in an Information Society*, London: Sage.
Heath, R. and Ryan, M. (1989) 'Public relations' role in defining corporate social responsibility', *Journal of Mass Media Ethics* 4(1): 21–38.
Herbst, S. (1993) 'The meaning of public opinion: citizens' constructions of political reality', *Media, Culture and Society* 15: 437–54.
Hiebert, R.E. (1966) *Courtier to the Crowd: The Story of Ivy Lee and the Development of Public Relations*, Ames, IO: Iowa State University Press.
Hiebert, R. (ed.) (1988) *Precision Public Relations*, London: Longman.

Hill, C. and Beshoff, P. (eds) (1994a) *Two Worlds of International Relations*, London: Routledge.

Hill, C. and Beshoff, P. (1994b) 'The two worlds: natural partnership or necessary distance?', in C. Hill and P. Beshoff (eds) *Two Worlds of International Relations*, London: Routledge.

Hirst, P. and Zeitlin, J. (1991) 'Flexible specialisation versus post-Fordism', *Economy and Society* 20(1): 1–56.

Hobbes, T. (1974) *Leviathan*, Glasgow: Collins/Fontana.

Hoffman, M. (1985) 'Normative approaches', in M. Light and A. Groom (eds) *International Relations: A Handbook of Current Theory*, London: Pinter.

Hoffman, M. (1994) 'Normative international theory: approaches and issues', in A.J.R. Groom and M. Light (eds) *Contemporary International Relations: A Guide to Theory*, London: Pinter.

Hoffman, W. and Moore, J. (1990) *Business Ethics: Readings and Cases in Corporate Morality*, New York: McGraw-Hill.

Hollinger, R. (1994) *Postmodernism and the Social Sciences*, London: Sage.

Hollingsworth (1991) *MPs for Hire*, London: Bloomsbury.

Homans, G.C. (1950) *The Human Group*, New York: Harcourt, Brace & World.

Honeth, A. and Hans, J. (1991) (eds) *Essays on Jürgen Habermas' The Theory of Communicative Action*, translated by J. Gaines and D. Jones, London: Polity Press.

Howard, W. (ed.) (1988) *The Practice of Public Relations*, London: Heinemann Professional Publishers.

Hume, D. (1980) *A Treatise of Human Nature*, Oxford: Oxford University Press.

Iannone, A. (ed.) (1989) *Contemporary Moral Controversies in Business*, New York: Oxford University Press.

Ind, N. (1990) *The Corporate Image: Strategies for Effective Identity Programmes*, London: Kogan Page.

Ingham, B. (1991) *Kill the Messenger*, London: Fontana.

International Public Relations Association (1990) 'Public relations education – recommendations and standards', Gold Paper no. 7.

Jablin, F., Putnam, L., Roberts, K. and Porter, L. (eds) (1987) *Handbook of Organizational Communication*, London: Sage.

Jakobson, R. (1960) 'Concluding statement on linguistics and poetics', in T. Sebeok (ed.) *Style in Language*, Cambridge, MA: MIT Press.

Jantsch, E. (1981) 'Autopoiesis: a central aspect of dissipative self-organization', in M. Zeleny (ed.) *Autopoiesis: A Theory of Living Organization*, New York: North Holland Publishers.

Jowett, G.S. and O'Donnell, V. (1986) *Propaganda and Persuasion*, London: Sage.

Kamekura, Y. (1966) *Trademarks and Symbols of the World*, London: Studio Vista.

Kant, I. (1983) *Perpetual Peace and other Essays*, translated by T. Humphrey, Indianapolis: Hackett Publishing.

Kapferer, J. (1992) *Strategic Brand Management*, London: Kogan Page.

Katz, D. and Kahn, R.L. (1966) *The Social Psychology of Organisations*, New York: John Wiley.

Katz, D., Cartwright, D., Eldersveld, S. and McClung Lee, A. (eds) (1954) *Public Opinion and Propaganda*, New York: Holt, Rinehart & Winston.

Katz. E. (1987) 'Communication research since Lazarsfeld', *Public Opinion Quarterly* 51: S25–S45.

Keen, C. and Warner, D. (eds) (1989) *Visual and Corporate Identity*, Banbury: HEIST.

Kelley, S. (1956) *Professional Public Relations and Political Power*, Baltimore: John Hopkins Press.

Kickert, W.J. (1993) 'Autopoiesis and the science of (public) administration: essence, sense and nonsense', *Organization Studies* 14(2): 261–78.

Kinder, D. and Sears, D. (1985) 'Public opinion and political action', in G. Lindzey and E. Aronson (eds) *The Handbook of Social Psychology*, 3rd edn, vol. 2.

Kinneir, J. (1980) *Words and Buildings: The Art and Practice of Public Lettering*, London: Architectural Press.

Kitto, H. (1986) *The Greeks*, London: Pelican.

L'Etang, J. (forthcoming) 'Issues management and psychological operations'.

Lacey, A. (1990) *A Dictionary of Philosophy*, London: Routledge.

Lasswell, H.D. (1927) *Propaganda Techniques in the World War*, New York: Smith.

Lauer, J. (1993) 'Rhetoric and composition studies: a multimodal discipline', in T. Enos and S.C. Brown (eds) *Defining the New Rhetorics*, London: Sage.

Lawrence, P. and Lorsch, J. (1967) *Organizations and Environment*, Cambridge, MA: Harvard Graduate School of Business Administration.

Lazarsfeld, P. (1981) 'Public opinion and the classical tradition', in M. Janowitz and P. Hirsch (eds) *Reader in Public Opinion and Mass Communication*, 3rd edn, New York: Free Press.

Lechte, J. (1994) *Fifty Contemporary Thinkers*, London: Routledge.

Leff, M. (1978) 'In search of Ariadne's thread: a review of the recent literature on rhetorical theory', *Central States Speech Journal* 29: 73–91.

Lessnoff, M. (1986) *Social Contract*, Basingstoke: Macmillan Education.

Lippmann, W. (1922) *Public Opinion*, New York: Macmillan.

Lippmann, W. (1925) *The Phantom Public*, New York: Harcourt, Brace.

Lippmann, W. (1954) 'The image of society', in D. Katz, D. Cartwight, S. Eldersveld and L. McClung Lee (eds) *Public Opinion and Propaganda*, New York: Reinhart & Winston (originally published 1922, *Public Opinion*, New York: Macmillan Co.).

Lippmann, W. (1954) *Public Opinion*, New York: Macmillan.

Lippmann, W. (1954) 'The image of democracy', in D. Katz, D. Cartwright, S. Eldersveld and A. McClung Lee (eds) *Public Opinion and Propaganda*, New York: Holt, Rinehart & Winston.

Lodge, G.C. (1986) 'The large corporation and the new American ideology', in R.B. Dickie and L.S. Rouner (eds) *Corporations and the Common Good*, University of Notre Dame Press.

Luhmann, N. (1984) *Soziale Systeme*, Frankfurt: Suhrkamp.

Luhmann, N. (1986) 'The autopoiesis of social systems', in F. Geyer and J. van der Zouwen (eds) *Sociocybernetic Paradoxes*, London: Sage.

Luttberg, N. (1974) *Public Opinion and Public Policy: Models of Political Linkage*, Homewood, IL: Dorsey Press.

Lyotard, J. (1977) 'The unconsious as mise-en-scène', in M. Benamou and C. Caramello (eds) *Performance in Postmodern Culture*, Wisconsin: Center for Twentieth Century Studies and Coda Press.

Lyotard, J.F. (1984) *The Postmodern Condition: A Report on Knowledge*, Manchester: Manchester University Press.

Macarthur, J.(1992) *Second Front: Censorship and Propaganda in the Gulf War*, New York: Hill & Wang.

McBride, G. (1989) 'Ethical thought in public relations history: seeking a relevant perspective', *Journal of Mass Media Ethics* 4(1): 5–20.

McCulloch, A. and Shannon, M. (1977) 'Organization and protection', in S. Clegg and D. Dunkerley (eds) *Critical Issues in Organizations*, London: Routledge & Kegan Paul.

Machiavelli, N. (1981) *The Prince*, Harmondsworth: Penguin Classics.

Machiavelli, N. (1983) *The Discourses*, Harmondsworth: Penguin Classics.

McNair, B. (1988) *Images of the Enemy*, London: Routledge.

McNair, B. (1989) 'Television news and the 1983 election', in C. Marsh and C. Fraser (eds) *Public Opinion and Nuclear Weapons*, London: Macmillan.

McNair, B. (1991) *Glasnost, Perestroika and the Soviet Media*, London: Routledge.

McNair, B. (1995) *An Introduction to Political Communication*, London: Routledge.

McNeil, K. (1978) 'Understanding organizational power: building on the Weberian legacy', *Administrative Science Quarterly* 23(1): 65–90.

Macpherson, C. (1976) *The Life and Times of Liberal Democracy*, Oxford: Oxford University Press.

McQuail, D. (1987) *Mass Communication Theory: An Introduction*, 2nd edn, London: Sage.

Maeckling, C. (1983) 'The future of diplomats', in W. Olson (ed.) *The Theory and Practice of International Relations*, Englewood Cliffs, NJ: Prentice-Hall.

Mannheim, J.B. and Pratt, C.B. (1989) 'Communicating corporate social responsibility', *Public Relations Review* 15(2): 9.

Marsh, K. and Fraser, C. (eds) (1989) *Public Opinion and Nuclear Weapons*, London: Macmillan.

Matrat, L. (1990) 'Good citizenship and public relations', *International Public Relations Review* 13(2): 8–12.

Maturana, H. and Varela, F. (1980) *Autopoiesis and Cognition: The Realization of the Living*, London: Reidl.

May, L. (1986) 'Corporate property rights', *Journal of Business Ethics* 5.

Mayo, E. (1933) *The Human Problems of Industrial Civilisation*, New York: Macmillan.

Mercer, D., Mungham, G. and Williams, K. (1987) *The Fog of War*, London: Heinemann.

Miliband, R. (1973) *The State in Capitalist Society*, London: Quartet.

Mill, J.S. (1975) *Three Essays*, London: Oxford University Press.

Mill, J.S. and Bentham, J. (1987) *Utilitarianism and Other Essays*, Harmondsworth: Penguin.

Miller, C. (1991) *Lobbying: Understanding and Influencing the Corridors of Power*, Oxford: Blackwell.

Miller, D. (1994) *Don't Mention the War*, London: Pluto.

Miller, G. (1989)''Persuasion and public relations: two "Ps" in a pod', in C. Botan and V. Hazleton (eds) *Public Relations Theory*, Hillsdale, NJ: Lawrence Erlbaum.

Miller, J. (1981) *The World of States*, London: Croom Helm.

Mills, C. (1975) *The Power Elite*, New York: Oxford University Press.

Mintzberg, H. (1983) *Power in and around Organizations*, Englewood Cliffs, NJ: Prentice-Hall.

Mintzberg, H., Reisinghani, D. and Theoret, A. (1976) 'The structure of unstructured decision processes', *Administrative Science Quarterly* 21: 246–75.

Mitnick, B. (1993) *Corporate Political Agency: The Construction of Competition in Public Affairs*, London: Sage.

Moffitt, M. (1994) 'A cultural studies perspective toward understanding corporate image: a case study of state farm insurance', *Journal of Public Relations Research* 6(1): 41–66.

Morgan, G. (1986) *Images of Organization*, Newbury Park/London: Sage.

Morgan, G. (1989) *Creative Organization Theory*, London: Sage.

Morgan, G. (1990) *Organisations in Society*, London: Macmillan.

Morgan, G. (1992) *Imaganization*, London: Sage.

Morris, D. (1994) 'Public relations in the UK: an overview of the marketing/public relations debate', unpublished master's dissertation, University of Stirling.

Murray, R. (1955) *Red Scare: A Study of National Hysteria, 1919–20*, Westport: Greenwood Press.

Myerson, G. (1994) *Rhetoric, Reason and Society: Rationality as Dialogue*, London: Sage.

Naisbett, J. (1982) *Megatrends*, New York: Warren Books.

Nardin, T. and Mapel, D. (eds) (1992) *Traditions of International Ethics*, Cambridge: Cambridge University Press.

Nash, L. (1990) 'Ethics without the sermon', in W.M. Hoffman and J.M. Moore (eds) *Business Ethics: Reading and Cases in Corporate Morality*, 2nd edn, New York: McGraw-Hill.

Nelson, R. (1990) 'Bias versus fairness: the social utility of issues management', *Public Relations Review* 16(2): 98–104.

Nelson, R. (1994) 'Issues communication and advocacy: contemporary ethical challenges', *Public Relations Review* 20(3): 225–33.

Newcomb, T. (1953) 'An approach to the study of communicative arts', *Psychological Review* 60: 393–404.

Newman, W. (1993) 'New words for what we do', *Institute of Public Relations Journal* (October): 12–15.

Nicolson, H. (1954) *The Evolution of the Diplomatic Method*, London: Constable & Co.

Noelle-Neumann, E. (1979) 'Public opinion and the classical tradition: a re-evaluation', *Public Opinion Quarterly* 43: 143–56.

Nozick, R. (1990) *Anarchy, State and Utopia*, Oxford: Blackwell.

O'Keefe, D. (1990) *Persuasion: Theory and Research*, London: Sage.

O'Sullivan, T., Hartley, J., Saunders, D., Montgomery, M. and Fiske, J. (eds) (1994) *Key Concepts in Communication and Cultural Studies*, London: Routledge.

Olins, W. (1978) *The Corporate Personality*, London: Design Council.

Olins, W. (1989) *Corporate Identity*, London: Thames & Hudson.

Parker, I. (1992) *Discourse Dynamics: Critical Analysis for Social and Individual Psychology*, London: Routledge.

Parker, M. (1992) 'Post-modern organizations or postmodern organization theory', *Organization Studies* 13(1): 1–17.

Parsons, T. (1951) *The Social System*, London: Free Press.

Parsons, T. (1959) *Economy and Society*, London: Routledge & Kegan Paul.

Parsons, T. (1960) *Structure and Process in Modern Societies*, New York: Free Press.

Paton, H.J. (1948) *The Moral Law: Kant's Groundwork of the Metaphysic of Morals*, London: Hutchinson.

Pavlik, J. (1987) *Public Relations: What Research Tells Us*, Newbury Park: Sage Commtext.

Pearson, R. (1989a) 'Beyond ethical relativism in public relations: co-orientation, rules and the idea of communication symmetry', in J.E. Grunig and L.A. Grunig (eds) *Public Relations Research Annual*, vol. 1, Hillsdale, NJ: Lawrence Erlbaum.

Pearson, R. (1989b) 'Business ethics as communication ethics: public relations practice and the idea of dialogue', in C.H. Botan and V. Hazleton (eds) *Public Relations Theory*, Hillsdale, NJ: Lawrence Erlbaum.

Pearson, R. (1990) 'Ethical values or strategic values? Two faces of systems theory in public relations', in L. Grunig and J. Grunig (eds) *Public Relations Research Annual*, vol. 2, Hillsdale, NJ: Lawrence Erlbaum.

Pearson, R. (1992) 'Perspectives in public relations history', in E. Toth and R. Heath (eds) *Rhetorical and Critical Approaches to Public Relations*, Hillsdale, NJ: Lawrence Erlbaum.

Perrow, C. (1961) 'The analysis of goals in complex organizations', *American Sociological Review* 32: 194–209.

Perloff, R.M. (1993) *The Dynamics of Persuasion*, Hillsdale, NJ: Lawrence Erlbaum.

Peters, T. (1987) *Thriving on Chaos*, London: Macmillan.

Peters, T. and Waterman, R. (1982) *In Search of Excellence*, New York: Harper & Row.

Pettigrew, A. (1973) *The Politics of Organizational Decision-Making*, London: Tavistock.

Pfeffer, J. (1981) *Power in Organizations*, Boston: Pitman Press.

Pfeffer, J. and Salancik, G. (1978) *The External Control of Organizations: A Resource Dependence Perspective*, New York: Harper & Row.

Piore, M. and Sabel, C. (1984) *The Second Industrial Divide*, New York: Basic Books.

Plato (1986) *Phaedrus*, Harmondsworth: Penguin.

Plato (1988) *Gorgias*, translated and with an introduction by W. Hamilton, Harmondsworth: Penguin.

Plato (1989) *Gorgias*, translated with notes by T. Irwin, Oxford: Clarendon.

Pollert, A. (1988) 'Dismantling flexibility', *Capital and Class* 34: 42–7.

Porter, J. (1993) 'Developing a postmodern ethics of rhetoric and composition', in T. Enos and S.C. Brown (eds) *Defining the New Rhetorics*, London, Sage.

PR Week (23 September 1993): 16.

Price, J.L. (1968) *Organizational Effectiveness: An Inventory of Propositions*, Homewood, IL: Irwin.

Price, V. (1992) *Public Opinion*, Newbury Park: Sage.

Pusey, M. (1987) *Jürgen Habermas*, London: Ellis Harwood.

Quinn, R.E. and Hall, R.H. (1983) 'Environments, organizations and policymakers: towards an integrative framework', in R.H. Hall and R.E. Quinn (eds) *Organizational Theory and Public Policy*, Beverly Hills, CA: Sage.

Radcliffe-Brown, A. (1952) *Structure and Function in Primitive Society*, London: Cohen & West.

Rafalko, R.J. (1989) 'Corporate punishment: a proposal', *Journal of Business Ethics* 8: 923.

Rapoport, A. (1968) 'General systems theory', in Sills (ed.) *International Encyclopedia of Social Sciences*, New York: Macmillan Co./Free Press.

Rasmussen, D.M. (1990) *Reading Habermas*, Oxford: Blackwell.

Rawls, J. (1988) *A Theory of Justice*, Oxford: Oxford University Press.

Ray, L. (1993) *Rethinking Critical Theory*, London: Sage.

Reardon, K.K. (1991) *Persuasion in Practice*, London: Sage.

Reed, M. (1992) 'Introduction', in M. Reed and M. Hughes (eds) *Rethinking Organization*, London: Sage.

Reed, M. (1993) 'Organizations and modernity: continuity and discontinuity in organization theory', in J. Hassard and M. Parker (eds) *Postmodernism and Organizations*, London/Newbury Park/New Delhi: Sage.

Regan, T. (ed.) (1984) *Just Business: New Introductory Essays in Business Ethics*, New York: Random House.

Reynolds, P. (1980) *An Introduction to International Relations*, 2nd edn, London: Longman.

Richmond, S.B. (1968) *Operations Research for Management Decisions*, New York: Ronald Press.

Robison, W., Pritchard, M. and Ellin, J. (eds) (1983) *Profits and Professions: Essays in Business and Professional Ethics*, Clifton, NJ: Humana Press.

Rocher, G. (1974) *Talcott Parsons and American Sociology*, translated by B. Mennell and S. Mennell, London: Nelson.

Rousseau, J.-J. (1968), *The Social Contract*, Harmondsworth: Penguin.

Rowland, R.C. and Womack, D.F. (1985) 'Aristotle's view of ethical rhetoric', *Rhetoric Society Quarterly* 15: 13–31.

Ruse, M. (1993) *The Darwinian Paradigm: Essays on its History, Philosophy and Religious Implications*, London: Routledge.

Scott, R. (1993) 'Rhetoric is epistemic: what difference does that make?', in T. Enos and S.C. Brown (eds) *Defining the New Rhetorics*, London: Sage.

Sharpe, M. (1990) 'Harmonizing ethical values in the global village: the public relations professional challenge!', *International Public Relations Review* 13(3): 21–5.

Shaw, E. (1993) *The Labour Party Since 1979*, London: Routledge.

Signitzer, B. and Coombs, T. (1992) 'Public relations and public diplomacy: conceptual convergences', *Public Relations Review* 18(2): 137–47.

Silverman, D. (1970) *The Theory of Organizations*, London: Heinemann.

Silverman, D. and Jones, J. (1976) 'Getting in: the managed accomplishments of "correct" selection outcomes', in J. Child (ed.) *Man and Organisation*, London, George Allen & Unwin.

Smith, A. (1987) *The Wealth of Nations*, books I–III, Harmondsworth: Penguin.

Smith, C. (1989) 'Flexible specialization, automation and mass production', *Work, Employment and Society* 3(2): 203–20.

Smith, M.J. (1982) *Persuasion and Human Action: A Review and Critique of Social Influence Theories*, Belmont, CA: Wadsworth.

Sorell, T. (1991) 'Ethics and public relations', *Business Ethics*, University of Stirling.

Speier H. (1980) 'The rise of public opinion', in H. Lasswell, D. Lerner and H. Speier (eds) *Propaganda and Communications in World History*, vol. 2, Honolulu: University Press of Hawaii.

Steiner, G.A. (1983) *The New CEO*, New York: Macmillan.

Stout, D.A. (1990) 'Internal process of corporate advocacy', *Public Relations Review* (Spring): 52–62.

Strauss, A. (1978) *Negotiations*, New York: Wiley.

The Sunday Times (5 February 1989) 'Making a mark is big business'.

Taylor, T. (ed.) (1978) *Approaches to Theory in International Affairs*, Longman: New York.

Terry, K.E. (1989) 'Educator and practitioner differences on the role of theory in public relations', in C.H. Botan and V. Hazleton (eds) *Public Relations Theory*, Lawrence Erlbaum.

The Place of Public Relations in Management Education (1991) Public Relations Education Trust.

Thomas, C. and Webb, E. (1994) 'From orality to rhetoric: an intellectual transformation', in I. Worthington (ed.) *Persuasion: Greek Rhetoric in Action*, London: Routledge.

Thompson, K. (1983) 'The moral dilemma of diplomacy', in W. Olson (ed.) *The Theory and Practice of International Relations*, Englewood Cliffs, NJ: Prentice-Hall.

Thompson, P. (1993) 'Postmodernism: Fatal Attraction', in J. Hassard and M. Parker (eds) *Postmodernism and Organizations*, London/Newbury Park/ New Delhi: Sage.

Thucydides (1987) *History of the Peloponnesian War*, Harmondsworth: Penguin Classics.

Toth, E. (1992) 'The case for pluralistic studies of public relations; rhetorical, critical and systems perspectives', in E. Toth and R. Heath (eds) *Rhetorical and Critical Approaches to Public Relations*, Hillsdale, NJ: Lawrence Erlbaum.

Toth, E. and Heath, R. (eds) (1992) *Rhetorical and Critical Approaches to Public Relations*, Hillsdale, NJ: Lawrence Erlbaum.

Traverse-Healy, T. (1988a) 'Public relations and propaganda: values compared', International Public Relations Association Gold Paper No. 6.

Traverse-Healy, T. (1988b) 'The credibility factor and diplomacy: a public relations perspective on public affairs', Koeppler Memorial Lecture, Baylor University, Waco, TX, 15 November, unpublished lecture.

Traverso, M. and White, J. (1990), 'The launch of the Prudential's corporate identity', in D. Moss (ed.) *Public Relations in Practice*, London: Routledge.

Tsoukas, H. (1992) 'A reply to Martin Parker', *Organization Studies* 13(4): 643–650.

Tsoukas, H. (ed.) (1994) *New Thinking in Organizational Behaviour*, Oxford: Butterworth-Heinemann.

Turner, B. (1986) *Citizenship and Capitalism: The Debate over Reformism*, London: Allen & Unwin.

Turner, B. (1990) 'The rise of organizational symbolism', in J. Hassard and D. Pym (eds) *The Theory and Philosophy of Organizations*, London: Routledge.

Velasquez, M.G. (1983) 'Why corporations are not morally responsible for anything they do', *Business and Professional Ethics Journal* 11.

Vidal, J. and Cordahi, C. (1995) 'A question of guilt', *The Guardian* (23 August): 5.

Von Bertalanffy, L. (1950) 'The theory of open systems in physics and biology', *Science* 3.

Von Bertalanffy, L. (1956) 'General systems theory', *General Systems* 1: 1–10.

Von Bertalanffy, L. (1972) 'General systems theory – a critical review', in J. Beishon and G. Peters (eds) *Systems Behaviour*, London: Harper Ross for the Open University Press.

Wakefield, G. and Cottone, L. (1992) 'Public relations executives' perceptions of disciplinary emphases important to public relations practice for the 1990s', *Public Relations Review* 18(1): 67–79.

Wartick, S.L. and Rude, R.E. (1986) 'Issues management: corporate fad or corporate function?', *California Management Review* (fall): 124–40.

Wathen, M. (1987) 'Names people play', *Public Relations Journal* (May): 14–16.

Weick, K. (1969) *The Social Psychology of Organising*, Reading, MA: Addison-Wesley.

Weick, K. (1979) 'Cognitive processes in organizations', *Research in Organizational Behaviour* 1: 41–74.

Wells, C. (1989) 'The decline and rise of English murder: corporate crime and individual responsibility', *Criminal Law Review* (March).

Wells, C. (1993) *Corporations and Criminal Responsibility*, Oxford Monographs on Criminal Law and Justice, Oxford: Clarendon Press.

Wetherbee Phelps, L. (1993) 'Writing the new rhetoric of scholarship', in T. Enos and S.C. Brown (eds) *Defining the New Rhetorics*, London: Sage.

White J. and Mazur, L. (1995) *Strategic Communications Management: Making Public Relations Work*, Wokingham: Addison Welsey.

White, J. and Blamphin, J. (1994) 'Priorities for research into public relations practice in the United Kingdom', unpublished report from a Delphi study carried out among UK practitioners and public relations academics in 1994.

White, J. (1991) *How to Understand and Manage Public Relations*, London: Business Books.

White, S. (1990) *The Recent Work of Jürgen Habermas*, Cambridge: Cambridge University Press.

Wight, M. (1994) *International Theory: The Three Traditions*, Leicester: Leicester University Press for the Royal Institute for International Affairs.

Wilcox, D. Ault, P. and Agee, W. (1988) *Public Relations: Strategies and Tactics*, New York: Harper & Row.

Williams, J. and Beaver, W. (1990) 'Barnados: relaunching Britain's biggest children's charity', in D. Moss (ed.) *Public Relations in Practice*, London: Routledge.

Williams, R. (1976) *Keywords*, Glasgow: Fontana/Croom Helm.

Wilson, L.J. (1990) 'Corporate issues management: an international view, *Public Relations Review* (Spring): 40–51.

Wolfers, A. (1966) *Discord and Collaboration: Essays in International Politics*, Baltimore: John Hopkins University Press.

Worthington, I. (ed.) (1994) *Persuasion: Greek Rhetoric in Action*, London: Routledge.

Wright, D.K. (1979) 'Professionalism and social responsibility', *Public Relations Review*: 20–33.

Young, K. (1954) 'Comments on the nature of "public" and "public opinion"', in D. Katz, D. Cartwright, S. Eldersveld and A. McClung Lee (eds) *Public Opinion and Propaganda*, New York: Holt, Rinehart & Winston (originally published 1948, *International Journal of Opinion and Attitude Research* 2: 385–92).

Zeitz, G. (1975) 'Interorganizational relationships and social structure: a critique of some aspects of literature', in A.R. Negandhi (ed.) *Interorganizational Theory*, Kent, OH: Kent State University Press.

Zeller, J. (1992) *The Nature and Origins of Mass Opinion*, Cambridge: Cambridge University Press.

INDEX